FACETS OF THE CONFLICT IN NORTHERN IRELAND

Facets of the Conflict in Northern Ireland

Edited by

Seamus Dunn
Professor of Education
Director, Centre for the Study of Conflict
University of Ulster, Coleraine

St. Martin's Press

First published in Great Britain 1995 by
MACMILLAN PRESS LTD
Houndmills, Basingstoke, Hampshire RG21 2XS
and London
Companies and representatives
throughout the world

A catalogue record for this book is available
from the British Library.

ISBN 0–333–60717–1 hardcover
ISBN 0–333–64252–X paperback

10	9	8	7	6	5	4	3	2	1
04	03	02	01	00	99	98	97	96	95

Printed and bound in Great Britain by
Ipswich Book Co. Ltd
Ipswich, Suffolk

First published in the United States of America 1995 by
Scholarly and Reference Division,
ST. MARTIN'S PRESS, INC.,
175 Fifth Avenue,
New York, N.Y. 10010

ISBN 0–312–12280–2

Library of Congress Cataloging-in-Publication Data
Facets of the conflict in Northern Ireland / edited by Seamus Dunn.
p.   cm.
Includes index.
ISBN 0–312–12280–2
1. Northern Ireland—History—1979–   2. Social conflict—Northern
Ireland.   I. Dunn, Seamus, 1939– .
DA990.U46F27   1995

To the memory of Annie Dunne, 1904–84

Contents

Acknowledgements

I am indebted to all my colleagues, present and past, in the Centre for the Study of Conflict, for their cooperation and support during the planning and writing of this book. Particular thanks are due to Pat Shortt who provided moral and administrative support at all stages and to Valerie Feeney who helped create the reference lists.

The Contributors

Ed Cairns   Professor of Psychology and Research Associate, Centre for the Study of Conflict, University of Ulster.

Tara Cairns   Postgraduate Student, Psychology Department, University College Swansea.

John Darby   Professor of Ethnic Studies, University of Ulster and Director of the Joint International Programme on Conflict Resolution and Ethnicity, United Nations University/University of Ulster.

Brice Dickson   Professor of Law, Department of Public Administration and Legal Studies, University of Ulster.

Seamus Dunn   Professor of Education and Director of the Centre for the Study of Conflict, University of Ulster.

Grace Fraser   Research Officer, Faculty of Education, and former Research Officer, Centre for the Study of Conflict, University of Ulster.

Anthony M. Gallagher   Lecturer in Educational Research, Queen's University, Belfast, and former Research Officer, Centre for the Study of Conflict, University of Ulster.

Adrian Guelke   Professor of Politics, University of Witwatersrand, South Africa, formerly of Queen's University, Belfast.

Andrew Hamilton   Lecturer in Social Administration, University of Ulster, and Research Associate, Centre for the Study of Conflict.

Joanne Hughes   Lecturer, Public Administration and Legal Studies, University of Ulster and former Research Officer, Centre for the Study of Conflict.

Colin Knox   Senior Lecturer, Public Administration and Legal Studies, University of Ulster.

Sally McClean   Professor of Mathematics, University of Ulster.

Martin Melaugh   Research Officer, Centre for the Study of Conflict, University of Ulster.

Linda Moore   Lecturer, Department of Crime and Justice, Edgehill College, and former Research Officer, Centre for the Study of Conflict, University of Ulster.

Valerie Morgan   Professor of Education, University of Ulster, and Research Director of the Joint International Programme on Conflict Resolution and Ethnicity, United Nations University/University of Ulster.

Duncan Morrow   Lecturer in Politics and former Research Officer, Centre for the Study of Conflict, University of Ulster.

Dominic Murray   Professor of Peace Studies, University of Limerick.

Ciarán Ó Maoláin   Information Officer, Centre for the Study of Conflict, University of Ulster.

Alan Smith   Research Fellow, Centre for the Study of Conflict, University of Ulster.

John Sugden   Senior Lecturer, Sport and Leisure Studies, University of Ulster.

Jerry Tyrrell   Research Officer, Centre for the Study of Conflict, University of Ulster.

Derick Wilson   Research Fellow, Centre for the Study of Conflict, University of Ulster.

List of Abbreviations

ACT	All Children Together
AVP	Alternatives to Violence Project
BAN	Belfast Areas of Need
BELB	Belfast Education and Library Board
CAJ	Committee on the Administration of Justice
CCMS	Council for Catholic Maintained Schools
CCRU	Central Community Relations Unit
CES(NI)	Charities Evaluation Service (Northern Ireland)
CMRS	Conference of Major Religious Superiors
CRC	Community Relations Commission (1969–74)
CRC	Community Relations Council (1990–)
CRO	Community Relations Officer
CSC	Centre for the Study of Conflict, University of Ulster
CWIS	Campus-Wide Information Service (within University of Ulster)
DENI	Department of Education, Northern Ireland
DFP	Department of Finance and Personnel
DHAC	Derry Housing Action Committee
DHSS	Department of Health and Social Services
DoE	Department of the Environment
DUP	Democratic Unionist Party
EC	European Community
EEC	European Economic Community
EMU	Education for Mutual Understanding
EOCNI	Equal Opportunities Commission for Northern Ireland
EPA	Emergency Provisions Act
ESRC	Economic and Social Research uncil (UK)
ESRI	Economic and Social Research Institute (Ireland)
EU	European Union
FAI	Football Association of Ireland (mainly Republic of Ireland)
FAIT	Families Against Intimidation and Terror
FEA	Fair Employment Agency (1976–89)
FEC	Fair Employment Commission (1989–)
FES	Family Expenditure Survey
FET	Fair Employment Tribunal
GAA	Gaelic Athletic Association

ICC	Irish Council of Churches
ICJP	Irish Commission for Justice and Peace
ICPC	Independent Commission for Police Complaints
IDB	Industrial Development Board
IFA	Irish Football Association (Northern Ireland)
INCORE	Joint International Programme on Conflict Resolution and Ethnicity (based at the University of Ulster)
INLA	Irish National Liberation Army
INNATE	Irish Network for Nonviolent Action, Training and Education
IPLO	Irish People's Liberation Army
IRA	Irish Republican Army (referred to as Provisional IRA)
IRSP	Irish Republican Socialist Party
LEDU	Local Enterprise Development Unit
LFS	Labour Force Survey
MBW	Making Belfast Work
NCBI	National Coalition Building Institute
NCCL	National Council for Civil Liberties (now called Liberty)
NEELB	North Eastern Education and Library Board
NICC	Northern Ireland Curriculum Council
NICED	Northern Ireland Council for Educational Development
NICHS	Northern Ireland Children's Holiday Scheme
NICIE	Northern Ireland Council for Integrated Education
NICMA	Northern Ireland Conflict and Mediation Association
NICRA	Northern Ireland Civil Rights Association
NICRC	Northern Ireland Community Relations Commission
NICRC	Northern Ireland Community Relations Council
NICS	Northern Ireland Civil Service
NICTU	Northern Ireland Congress of Trade Unions
NIHE	Northern Ireland Housing Executive (1971–)
NIHT	Northern Ireland Housing Trust (1945–71)
NILP	Northern Ireland Labour Party
NIMMA	Northern Ireland Mixed Marriage Association
NIO	Northern Ireland Office
NIRRL	Northern Ireland Regional Research Laboratory
NISAS	Northern Ireland Social Attitudes Survey
NUM	New Ulster Movement
OUP	Official Unionist Party (synonymous with UUP)
PACE	Protestant and Catholic Encounter
PACE	Police and Criminal Evidence

PANI   Police Authority for Northern Ireland
PIRA   Provisional Irish Republican Army (usually IRA)
PPRU   Policy, Planning and Research Unit
PRI   Policy Research Institute
PSI   Policy Studies Institute
PTA   Prevention of Terrorism Act
QPEP   Quaker Peace Education Project
RIR   Royal Irish Regiment
RTU   Regional Training Unit
RUC   Royal Ulster Constabulary
RUCR   Royal Ulster Constabulary Reserve
SACHR   Standing Advisory Commission on Human Rights
SAS   Social Attitudes Survey (also NISAS)
SAS   Special Air Service
SDLP   Social Democratic and Labour Party
SELB   Southern Education and Library Board
SEELB   South Eastern Education and Library Board
SOC   Standard Occupational Classification
TSN   Targeting Social Need
UDA   Ulster Defence Association
UDP   Ulster Democratic Party
UDR   Ulster Defence Regiment
UFF   Ulster Freedom Fighters
UK   United Kingdom
UPC   Ulster Peoples College
UPNI   Unionist Party of Northern Ireland
USC   Ulster Special Constabulary (B Specials)
UUP   Ulster Unionist Party
UVF   Ulster Volunteer Force
UWP   Ulster Workers Council
YCNI   Youth Council for Northern Ireland
WAVE   Widows Against Violence
WELB   Western Education and Library Board

Part One
Context

1 The Conflict as a Set of Problems

Seamus Dunn

INTRODUCTION

On 1 September 1994, the Provisional Irish Republican Army (PIRA) declared a 'complete cessation of military operations'. As I write this in September 1994 the equivalent loyalist paramilitary groupings are considering their position. All the current evidence however suggests that, after 25 years of violence, the sounds of guns and bombs are about to disappear from the streets of Northern Ireland. The overall impact of this change in economic and social terms is not easy to predict, but the effect of a cease-fire on the conflict – in its widest sense – requires careful analysis. To begin with, it is a defining characteristic of all internal conflicts that they are never completely solved. The cease-fire suggests that one facet has been, for the moment, resolved and it is probable that this will be followed by the emergence of new democratic structures and institutional forms.

The purpose of this book is to illustrate that the end end of violence and the accompanying political accommodations are only the first steps in a long-term process of social reconstruction. Clearly these developments are a necessary and deeply significant part of any process of normalisation but they are not enough in themselves. The range of the problems that contribute to the conflict is very large and complex, and political accommodations, although they are a very good start, will not deal with all the issues. The book therefore examines a wide spread of social and political themes and provides detailed support for the general view that such 'internal' conflicts are varied, intricate and multi-dimensional and so are unresponsive to simple dogmatisms. Much of the book's contents results from the researches carried out at the Centre for the Study of Conflict in the University of Ulster during the past 17 years.

It has become almost a cliché to say that conflicts arising from inter-group – or inter-ethnic, or inter-community, or internal – disputes now represent the most striking and salient examples, all round the world, of modern brutality and violence, if not actual war. In many of these quarrels the initial sources of the mutual antagonisms are of great age, and the determination of the causes of recent outbreaks a matter of dispute. For example, the many violent conflicts in Eastern Europe filling the pages of newspapers in the early 1990s reflect long-standing fears, separations and hostilities and did not just emerge suddenly, without a past. Their persistence and virulence suggest that they will not be transformed by any simple remedy.

The origins of these disputes are usually connected with one or more of a set of fundamental forms of human association (and therefore separateness) such as religion, politics, race, ethnicity and culture. Such associations and divisions are of great power and significance because they relate to the ways in which people identify themselves and their individual places in the world. The determination to remain distinctive and separate leads to drawing of boundaries or building of walls, to marking out territories and to a physical and emotional distancing from others. One consequence of this process is called nationalism.

In Northern Ireland (although, as we are coming to realise, not uniquely in Northern Ireland) all these issues are available and part of the discourse. For a time it seemed as if the conflict here was distinctive in its atavism, a throwback to earlier European times. For this reason, among others, it attracted and continues to attract a remarkable amount of both academic and popular attention. (In the final chapter of this book we refer to the extraordinary range of existing literature, academic work and research that the conflict has stimulated.) The conflicts in Eastern Europe, along with the emergence of a higher profile for inter-group conflict generally, have combined to place some emphasis on the question of the extent to which the Northern Ireland conflict is unique and different. It is relatively easy to find common features with Israel, Sri Lanka, even with Bosnia. But the substance of these commonalities, their congruence and their powers of explanation are less clear. The urge to find common features, however, is strong and is motivated by two instincts. The first is that experiences in other places may be helpful in Northern Ireland in generating positive developments. The second arises from an attempt to examine all conflicts in search of general features that can be clarified and analysed. Certainly the longevity of the conflict here, and the quantity of research and writing about it, have the potential to provide insights into and understandings of conflict generally, and to counter a tendency towards quick answers and simple remedies.

For many observers the Northern Ireland conflict is impossible to get to grips with. It seems to be endlessly confused and confusing, and all explanations are immediately seen to be partial, so that those who seek to encapsulate it in one thesis must have the capacity to live with contradiction. For example, there are two apparently contradictory ways of describing social and community life in Northern Ireland, both of which are partially true. An examination of these contradictory truths helps to illustrate the need for care and caution when making judgements. The first description says that the two peoples in Northern Ireland live closely and intimately with each other; they do not live in segregated cities or compounds; they work together, shop together, go to football matches together, attend the same universities; they cannot tell from looking or listening which group the other belongs to; there are no distinguishing marks such as colour or language, no accents distinctive to one side, no recognisable physical traits. Immediately it has to be said that, while all these things are undoubtedly true, few of them are completely true. For example, the level of residential segregation within Northern Ireland is a matter of current debate. But, whatever the real level turns out to be for any particular town or housing estate or street, that example can be countered by many other examples where the separation is less complete. And even for those places that appear to be completely segregated, this is never a permanent state and the continuing process of change, movement and social interaction acts against its permanency. Therefore, despite the anecdotal evidence about Protestants who never meet Catholics, or vice versa, this is not the normal experience of a very large proportion of the population. The simple daily activities of buying petrol for a car, visiting a government office or sitting in a bus make such isolation unlikely.

The second, and contradictory, description says that the two peoples of Northern Ireland live separate lives in a number of significant ways. For the most part they attend separate schools, worship in separate churches, read different newspapers, play different games, and belong to different social and sporting clubs. And again, this must be qualified by saying that the degree to which any or all of these is true varies considerably with respect to such variables as geographical location, social class, levels of residential segregation and levels of employment/unemployment.

The violence, maintained for a quarter of a century, clearly arose out of a set of separations, both metaphorical and real, and this may help to explain the paradox. Such separations are complex, changeable and full of contrasts. Not surprisingly, perhaps, this complexity leads to confusion and makes it possible for evidence to be presented to support particular analyses and proposed solutions. One response, for example, is to attribute the violence to a small group of unrepresentative 'terrorists' who are essentially criminals and degenerates. Some go so far as to comfort themselves with the view that these people are mindless and stupid. Another, almost opposite response, is to hold the view that all the people of Northern Ireland are prepared to use or support violence when their own position is threatened, and therefore that all are to blame. Like most simplifications there are elements of truth in both of these – but only elements.

Perhaps the most vital and (apparently) logical point of entry for many is the political one. It is frequently argued that the conflict arose purely and simply from a political and constitutional separation: and that, if the politicians could sit down together and hammer out a form of government for Northern Ireland acceptable to all the parties, then the cause of the conflict would have been removed, and the violence would disappear. Interestingly, these two elements – politics and violence – are included or are implicit in the recent ceasefire, but the order seems to have been reversed. Recent events in the Middle East and in South Africa have been cited as examples of how progress can be made; but prior to that the examples were likely to be the re-creation of friendly inter-state relationships in post-world-war Europe. Indeed, in the early years of the conflict other examples of 'successful' political settlements were often cited for emulation – such as Lebanon and Sri Lanka.

It is obviously true that such a political settlement in Northern Ireland is necessary if peace is to be established. But if the other separations (economic, social, cultural, historical) remain, it is at least likely that they will serve to keep the two communities apart, reinforce and emphasise their differences, and maintain a potential for the resumption of violence. So, while necessary and of the deepest importance, a political settlement may not be sufficient. It might be as well to remember that the power sharing Executive of 1973 was an agreed political settlement.

In contrast with the emphasis on political settlements, surprisingly little research on conflict looks at practical domestic issues at the level of internal social institutions. The concern is often with the larger issues of political structures, armed forces and international relations, and so institutions like education or churches or housing are neglected. The implication seems to be that these can be dealt with after, and as a consequence of, political and military agreements. The power, or the potential, of such internal changes to contribute to the social and psychological atmosphere that might allow conflict to be reduced is rarely examined. As often as not it is simply dismissed as unimportant.

Most of the research also ignores the dynamic and evolutionary nature of many ethnic conflicts, where there are stages that allow different and progressively more detailed approaches to be attempted. In the early or undeveloped stages, the emphasis is on the wider issues such as nationality, boundaries or the search for acceptable forms of political accommodation. The opposing groups are convinced of their differences, of the unlikelihood of common ground; there is much appeal to particular versions of history, to the unbridgeability of religious and, often, linguistic differences and to abstract, but often very powerful, notions of ethos and culture. Both sides believe that there is a solution which will advantage them and disadvantage the others. This might be thought of as the 'naive' stage, when relatively advanced, socially reconstructive, notions like integrated schools, or ecumenical church activities, or revisionist history are perceived as impossible and fanciful – or not necessary, since one side will 'win'. Separate schools, religious purity, and partial, often romanticised, history are necessary to maintain the equivalent of 'the spirit of the nation'. It is only at a much later, more developed, stage, when the impossibility of simple solutions is acknowledged, and the realisation that winning is impossible is established, that the social institutions which both reinforce and symbolise separation become legitimate subjects for discussion and action. There are of course many intervening stages. For example, there is the psychological approach which stresses the need to unfreeze attitudes before change is possible.

PART ONE: THE CONTEXT

This book therefore represents a view that there is not so much a single Northern Ireland problem, easily characterised and classified, as a set of interlocked and confused problems. The book is intended to provide a contrast with what are seen as simple and ingenuous explanations. So the sort of arcane debates that try to establish, for example, whether it is a religious problem, or an economic problem, or a social problem, or a political problem are thought to be pointless, since it is all of these, and others as well. The most important consequence of this analysis is the view that most if not all the separations within the society are important in understanding the dispute, and that all of them must be analysed, worked at and given energy. It resists the temptation to plump for any singular one-dimensional analysis (if only the troublemakers had jobs), or to accept simple, easy answers (lock up the few hundred terrorists).

The first part of the book is about context and includes this introductory chapter, and one other on the 'background to the conflict'. Taken together these two chapters are an attempt to place the conflict in a social and historical context. This includes reference to the vagaries of Anglo-Irish relationships down the centuries right up to the beginning of the current stage of the conflict in 1969. Other forms of contextualisation include a description of the main political groupings in Northern Ireland and an analysis of the range of attitudes to and positions on the United Kingdom/Irish connection.

Finally, this first part examines the sequence of attempts to find a political structure for the region. These have been unending and often ingenious; they have included a proposal to reform Stormont in 1971; direct rule from Westminster in 1972 (a development that prompted Liam de Paor to write that it replaced a system that had failed for fifty years with one that had failed for five hundred years); a power-sharing Executive in 1973; a Constitutional Convention in 1975; the Northern Ireland Assembly in 1982; the Anglo-Irish Agreement in 1985; attempts to establish inter-party talks, begun by the then Secretary of State Peter Brooke in 1990 and continued by his 1992 successor Patrick Mayhew; and, finally, the Joint Declaration by the Irish and British governments in 1993.

PART TWO: GOVERNMENT AND LAW

The second part of the book examines aspects of government policy within Northern Ireland, especially those policies likely to have an impact on the violence.

There were periods – especially in the early to mid-seventies – when issues associated with civil and human rights were a high priority: these included matters to do with the franchise, housing and local government, all of which were reformed during that period, and, it is agreed, with some success. Activity in this area, however, declined in the late seventies and early eighties, but revived in the mid-eighties when there was a new and more sophisticated awareness within the Westminster administration, the Northern Ireland Office and the Northern Ireland Civil Service of the intricate and entangled nature of social structures and social relations in Northern Ireland. This enhanced awareness began to have influence – perhaps because the simple answers do not seem to have achieved much. The new focus was on plurality and therefore on equity as between the two communities, on inter-community relations and on cultural diversity – that is on bringing the solvent of concepts like heritage, tradition and history into play. There was, it was argued, a need to generate a more generous sense of the past, to become aware of and understand the fault-lines in Irish culture. Considerable support now exists therefore for the interpretation that Northern Ireland is a pluralist society and that the separate parts of that society have not in the past been given equal esteem, equal resources or equal opportunity. It is surmised, further, that this past absence of equity has helped to buttress and support social and political divisions. The evidence for this new acceptance of plurality can be found in government public statements, and, more importantly, in a number of new structures, and in new legislation.

The theory underlying these developments is rarely spelt out clearly, but, at its lowest, it reflects a view that such an approach will have a redemptive quality and begin to remove causes of social disaffection and encourage the two main communities to understand each other better. At its highest it is hoped that new policies will remove public support from violence. Implicit in it also is a belief that men of violence only thrive with the support of their communities.

A very specific, but highly significant, approach to community relations has been through local government, an area which, in the past in Northern Ireland, has not always been characterised by tolerance and mutual respect. The work has involved the provision of extra finance to district councils to allow them to employ community relations officers with a view to maximising the contribution that can be made at local level to the promotion of contact, joint activities, cultural events and so on.

Perhaps the most serious and difficult dilemma posed for government is the need for just security procedures. Like many aspects of the problem, this has a long history and has almost always concerned special legislation. Belief in a military solution is always at least a subtext, although its power to influence events appears to be dependent on a variety of matters such as the level of interest internationally and in the media, and the degree of paramilitary activity. Despite assertions to the contrary, there has always been an acceptable level of violence, which is itself variable but nonetheless real. Security activity becomes more obvious when the current level of acceptability is exceeded. Certainly if it is assumed that the security forces are restrained from draconian military actions which would themselves be unacceptable in moral and political terms, or which would be likely to be counter-productive, then there is little evidence that the security forces acting alone could defeat the various paramilitary groups. Not surprisingly this generates enormous bitterness and frustration and a desire for quick remedies, which, if acceded to, adds to the perpetual cycle.

PART THREE: SUBGROUPS

The third part of the book is about subgroups in the society and about differentials between them with regard to provision and status. There are many of these, but the book focuses on women, children and paramilitaries, as well as on the differentials of provision in housing, health and unemployment as between Protestants and Catholics.

The position of women in a society experiencing inter-group conflict is far from clear. For example, one common assumption is that women are the peace-makers with an unwavering and unanalysed commitment to peace at all costs. This is an oversimplified view and does not take account of the range and subtlety of women's responses. In a society as conservative and male-dominated as Northern Ireland, many women are allocated the role of preserver and defender of the family and of family unity, and not surprisingly, they will try to defend their family from the impact of violence. But there is evidence that women have developed views and obligations of their own with respect to the wider community outside their homes and that these cover the full range of responses, from support for violence to support for community integration.

The role of children in the conflict and, more importantly, the effect on them of the continuing violence is of great significance. In particular there has always been an expressed anxiety that children will grow up likely to use force or criminal methods in pursuit of their own needs; or that the cumulative effects of the experience of violence will be seen in increased overall levels of mental illness. Neither of these anxieties have, it seems, been realised but there is a view that the continuing levels of unemployment, low wages, and resulting high levels of poverty may have had a more subtle effect on children and on their lives. One particular consequence has been a steadily growing brain drain of young people out of Northern Ireland, and this will have a long-term effect on all aspects of society in Northern Ireland even when the troubles do come to an end.

One of the more remarkable results of the conflict has been the growth in illegal paramilitary bodies on both sides, committed to the use of violence in pursuit of their ends. The majority of these organisations, especially in their modern developed form, grew out of the troubles, and the history of their development, and their influence on and contribution to historical events since 1968, are of great interest and are for the most part in the public domain. The more problematic question is about the relationships between paramilitaries and the communities within which they live, not to mention the wider community from which they come. The largely non-rational effect of the hunger strikes (1980–1) on how people in the nationalist community talked and felt about 'political prisoners' is a perfect example of that confusion. This is equally true of the relationship between the Protestant paramilitaries and the unionist community, and may well relate to a wider and more general question about ethnicity and the violence that often accompanies ethnic resurgence. In a sense the person who engages in violence can be dealt with as a category, and so disposed of. But the community out of which he or she emerges is less easy to deal with or categorise, with its ambivalences, its qualified allegiances, its openness to influences and its emotional swings.

There is also an almost inevitable desire to demonise or to dehumanise members of organisations like the IRA. This desire should be resisted for two reasons. First because it indulges the temptation to separate them from the rest of the community as a special caste whose destruction would solve the problem. They are part of the body of the community, however abhorrent or pathological, and – to continue the medical analogy – progress will only be made through medicine not surgery. The second reason is because dehumanisation removes from us the responsibility to try to find out who and what they are. Despite all the research, little is actually known about the perpetrators of violence in Northern Ireland. There are no organised sets of social data about such matters as the sort of schools they went to, their academic record, the homes they came out of, the age when they became involved, their prison experiences, their ideology, hopes, ambitions and religious fervour. Undoubtedly a lot of relevant data exist in such places as the courts, the police records, the prisons, the probation service, not to mention intelligence files. But there has been no public attempt to organise and analyse these data. Obviously there are difficulties relating to access, confidentiality, security, ethics, but nonetheless it would seem obvious that such information would be an important contribution to our current limited knowledge of the people at the heart of paramilitary violence.

PART FOUR: INSTITUTIONS

The fourth part of the book is about institutional forms in Northern Ireland and the extent to which these contribute to the promotion of peace and to cross-community contact. It is difficult to be absolutely clear about the influence or impact of divided social structures. Some forms of division, such as the separate churches, are so manifest and obvious that they are thought by some to be the foundation cause of the conflict. There can be no doubt that much of the resonance and colour of the social division in Northern Ireland finds its source in the differing cultural and ideological world-views characteristic of Catholicism and Protestantism. The close and intimate connection between everyday culture and community life and religious affiliation is, especially in rural parts, profound and deeply rooted. When unionists talk about their culture and heritage and way of life, much of this involves Protestant culture and heritage and way of life. On the other hand, the old Gaelic world was and to some extent the Northern nationalist milieu remains Catholic in the vernacular details of its daily life. The dilemma for the churches is to resolve the social and sometimes harmful separations that result while maintaining and supporting all that is important, remarkable and valuable in their religious cultures.

The divided educational system is perhaps the most researched and investigated of all aspects of institutional life in Northern Ireland, and is certainly the institution that is most often cited as influential and significant in the continuing separation. However, despite the emphasis placed on it, its reform is rarely thought of as being enough in itself, or as being other than a long-term strategy with effects that will become obvious in future generations.

The issue of policing is of course extremely important. It is generally agreed that Northern Ireland needs a police force that is perceived as impartial and generally acceptable, but that some parts of the community do not give the RUC their full confidence. There is certainly an awareness by the authorities of the need to try to improve community–police relations and to be sure that the administration of justice has no conscious or unconscious bias. There have been continuing developments in these matters including attempts to increase recruitment from the Catholic community, assessments of and changes in the relationships between the police and the army, codes of conduct, police–community liaison committees and an Independent Commission for Police Complaints. Despite these, the problem of policing a divided society remains, and demands thinking that is flexible and imaginative, and there is not much evidence to suggest the existence of this sort of creative thinking.

Other forms of division, such as in sport, are often most experienced at a micro level and are therefore structural and taken for granted to the extent that they are, in a sense, invisible. Even when teams from the two communities are playing the same game – such as soccer – more often than not the membership of each team represents one side only. Local sports teams normally have a valuable and positive capacity as a source of unity and community coherence; but when the community is divided, and sport parallels and reinforces the division, then it can become a negative force. Those involved in the management and administration of large national and international sporting bodies therefore have a responsibility to ensure that as much as possible is done to ensure that the sport's capacity to reinforce division is minimised.

There are, of course, a number of issues which do not receive enough attention and where not enough research is carried out. For example, economic issues associated with the violence have received surprisingly little attention from researchers on the conflict, although this may now change as the effects of the cease-fire begin to be felt. The impact of the Thatcher-style 'enterprise culture' on thinking about economic regeneration in Northern Ireland has been substantial, although the unique features of its regional economy ensured that Northern Ireland did not participate in the period of rapid growth experienced by the rest of the national economy between 1983 and 1989. However, there have been strong attempts to attract new investment and to rebuild (some would say build) the Northern Ireland economy. In particular this has placed some emphasis on those parts of Belfast where violence originates, and has involved projects such as Making Belfast Work, injections of capital from the International Fund for Ireland, attempts to lure more multinationals into the province and attempts to generate an indigenous enterprise culture. All of this has had no very dramatic effect on the highest unemployment figures in the UK.

The relationships between these features and the conflict are not well understood. For example there has been no ongoing comparative attempt to measure the costs of the violence. At least part of the unstated agenda associated with some aspects of economic policy has been the desire to undermine violence by improving the economic character of the regions from which it comes. There has not, however, been any research which attempts to evaluate this process generally, or to develop an understanding of the association, if any, between these programmes and the feelings and attitudes of the people of these areas.

PART FIVE: SOURCES OF INFORMATION

Anyone wishing to study or write about the Northern Ireland conflict is faced with a great deal of choice, and this last chapter is an attempt to provide some guidance and to indicate where information can be found. Obviously in such a short essay it cannot be exhaustive and has to make choices about what to omit. But the reader will at least be set out on the trail and can decide where to go thereafter.

The chapter is in three sections, the first dealing with publications, mainly books and booklets. Since this is the area where there is the greatest glut of material it is therefore bound to be the most selective, and the most important selection criterion used is that the material referred to in John Whyte's book *Interpreting Northern Ireland* is not referred to here again. This means that books from about mid-1989 are examined. However, an attempt is made to refer to both general books and to particular areas of study such as history, education, the churches, and so on.

The second section is about research and deals with how to find out what research is being done and also where to go for information if involved in or wishing to pursue research. It provides information on research registers and other listings, on libraries, archives and special collections, and on the existence and accessibility of official papers, the papers of various institutions – such as the political parties – and a range of information services.

The third section looks at data sources, especially statistical data. A great many of these are government publications and compilations but the range of sources is extensive and somewhat confusing and this section will allow those trying to examine and collect data for research or other reasons at least to begin the process.

2 Conflict in Northern Ireland: A Background Essay
John Darby

This chapter is in three sections; first, an outline of the development of the Irish conflict; second, brief descriptions of the main contemporary parties and interests in conflict; and third, an overview of approaches to managing or resolving the conflict.

1. DATES AND SLOGANS

Dates are important in Ireland. This section will select four critical dates, each of which represents a major lurch in the already unstable chronicle of Anglo-Irish relationships. What follows, therefore, is not an abbreviated history but an attempt to identify a succession of themes.

1170: The Norman Invasion

More than a century after the Norman Conquest of England, Henry II of England claimed and attempted to attach Ireland to his kingdom. He succeeded in establishing control in a small area around Dublin known as the Pale. Over the next four centuries this area was the beachhead for the kingdom of Ireland, adopting English administrative practices and the English language and looking to London for protection and leadership. A number of attempts were made to extend English control over the rest of Ireland, but the major expansion of English dominion did not take place until the sixteenth century. For the Irish clans who disputed the rest of the island with each other, England became the major external threat to their sovereignty and customs.

1609: The Plantation of Ulster

By the end of Queen Elizabeth's reign, military conquest had established English rule over most of the island of Ireland, with the

15

principal exception of the northern province of Ulster. The Ulster clans, under Hugh O'Neill, had succeeded in overcoming their instinctive rivalries to create an effective alliance against Elizabeth's armies. After a long and damaging campaign, Ulster was eventually brought under English control and the Irish leaders left the island for Europe. Their land was confiscated and distributed to colonists from Britain. By 1703, less than 5 per cent of the land of Ulster was still in the hands of the Catholic Irish.

The Plantation of Ulster was unique among Irish plantations in that it set out to attract colonists of all classes from England, Scotland and Wales by generous offers of land. Essentially it sought to transplant a society to Ireland. The native Irish remained, but were initially excluded from the towns built by the Planters, and banished to the mountains and bogs on the margins of the land they had previously owned. The sum of the Plantation of Ulster was the introduction of a foreign community, which spoke a different language, represented an alien culture and way of life, including a new type of land tenure and management. In addition, most of the newcomers were Protestant by religion, while the native Irish were Catholic. So the broad outlines of the current conflict in Northern Ireland had been sketched out within fifty years of the plantation: the same territory was occupied by two hostile groups, one believing the land had been usurped and the other believing that their tenure was constantly under threat of rebellion. They often lived in separate quarters. They identified their differences as religious and cultural as well as territorial.

The next two centuries consolidated the differences. There were many risings. The Dublin-based institutions of government – an Irish monarchy, parliament and government, reflecting those in Britain – enforced a series of penal laws against Catholics and, to a lesser extent, Presbyterians. In 1801, in an attempt to secure more direct control of Irish affairs, the Irish parliament and government were abolished by an Act of Union and its responsibilities taken over by Westminster. During the nineteenth century a succession of movements attempted to overthrow the union. Some of these movements, including the Repeal movement in the 1840s and the Home Rule movement from the 1870s, were parliamentary. Others, like the Fenians and the Irish Republican Brotherhood, were dedicated to overthrowing the union by the use of physical force. It is probable that the union would have been repealed by a Home Rule act but for the intervention of the First World War. During the war an armed rising was attempted in Dublin during Easter week, 1916. The rising failed and the leaders were executed, creating a wave of sympathy for the IRA and its political wing, Sinn Féin. In the 1918 election Sinn Féin effectively replaced the old Irish Parliamentary Party and established its own Irish parliament. The resulting War of Independence between Britain and the IRA was eventually ended by a treaty and the Government of Ireland Act in 1920.

Since the 1880s, many Ulster Protestants had become increasingly concerned about the possible establishment of home rule for Ireland. They prepared for resistance. In 1912 a civil war seemed imminent, but the focus was shifted from Ulster by the start of the First World War and by the Easter rising. From 1918, Ulster Protestants increasingly settled for a fall-back position and set out to ensure that the northern counties of Ireland, at least, should be excluded from any Home Rule arrangements. The 1920 Government of Ireland Act, which came into effect in the following year, recognised and confirmed their position by partitioning the island.

1921: Partition

The 1921 settlement precipitated a civil war in the southern 26 counties, between those willing to accept the settlement and those who believed it was a betrayal. Northern Ireland, the name given to the new six-county administration, had been created through demographic compromise. It was essentially the largest area which could be comfortably held with a majority in favour of the union with Britain. The new arrangements established a bicameral legislature, and a subordinate government in Belfast with authority over a number of devolved powers, including policing, education, local government and social services. London retained ultimate authority, and Northern Ireland sent MPs to Westminster.

The establishment of these institutions was a challenge to what some Irish republicans saw as unfinished business. The objective of securing a united independent Ireland, by force if necessary, remained, and there were IRA campaigns in the 1920s, 1940s and 1950s. For many unionists the new arrangements and the union itself could only be maintained with constant vigilance. Emergency legislation was introduced on a permanent basis; a police force and police reserve was established which was almost exclusively Protestant; local government electoral boundaries were openly gerrymandered, a stratagem also used by nationalists when they were able to do so; and a system of economic discrimination was introduced against the Catholic minority in Northern Ireland. This minority formed about one-third of the population for most of the twentieth century, and currently represents around 40 per cent.

A number of Westminster-led social changes after the Second World War, including the introduction of free secondary education for all, led during the 1950s to the emergence of a Catholic middle class. It was their growing dissatisfaction that led to the civil rights campaign of the 1960s.

Civil Rights and After: 1969

By the 1950s there were growing signs that some Catholics were prepared to accept equality within Northern Ireland rather than espouse the more traditional aim of securing a united Ireland. In 1967 the Northern Ireland Civil Rights Association was formed to demand liberal reforms, including the removal of discrimination in the allocation of jobs and houses, permanent emergency legislation and electoral abuses. The campaign was modelled on the civil rights campaign in the United States, involving protests, marches, sit-ins and the use of the media to publicise minority grievances. The local administration was unable to handle the growing civil disorder, and in 1969 the British government sent in troops to enforce order. Initially welcomed by the Catholic population, they soon provided stimulus for the revival of the republican movement. The newly-formed Provisional IRA began a campaign of violence against the army. By 1972 it was clear that the local Northern Irish government, having introduced internment in 1971 as a last attempt to impose control, was unable to handle the situation. Invoking its powers under the Government of Ireland Act, the Westminster parliament suspended the Northern Ireland government and replaced it with direct rule from Westminster. This situation continued into the 1990s.

On paper the civil rights campaign had been a remarkable success. Several of its objectives had been conceded by the end of 1970. By that time, however, proceedings had developed their own momentum. The IRA campaign developed strongly from 1972. Instead of the riots between Catholics and Protestants which had characterised 1969 and 1970, the conflict increasingly took the form of violence between the Provisional IRA and the British Army, with occasional bloody interventions by loyalist paramilitaries. The violence reached a peak in 1972, when 468 people died. Since then it has gradually declined to an annual average of below 100.

Themes

Since the twelfth century therefore, it is possible to discern significant shifts in the Irish problem. Until 1921, it was essentially an Irish–English problem and focused on Ireland's attempt to secure independence from Britain. From 1921 the emphasis shifted to relationships within the island of Ireland, between what later became the Republic of Ireland and Northern Ireland; this issue has somewhat revived since the signing of the Anglo-Irish agreement in 1985. Finally, since 1969, attention has focused on relationships between Catholics and Protestants within Northern Ireland.

2.   THE MAIN PARTIES

Unionists

Unionists are the successors of those who opposed Home Rule in the nineteenth century, and eventually settled for the state of Northern Ireland. The main unionist parties are the Ulster Unionist Party (OUP), which formed all governments from 1921 to 1972; and the more recently established Democratic Unionist Party (DUP), which is more populist, more anti-nationalist, but less popular in electoral support. Both are opposed to the involvement of the Irish Republic in Northern Ireland, and are unwilling to share executive power with non-Unionist parties. They also share a suspicion of Britain's commitment to the union. The DUP holds all these positions more extremely than the UUP, and also is more preoccupied with the power of the Catholic church. In 1994 the leader of the UUP was James Molyneaux, and Ian Paisley led the DUP.

Nationalists

The basic tenet of nationalists is the aspiration to unify the island of Ireland. The main constitutional party is the Social Democratic and Labour Party (SDLP), which contests the nationalist vote with Sinn Féin, generally accepted to be the political arm of the IRA. The SDLP campaigns for internal reforms, and has accepted that unity must await the support of the majority in Northern Ireland. Sinn Féin argues that force is necessary to remove the British presence, and that its mandate is historical. Sinn Féin has refused to condemn the IRA, and has not been included in any official political talks. John Hume led the SDLP in 1994, and Gerry Adams Sinn Féin.

The Paramilitary Organisations

The republican paramilitary organisations, of which the IRA is by far the most important, believe that only force will remove the British from Ireland. Initially they saw themselves as defenders of the Northern Catholic minority, but later spread their military activities throughout Northern Ireland, Britain and Europe. There is disagreement about whether loyalist violence is essentially reactive, but certainly the pattern of loyalist violence has shadowed republican violence. There has been a major shift in the form of violence since 1990, with loyalists for the first time killing more victims than republicans. It has been speculated that this rise in loyalist violence may be connected to the failure of recent political talks.

The United Kingdom

The official British position is that Northern Ireland is part of the United Kingdom. This is shared by all parties, although the Labour Party favours Irish unity, when the majority in Northern Ireland support it. Until 1993 most political talks have aimed to restore a devolved government, with power shared between unionists and nationalists. The 1985 Anglo-Irish Agreement between the British and Irish governments accepted that the Dublin government had the right to be consulted on Northern Irish affairs.

The Irish Republic

Articles 2 and 3 of the Irish constitution lay claim to the 32 counties of Ireland, somewhat modified by the Irish government's acceptance in the Anglo-Irish Agreement that any move towards unity required the agreement of a majority in Northern Ireland. The same agreement assures the Irish government a role in Northern Irish affairs, which tends to be primarily an advocacy one for Northern nationalists.

3. THE MANAGEMENT AND RESOLUTION OF CONFLICT

'The Northern Irish problem' is a term widely used in Northern Ireland and outside as if there were an agreed and universal understanding of what it means. It is more accurate, and more productive, to consider the issue, not as a 'problem' with the implication that a solution lies around the corner for anyone ingenious enough to find it, but as a tangle of interrelated problems:

— There is a central constitutional problem: what should be the political context for the people of Northern Ireland? Integration with Britain? A united Ireland; independence?
— there is a continuing problem of social and economic inequalities, especially in the field of employment;
— there is a problem of cultural identity, relating to education, to the Irish language and to a wide range of cultural differences;
— there is clearly a problem of security;
— there is a problem of religious difference;
— there is certainly a problem of the day-to-day relationships between the people who live in Northern Ireland.

All of these are elements of the problem, but none can claim dominance. Each affects the others. Any approach to change needs to take into account all elements of the problem. Viewed against this broader context, an evaluation of conflict relations policy over the last 20 years can point to some successes: discrimination in the allocation of housing, a major grievance in 1969, has been removed; integrated schooling has been encouraged, and the segregated schools attended by the vast majority of children are required to introduce the concepts of cultural diversity and mutual understanding; minority cultural expression, especially through the use of the Irish language, has been allowed and even encouraged through the acceptance of a small number of Irish-language schools. At local government level, 11 of Northern Ireland's 26 councils were in 1993 operating a power-sharing regime, often involving rotation of the chair, and 18 had agreed to implement a community relations programme with specific and binding requirements.

On the other side of the balance, a number of major problems remain. Catholics are much more likely to be unemployed than are Protestants, more than twice as likely in the case of males. The problem of violence remains as persistent as ever. Progress towards a more general political solution has been disappointing. Since the introduction of direct rule from Westminster in 1972 there have been six attempts to reach a political accord. All have failed.

1973–74: The power-sharing Executive, which lasted for three months, remains Northern Ireland's only experience of a government shared by Catholics and Protestants. It attempted to construct a devolved system based on power-sharing between Protestants and Catholics, and on a Council of Ireland to regulate affairs between the two parts of Ireland. It was opposed by the Democratic Unionist Party and most of the Ulster Unionist party, but eventually was brought down through a Protestant workers' strike in May 1974.

1975–76: A Constitutional Convention was convened to enable elected representatives from Northern Ireland to propose their own solution. The majority unionist parties proposed a return to majority rule, modified by a committee system with some minority rights inbuilt. It was rejected by both the British and the minority SDLP.

1977–78 and 1980: Two attempts to set up devolved institutions were initiated by two Northern Ireland secretaries of state, Roy Mason and Humphrey Atkins. Neither got to first base. They were opposed, for different reasons, by the SDLP and the UUP, but both simply petered out. As a measure of the cultural gap between the two sides, two bars were set up in Stormont during the Atkins talks of 1980, one serving only non-alcoholic beverages. Students of national stereotyping may guess which bar was designed for which political parties.

1982–84: Rolling Devolution, introduced by James Prior, was perhaps the most ingenious proposal, again involving an elected assembly and a committee system. This envisaged a gradual return to power by elected representatives, but only if the proposed powers had 'widespread acceptance', defined as 70 per cent agreement. In other words, the amount of power allowed to local political parties depended on their ability to agree, and would roll along at the speed of progress determined by them. It was boycotted by the SDLP because it did not guarantee power-sharing.

1991–92: The Brooke-Mayhew initiatives sought to introduce phased talks, involving the Northern Irish parties first and the Dublin government at a later stage. This initiative followed the introduction of the Anglo-Irish Agreement in 1985, an agreement signed by the governments of the United Kingdom and the Irish Republic, but which did not involve local politicians and has been bitterly opposed by unionists. A major survey in 1990 confirmed that, for Protestants, the Anglo-Irish Agreement is still perceived to be the biggest single obstacle to peace.

Prior to 1993 Sinn Féin was excluded from all major political talks, mainly because unionist parties refused to talk with terrorists. In 1988 and 1993, however, those whom they regarded as the leaders of the SDLP and Sinn Féin held two series of bilateral talks. The consequences remain to be seen.

1993: The Downing Street Declaration, jointly announced by the Prime Minister of the United Kingdom, John Major, and the Irish Taoiseach, Albert Reynolds, introduced for the first time the possibility of Sinn Féin becoming involved in talks. The condition was an ending of violence for at least three months. In return, the Irish government accepted that any constitutional change in the status of Northern Ireland required the support of a majority within Northern Ireland. At the time of writing, three months after the Declaration, the unionist parties were divided on the initiative and Sinn Féin was still considering it. The Declaration offered, for the first time, the possibility of addressing the constitutional and security problems together as part of a peace package.

In summary, then, if a broader definition of conflict management or resolution is accepted, Northern Ireland has experience of a wide variety of approaches:

— Majority domination, from 1921 to 1972;
— Integration, for a three-month period in 1974 when a power-sharing executive was formed and failed;
— Administrative reforms, since 1969, when legislative changes covering housing, employment, social and educational reforms were introduced, with varying results;
— 'Holding the fort' with a standing army, since 1969;
— Political talks, as detailed above;
— Superordinate agreement between the two main governments, as with the Anglo-Irish Agreement in 1985.

Part Two
Government and Law

3 The Approach of Government: Community Relations and Equity

Anthony M. Gallagher

INTRODUCTION

Over 25 years ago – for the present author almost a lifetime – the present wave of violence broke out in Northern Ireland. Since that time over 3000 people have been killed and ten times that number have been injured. There been over 34 000 recorded shooting incidents and over 14 000 bombs planted: over 100 tons of explosives have been seized and a greater weight is estimated to have been exploded. Between 1972 and 1992, 15 615 people were charged with terrorist offences. Viewed from the outside the absolute level of deaths in Northern Ireland can look modest, but a more considered examination of the data should highlight the deep sense of pain and bitterness felt by many. Perhaps most starkly of all, survey evidence suggests that almost one in two people in Northern Ireland have had a friend or acquaintance killed in the violence, and almost one in ten have had a member of their family killed (Smith, 1987). Whatever the state of relations between the Protestant and Catholic communities prior to the violence, there should be no doubt that there exists a deep well of bitterness that has poisoned, and has the potential to continue poisoning, community relations. If this chapter begins by painting a pessimistic scenario, it is motivated rather by an attempt to inject a hard sense of realism. Even if the violence were to end overnight, the emotional and psychological consequences would remain with us for many years to come and this is a reality from which we should not flinch. That said, an acknowledgement of the severity of the problem should not lead us to wallow in despair: to paraphrase a famous aphorism of Antonio Gramsci, we should maintain a realistic sense of the difficulties we face while at the same time retaining an optimistic sense that they can, in time, be overcome. This is certainly the spirit in which this chapter is written.

The chapter is concerned with the specific area of community relations policy in Northern Ireland. It will examine the two main phases when government has appeared to place a priority (and perhaps more importantly, has spent money) on this area of policy. The first phase formed part of the wave of reforms which followed the outbreak of violence, but which spluttered and died in the cul-de-sac of militarism, both legal and illegal. We are still in the second phase and the consequences or effects of this policy emphasis remain unclear. A degree of optimism had seemed justified until autumn 1993, but this appeared to dissipate almost overnight following the Shankill bombing and the attack on a public house in Greysteel in October 1993. In the immediate aftermath, however, it became clear that various lines of communication had been operating between the British and Irish governments, and the IRA, in an attempt to create conditions for a cessation of violence. Twenty-three deaths in a fortnight shocked the community and appear to have speeded up the deliberations of the various participants to these talks, culminating in the Downing Street Declaration (15 December 1993). As this chapter was being written a definitive response from the paramilitary organisations to the declaration was awaited.

INITIAL STEPS

Following the outbreak of violence and a virtual descent into anarchy in Northern Ireland, the British government sent in troops in August 1969 to restore order. Direct involvement of the British soldiers was inevitably followed by direct involvement of British politicians and ministers: hitherto a convention had been established in Westminster such that all Northern Ireland business, apart from a few limited areas of policy, was within the purview of the region's parliament in Belfast. This is turn led to a wave of reform measures, from 1969 onwards, designed to address some of the most grievous inequities that had inspired the Northern Ireland civil rights campaign. Inter alia these reform measures addressed such issues as the voting arrangements for local authorities, the procedures for determining electoral boundaries, the allocation of housing and the creation of procedures whereby citizens could seek redress for complaints of maladministration by public bodies. These measures were to be closely followed by the establishment of commissions to examine the causes and consequences of particular periods of violence, and to examine policing in Northern Ireland. The linchpin of this reform package was the agreed statement, known as the Downing Street Declaration (August 1969: *plus ça change!*), between the governments in London and Belfast that:

> in all legislation and executive decisions of Government every citizen of Northern Ireland is entitled to the same equality of treatment and freedom from discrimination as obtains in the rest of the United Kingdom irrespective of political views or religion. (House of Commons, Cmnd 4154 and 4158)

In the same month it was announced that a Community Relations Board (later Commission), was to be established, with half its members drawn from each community in Northern Ireland. The next month a Minister of Community Relations was appointed to the Belfast government, although he was to be the first of three ministers within a two-year period. The Community Relations Commission (CRC) was abolished and its functions taken over by the SDLP Minister of Community Relations in the power-sharing Executive in 1974. The ministry disappeared with the fall of the Executive and the establishment of direct rule from Westminster.

COMMUNITY RELATIONS COMMISSION

The CRC was closely modelled on the UK Commission formed to deal with 'race' issues in Britain. Its functions included the encouragement of bodies active in promoting improved community relations, advice to government, the provision of educational and other programmes, and the commissioning or carrying out of research on community relations themes.

In practice these formal terms of reference were pursued in a number of ways: the CRC supported activities designed to promote contact between Protestants and Catholics in Northern Ireland, not least because of the high level of social segregation in terms of housing and education. Perhaps more centrally, the CRC adopted a community development strategy designed to raise the self-confidence of local communities through voluntary organisations in the hope that, eventually, these local groups would feel sufficiently secure to begin dealing with people across the sectarian divide. A number of fieldworkers were employed to keep the CRC in touch with feelings on the ground as this was felt to be important if the Commission was to be able to advise government on the shifting state of community-relations at any time. In the area of education the CRC supported inter-school contact schemes, and supported a variety of publications and conferences. A number of research projects were supported in the local and other universities and a research team was established within the Commission to enable quick response to events.

MINISTRY OF COMMUNITY RELATIONS

The main executive function of the ministry was to administer the 'Social Needs Fund' through which resources could be directed at areas of relative social deprivation. Thereafter its primary role was to oversee the CRC. Maurice Hayes, the first Chair of the CRC, was critical of the very notion of a specific ministry: in a 1972 lecture, delivered after he had resigned his post in the CRC, he argued that:

> the problem of community relations, of ensuring that people can live together in a society ... [is the] central problem of Government. ... If it fails in that, government has failed. Neither is there such a thing as a separate 'community relations' policy. All the decisions of government, whether about education, location of industry, housing or law-enforcement, have an effect on relationships between the communities. (Hayes, 1972)

To locate governmental responsibility within a single, small ministry was, he argued, to marginalise the issue.

As indicated above, the effect was in fact somewhat more dramatic, in that the minister in the power-sharing Executive abolished the CRC altogether. The overt reason for this decision was that the political settlement of power-sharing had obviated the need for a community relations commission. At a more implicit level, however, it seems clear that politicians were suspicious of the community development strategy being promoted by the CRC, not least because a strengthened voluntary sector could provide an alternative basis for community leadership.

THE END OF THE BEGINNING

Whatever the direct reasons for the demise of the official community relations infrastructure, by the mid-1970s it was gone, although in many ways its disappearance was merely a symptom of how the head of steam had dissipated from the entire reform agenda. There was to be one more significant piece of reform legislation passed in 1976, the Fair Employment (Northern Ireland) Act, but the date of its passing is probably best explained by disruptions to the legislative agenda in Westminster because of domestic British political issues as by anything else.

By the mid-1970s the absolute level of violence, as measured by death-rates, had declined from its 1972 peak, but Northern Ireland appeared to face a 'stable' level of violence, self-contradictory though that notion seems. Nor was the only source of extra-legal violence now from the republican side: in response to apparent IRA successes, including the abolition of the local parliament in Belfast, loyalist paramilitaries had taken up the gun in a series of random sectarian assassinations. There was a period also when it appeared as if a military logic was driving government policy, with the twin strategies of 'criminalisation' and 'Ulsterisation' holding the promise of a military victory over the IRA. Such 'promise' as these strategies held reached their denouement with the hunger-strikes by republican prisoners in 1980–1 and the subsequent electoral rise of Sinn Féin.

In so far as a momentum had built up around community relations activity, this was dissipated as elements of the activity were spread out among various groups and organisations. Departmental responsibility devolved to the Department of Education for Northern Ireland (DENI), which provided financial support for community relations work in schools and through voluntary organisations. The role of the CRC field officers devolved to district councils which developed Community Services Departments and employed Community Services Officers. It seems clear, however, that the practice of these departments became less and less influenced by any community relations considerations and were limited even in the extent to which they contributed to community development:

> the majority of the money available to District Councils appears to have been spent on resources and community centres. The Community Services Officers are subsequently heavily weighed down with administrative and managerial duties, often at the expense of any community development work. (Frazer and Fitzduff, 1991)

Apart from the DENI contribution, perhaps the strongest thread of continuity in community relations work was that provided by reconciliation groups. The focus of many of these groups was to provide opportunities for Protestants and Catholics to meet in a situation where patterns of segregation were, if anything, becoming more profound. This theme of increasing contact across the sectarian divide was taken up particularly strongly by those who advocated religiously integrated schools. Throughout the 1970s a number of attempts were made to provide a legal context whereby the development of integrated schools would be encouraged, and also to encourage the churches to promote the conversion of existing schools into integrated schools. The lack of success in these attempts prompted one group to establish an integrated secondary school, Lagan College, in 1980 to serve as a model for others to follow.

There was some action also on economic issues. In 1983 the DENI funded the 'Belfast Areas of Need' (BAN) initiative to enable Belfast City Council to improve community relations. Unfortunately there was little clear sense in the programme of what community relations meant or of the relative effectiveness of different forms of action:

> The chief result from this was a general increase in the support for the principle of improving community relations, although many felt, in common with other groups attempting to work in this area, that adequate theory or practice to effectively fulfil their objectives were at present lacking. (Frazer and Fitzduff, 1991)

THE BEGINNING OF THE END?

This period of disparate action and conceptual confusion was to change fundamentally in the latter half of the 1980s. This change is best characterised by a number of features. First, government established a clear and explicit community relations policy which emphasised three objectives: (a) to increase opportunities for contact between Protestants and Catholics; (b) to encourage tolerance of cultural pluralism; and (c) to seek to achieve equality of opportunity for all citizens in Northern Ireland. Secondly, a community relations infrastructure was re-established with the creation of the Central Community Relations Unit (CCRU) in 1987, within the Central Secretariat of the NI Civil Service and of the Northern Ireland Community Relations Council (NICRC), in 1990; thirdly, new legislation to combat discrimination in employment and a set of education reforms came into effect in 1990: both pieces of legislation have significant community relations implications. Alongside these specific initiatives more government money was made available for community relations work.

The first question that might be asked of this apparent sea change in policy terms is: why did it happen? Although it is tempting to try to identify the single most important factor, in practice it seems likely that it was the confluence of a number of mutually reinforcing developments that provided the spur to action.

First, at a political level the post-hunger-strike period saw the electoral rise of Sinn Féin and the failure of one of the more imaginative attempts to provide a context for political agreement through the Northern Ireland Assembly and 'rolling devolution' (O'Leary, Elliott and Wilford, 1988). Alongside these political developments there seemed to be no end to the persistent level of violence.

Secondly, external pressure on the British government helped to spur action. This pressure can be seen from a number of sources. The MacBride Campaign (Equal Opportunities Review, 1986) against employment discrimination began to achieve some success in the United States and called into question government's stated commitment to eradicate discrimination. The 1985 Anglo-Irish Agreement (Hadden and Boyle, 1989) did not provide the Irish government with executive authority over Northern Ireland, but a new voice did begin to permeate policy discussions on Northern Irish issues: at the very least this will have widened the boundaries of the possible on policy options.

Thirdly, there was pressure also on the issue of fair employment from other quarters. In 1985 the Standing Advisory Commission on Human Rights (SACHR) initiated a review of the 1976 Fair Employment Act which included a series of research evaluations by the Policy Research Institute (Smith and Chambers, 1991). The results of this review were critical of the effectiveness of the 1976 Act and of the Fair Employment Agency (FEA). The SACHR added its voice to those who argued for additional and strengthened legislation.

A fourth factor was increased concern about the need for specific community relations activity. One of the more significant aspects of this resulted from a paper prepared for the Standing Advisory Commission on Human Rights by Hugh Frazer and Mari Fitzduff (Frazer and Fitzduff, 1991). The paper examined the history of community relations policy in Northern Ireland and considered ways in which community relations might be improved. Its main recommendation was for the creation of a new Community Relations

Agency, an idea to be taken up albeit with different nomenclature. Inter alia the successful independent activity of parents in establishing integrated schools can be seen as a further spur in this area: the parents proved that it could be done, but insisted that government support was necessary to underpin and accelerate the process (Moffat, 1993).

Outside observers of the Northern Ireland Civil Service (NICS) often perceive it as a homogeneous machine, constantly moving in a single, planned direction. While it is undoubtedly true that there are occasions where the NICS can and does close ranks, anyone who has worked closely with government departments will confirm that they are more often akin to a series of 'warring tribes', with the focus of disputes revolving round issues of resources or, on occasion, the demarcation of policy responsibility. The key point here is that a dynamic exists within the NICS and that much policy discussion is subject to argument and disagreement. The relevance for the present discussion is that this dynamic appears to be the fifth influence on the new policy emphasis on community relations. There is a fairly widespread consensus among researchers that the arrival of specific individuals in key positions within the NICS helped to strengthen the grounds for a policy shift: specifically, it would appear that some of these individuals both believed that something ought to be done and that something could be done. It is, of course, difficult to assess fully the importance of this factor because of the secrecy surrounding internal NICS policy discussions, but to neglect the potential role of this factor would be to work with an incomplete picture. Less speculative is the role of Dr Brian Mawhinney, to date the only Northern Ireland born MP to serve as a minister in the region. While some of Dr Mawhinney's views on community relations could be described as a little simplistic, it is undoubtedly true that he placed strong emphasis on the possible beneficial effects of increased contact between Protestants and Catholics and his views did have an impact on the development of policy.

Having examined the broad outlines of the new policy environment and some of the factors that seemed to have influenced its development, we now turn to an examination of some of the substantive measures that have been pursued. We will examine these under the three primary elements of the government's community relations policy, (a) Protestant/Catholic contact, (b) cultural pluralism and (c) equity. In addition we will look at the role of the CCRU within this policy environment.

PROTESTANT/CATHOLIC CONTACT

The government has taken on a commitment to encourage greater contact between Protestants and Catholics in Northern Ireland. Under the Education Reform Order (1989), which in broad terms mirrored the reform strategy in Britain, government adopted a commitment to support initiatives towards the development of planned integrated schools (Gallagher, Osborne and Cormack, 1993). In particular, it was made possible for an existing school to opt for integrated status through a parental ballot. On the basis that most pupils are likely to be educated in *de facto* religiously segregated schools for the foreseeable future, the Reform Order also provided that Education for Mutual Understanding (EMU) would form a compulsory cross-curricular theme in the new common curriculum. Although schemes involving contact between pupils in Protestant and Catholic schools are encouraged as part of EMU, this is not a compulsory part of EMU work. However, financial support is available from the DENI, through the Cross Community Contact Scheme, for schools which wish to incorporate contact activities as part of EMU.

More generally, government financial support is available to groups within the community that wish to engage in cross-community contact work. Initially these funds were provided by the CCRU but during 1993 responsibility for the disbursement of grant has devolved to the NICRC. In addition the NICRC provides advice and support through publications, conferences and its Development Officers.

CULTURAL PLURALISM

Under the Education Reform Order (1989) a second cross-curricular theme linked to community relations was established as part of the common curriculum: Cultural Heritage. This theme addresses the difficult, because often divisive, issues of history and culture. That history was taught differently in Protestant and Catholic schools prior to the outbreak of the present conflict was one of the first issues to be addressed in education, and this attention led to the development of new, improved history textbooks (Magee, 1970; Darby, 1974). The incorporation of Cultural Heritage in the common curriculum has provided a further spur to the publication of curricular materials on cultural and historical themes.

At a more general level, after the establishment of the CCRU a group of people were invited to form the Cultural Traditions Group in order to explore ways of enhancing tolerance of and respect for cultural pluralism in Northern Ireland. The Cultural Traditions Group was incorporated into the NICRC in 1990. Initially the Group sponsored three conferences on aspects of pluralism, but currently its role covers a wider range of schemes: there is financial support for projects and organisations working to generate wider understanding and appreciation of local cultural traditions; finance is available to support publications and other media dealing with cultural and historical themes; and a series of Cultural Traditions Fellowships has been established to support specific projects carried out by individuals.

EQUITY

Under the equity heading a number of initiatives can be identified, largely within the economic and employment spheres of policy. In July 1988 the government launched the Making Belfast Work (MBW) initiative in order to tackle urban decay, poverty, unemployment and social deprivation. Over the following five years a total of £124m was spent on MBW and a similar initiative was launched in Derry/Londonderry.

The Fair Employment Act (1989) significantly strengthened anti-discrimination legislation by mandating employers to monitor the religious composition of their workforce on an annual basis, outlawing indirect discrimination and providing a legal basis for affirmative action measures to ameliorate religious imbalances in workforces. In addition, the resources available to the Fair Employment Commission (FEC), which replaced the FEA, were increased, and a separate body, the Fair Employment Tribunal (FET), was established to judge alleged cases of individual discrimination.

These initiatives were set within a broader policy context by the announcement, in 1991, that Targeting Social Need (TSN) was to form the third public spending priority for government in Northern Ireland (Brooke, 1991). The rationale and purpose of TSN was set as twofold: on the one hand the strategy would imply that resources would be skewed towards areas of greatest social need in order to improve the social and economic conditions of the most disadvantaged areas and people in Northern Ireland. On the other hand, because of the economic and social inequities between the two communities to the disadvantage of Catholics, TSN-led decisions should, in principle, reduce community differentials.

Having outlined some of the policy initiatives that have been developed within the community relations policy, we now turn to a brief examination of the role taken by the CCRU.

THE ROLE OF THE CCRU

Within the context of declared government policy on community relations, the CCRU has three broadly defined roles: first, to ensure that policy decisions within government are informed by an evaluation of their possible effect on community relations; secondly, to review, periodically, the most important policies and programmes to assess their impact on community relations; and thirdly, to develop new ideas about improving community relations and supporting those working to improve relations and reduce prejudice. The overall thrust of these aims emphasises the role of CCRU within the governmental system. That said, until such time as a community relations infrastructure was developed, CCRU spent much of its time engaging with community and voluntary organisations.

As indicated above, in the early years of CCRU much of its time was devoted to grant-aiding groups and individuals engaged in community relations work, although this role has since lessened as NICRC has taken on much of this function. Despite this change, CCRU still funds specific projects among which the most notable is the district councils programme (see Chapter 4).

As the grant-awarding side of CCRU's activity reduces, the equity dimension to its work has become more important. Within this policy context CCRU has responsibility for carrying out the five-year review of the Fair Employment Act (1989), provides a lead on the TSN initiative, and has been coordinating proposals on the equal opportunity proofing of government policy and practice. In addition, CCRU has more recently taken a lead on discussions concerning the possible extension of British 'race' relations legislation to Northern Ireland. Much of this work is related to CCRU's role *vis-à-vis* government departments.

An additional feature of CCRU's work has been to support research. The unit's research strategy places a priority on research concerned with the evaluation of public policies and programmes, the dynamics of conflict, locality studies and comparative research. A review of CCRU's research strategy has been carried out and this is likely to lead to a new statement of research priorities in 1994.

WHERE ARE WE NOW?

In this final section of the chapter we will attempt briefly to assess the impact of community relations policy to date, beginning with the amount of activity generated in the community relations area. On this level the policy has clearly been successful: because of the new money and new expertise available in this area, the sheer amount of community relations activity that is currently being carried out in Northern Ireland is impressive. This enhancement of activity is aided by the NICRC and the networks it has provided, and by its general policy of directing funds towards new initiatives rather than activity which was already under way. Furthermore, the fact that government now requires that funded initiatives are evaluated seems likely to focus attention on the effectiveness of these activities. In education the arrival of the common curriculum and the mandatory cross-curricular themes of EMU and Cultural Heritage will ensure that, on some level at least, most young people will have an opportunity to gain some awareness of community relations issues, while over a third of all schools in Northern Ireland are now involved in contact activities. The Cultural Traditions programme has ensured a steady supply of ideas, books and teaching materials on historical issues. There has been a steady growth in the number of planned integrated schools. And on a somewhat different tack, the first years of the Fair Employment Act (1989) have been notably successful with an efficient and unproblematic implementation of religious monitoring, and the adoption by the Fair Employment Tribunal of a markedly robust stance (Rubenstein, 1993).

If we now move from the amount of activity generated by community relations policy to look at the impact of that activity, the picture is as yet unclear. We do not know, for example, the shape and form that EMU and Cultural Heritage are taking in the classroom, never mind what the consequences are for the attitudes and perceptions of school pupils. The limited evidence available on the impact of integrated schools is positive insofar as it suggests that the pupils in at least one school mix and work together, and that these friendship patterns are sustained beyond the school (Irwin, 1993). There appear to be some differences also on the desired or expected scope of integrated education even among the advocates and supporters of this strategy (compare, for example, the ambitions for integrated education expressed by Stephen, 1993, and Linehan, Kennedy and Sister Anna, 1993).

Analyses of the 1991 Northern Ireland Census suggest some evidence of an improvement in the occupational opportunities available to Catholics, although this is within the context of persisting broad patterns of employment differentials and, perhaps more importantly, a continuing unemployment gap to the disadvantage of Catholics (Cormack, Gallagher and Osborne, 1993; Gallagher, Osborne and Cormack, 1994). Furthermore, while the first few years of the Fair Employment Act (1989) appear to have been successful, it remains unclear what the nature and impact of affirmative action measures will be: this is particularly significant since affirmative action was identified as the main vehicle of change in the fair employment strategy. It would seem, therefore, that more experience and information will be needed before we can make a more considered judgement on the impact of aspects of community relations policy.

On another level, however, there does appear to be some indication of a more fundamental problem within community relations policy, although depending on one's viewpoint this could be described as either 'dynamic tension' or 'conceptual confusion'. This can be seen in a number of diverse areas and here we will illustrate the point by briefly examining issues that have arisen in the way people are coming to terms with the past; the SACHR research on education which highlighted the potential clash between integration and pluralism; and finally, the implementation of certain aspects of economic policy by government.

In the area of history it is unclear whether we are trying to achieve a sense of historical commonality or one of historical pluralism, or indeed both. There is a risk that some historical writing is predicated on an attempt to knock down the sacred cows of one tradition or another, a process that is relatively easy to do given the empirical fragility of nationalist and unionist conceptions of the past. It is true also, however, that the empirical fragility of long-held historical traditions is not solely a feature of Northern Ireland, but can be said to be true of almost all national histories. Moreover, if historical revisionism is seen to be directed at particular communities, or particular sections of the communities in Northern Ireland, it could serve to alienate people who feel their traditions are being devalued, ignored or denied, rather than providing a basis whereby all can come to celebrate the plurality of traditions and influences that shape our present circumstances.

In education the consequences of the SACHR research on the funding of Protestant and Catholic schools in Northern Ireland can be interpreted in a number of different ways (Gallagher, Osborne and Cormack, 1993). In essence, this research highlighted the consequences of differential funding arrangements for Protestant and Catholic schools and, in particular, linked this to the higher proportion of unqualified leavers from Catholic schools. Following the publication of the results the government announced additional resources to increase the number of places available in Catholic grammar schools, established a system to monitor the impact of policy and practice on the Protestant, Catholic and integrated school systems, and increased the level of capital grant available to Catholic schools to 100 per cent. One interpretation of these consequences would be to decry the underpinning of segregated schooling. An alternative view might suggest that government had demonstrated its commitment to equitable treatment of the different school systems and that this, in itself, underpins the legitimacy of pluralism.

The third area of economic policy is probably the most problematic. On the face of it the fact that TSN has been established as the third public spending priority in Northern Ireland is impressive. However, it is unclear whether the TSN approach is primarily geared towards reducing differentials between the two communities in Northern Ireland, or whether it is more of an anti-poverty programme geared towards objective levels of social need. In addition, it is difficult to identify any significant spending decision that can be independently attributed to the TSN priority. While the CCRU has played, and continues to play, a vital role in pushing the community relations agenda forward within government, it does appear to be understaffed at a time when its own policy agenda gets ever wider.

The tensions within community relations policy can be considered on a more general level: is it seeking to identify the factors we hold in common in Northern Ireland, or is it attempting to acknowledge, legitimate and, in the best of all possible worlds, celebrate the things we hold differently? Is it part of a process which seeks to isolate extremists, however they are defined, or is it seeking inclusive strategies to create ways in which as many people as possible can be included in a peaceful settlement?

Lest these questions be seen as unduly pessimistic, it should be kept in mind that evidence from the Northern Ireland Social

Attitudes Survey suggests that, at least until 1991, people did feel that community relations were improving in Northern Ireland and this was undoubtedly linked, to some degree, to the increased activity in this area from the mid-1980s onwards (Gallagher, 1992). In addition, the Opsahl process demonstrated the creativity and imagination in Northern Ireland that stands in marked contrast to the apparent stasis that has afflicted political discussions here for so many years (Pollak, 1993). The tensions within policy should perhaps obviate the fears of those who think they can discern a conspiratorial subtext to community relations policy: any effective conspiracy would seem to require a more clearly defined and unitary policy. But perhaps the tensions can be turned to positive effect as we recognise the difficult nature of the questions and options raised by the idea of community relations, and explore possible visions of what 'good' community relations would look like. After such a protracted period of violence which has touched so many people, tackling these questions and exploring these possibilities is perhaps more important than ever. It may well be, in fact, that the range of activities described and examined in these last few pages have helped create the conditions when it was possible to believe that an end to violence might occur. If there is any general lesson to be derived from this brief examination of community relations policy over the term of the present conflict it is that these questions slipped from the policy agenda once before. We must not let them slip through our hands again.

REFERENCES

Brooke, P. (1991) Opening Address, in *Review of Employment Equality in Northern Ireland*. Belfast, Central Community Relations Unit.

Cormack, R. J., A. M. Gallagher and R. D. Osborne (1993) *Fair Enough?* Belfast, Fair Employment Commission.

Darby, J. (1974) 'History in the Schools: a Review Article', *Community Forum*, 4: 2, 37–42.

Equal Opportunities Review (1986) 'The MacBride Principles', *Equal Opportunities Review*, 8, 16–21.

Frazer, H. and M. Fitzduff (1991) *Improving Community Relations*. Belfast, Northern Ireland Community Relations Council.

Gallagher, A. M. (1992) 'Community Relations in Northern Ireland' in *British Social Attitudes: the 9th Report*, ed. by R. Jowell, L. Brook, G. Prior and B. Taylor. Aldershot, Dartmouth.

Gallagher, A. M., R. D. Osborne and R. J. Cormack (1993) 'Community Relations, Equality and Education', in *After the Reforms: Education and Policy in Northern Ireland*, ed. by R. D. Osborne, R. J. Cormack and A. M. Gallagher. Aldershot, Avebury.

Gallagher, A. M., R. D. Osborne and R. J. Cormack. (1994) *Occupations, Industry and Religion in the 1991 Census*. Belfast, Fair Employment Commission.

Hadden, T. and K. Boyle (1989) *The Anglo-Irish Agreement: Commentary, Text and Official Review*. London, Sweet and Maxwell; Dublin, Edward Higel.

Hayes, M. (1972) *The Role of the Community Relations Commission in Northern Ireland*. London, Runnymede Trust.

Irwin, C. (1993) 'Making Integrated Education Work for Pupils' in *Education Together for a Change*, ed. by C. Moffat. Belfast, Fortnight Educational Trust.

Linehan, C., M. Kennedy and Sister Anna (1993) 'The Essential Role of the Churches in Supporting Integrated Education', in *Education Together for a Change*, ed. by C. Moffat. Belfast, Fortnight Educational Trust.

Magee, J. (1970) 'The Teaching of Irish History in Irish Schools', *Northern Teacher*, 10, 1, 15–21.

Moffat, C. (1993) *Education Together for a Change*. Belfast, Fortnight Educational Trust.

O'Leary, C., S. Elliott and R. Wilford (1988) *The Northern Ireland Assembly 1982–1986: a Constitutional Experiment*. London, Hurst.

Pollak, A. (1993) *A Citizens' Inquiry: the Opsahl Report on Northern Ireland*. Dublin, Lilliput Press; Belfast, Initiative 92.

Rubenstein, M. (1993) *Fair Employment Case Law*. Belfast, Fair Employment Commission.

Smith, D. J. (1987) *Equality and Inequality in Northern Ireland Part 3: Perceptions and Views*. London, Policy Studies Institute.

Smith, D. J. and G. Chambers (1991) *Inequality in Northern Ireland*. Oxford, Clarendon Press.

Stephen, F. (1993) 'Integrated Education in Northern Ireland: Current Provision and Legislation', in *Education Together for a Change*, ed. by C. Moffat. Belfast, Fortnight Educational Trust.

4 Local Government and Community Relations
Colin Knox and Joanne Hughes

THE CONTEXT FOR COMMUNITY RELATIONS IN LOCAL
GOVERNMENT

Local government and community relations could appear, to the
sceptical observer of events in Northern Ireland, as a contradiction
in terms. As early as 1922 the unionist government consolidated its
grip on local politics through the Local Government (NI) Act which
replaced proportional representation with majority voting, redrew
ward boundaries and altered the franchise by incorporating property ownership as a qualification for the vote (O'Dowd et al., 1980).
Such actions were hardly those of a government intent on living har-
moniously with the minority community. For civil rights campaigners of the late 1960s local authorities epitomised unionist
domination and abuse of power. Allegations of discrimination in
jobs and housing, alongside gerrymandering of local authority
boundaries and restricted franchise, precipitated the civil disturbances of 1968. In the wake of considerable violence, housing was
removed from the remit of local government and a centralised
agency, the Northern Ireland Housing Executive, created. This decision on housing shaped future administrative reforms, proposed in
the Macrory Report (1970). The report divided services into
regional (requiring large administrative units) and district (suitable
for small areas) services. The Stormont parliament was to take
responsibility for regional services and district councils would
administer local services. Macrory recommended the establishment
of 26 borough or district councils and the setting up of appointed
area boards to decentralise the administration of health and education services. The recommendations were subsequently passed into
law under the Local Government (NI) Act 1972. Macrory's proposals were overtaken by the suspension of Stormont in 1972, and the
responsibility for regional services now lies with the British government (direct rule) working administratively through the Northern

Ireland Office. Since the reorganisation of local government in 1973, the 26 district councils in Northern Ireland have been responsible for a limited range of public services, principally refuse collection, street cleaning and the provision of leisure and recreation facilities. Their relatively minor role is illustrated by a current expenditure budget of £170m (Department of the Environment, 1992) from a total public expenditure purse of £7 bn (Department of Finance and Personnel and H.M. Treasury, 1992).

Yet local authorities are important, apart from the executive functions they undertake. First, as the only democratically elected forum in Northern Ireland since the demise of the Northern Ireland Assembly in 1986, they are of symbolic significance. Secondly, in the absence of any devolved government, councillors are the most accessible source for constituents with concerns over education, health, housing and other mainstream services, over which local government has no direct control. Thirdly, councils employ about 9000 people in an economy which is noted for its high level of unemployment (14.2 per cent) (Department of Finance and Personnel and H.M. Treasury, 1992).

Given the lack of any other constitutional platform, local councillors indulge in political debate and occasionally skirmishes which have little to do with their executive functions. As observers have noted: 'While denuded of powers, the councils have functioned as the major indigenous arenas for politics during most of the direct rule period'(O'Leary, Elliott and Wilford, 1988: 63).

From 1973 to 1985 clashes with the British government occurred over security policy and resulted in a semi-boycott of council meetings in 1981. Acrimony heightened in 1985 when Sinn Féin councillors were elected to local authorities and the situation deteriorated further following the Anglo-Irish Agreement in November of the same year (Knox, 1990). Unionist-controlled councils became the vehicle for protests against the Agreement which included suspending council business and in some cases refusing to strike a district rate. After a sustained campaign of opposition, unionist councils drifted back to normal business due, inter alia, to concerns that their refusal to meet with government ministers had the potential to delay social and economic progress in their areas (Connolly and Knox, 1988). The local government elections of 1989 marked a turning point in council chambers with a degree of moderation not unrelated to the decline in representation from the political extremes. Dungannon District Council led the way with an experiment in 'responsibility sharing' prompted by its unanimous opposition to the

Enniskillen Remembrance Day bombing (November 1987). Other councils followed suit in the wake of the 1989 elections. Eight local authorities (Armagh, Derry, Down, Dungannon, Fermanagh, Limavady, Newry and Mourne, and Omagh) appointed mayors/ chairmen and deputies from both political traditions. A spirit of cooperation emerged in some councils which has proved useful in tackling issues arising from the Local Government (Miscellaneous Provisions) (Northern Ireland) Order 1992 – the introduction of compulsory competitive tendering and an increase in the role of councils in economic development. Such was the climate within which local councils became involved in the community relations initiative.

AN EMERGING COMMUNITY RELATIONS POLICY AGENDA

Before describing the details of the community relations programme it is important to locate the initiative within a broader approach by government designed to achieve equality and equity. Set alongside efforts at the macro level to achieve progress on the economic, social, political and security fronts, a series of equality and equity initiatives were devised by government to tackle the root causes of the underlying divisions and tensions in Northern Ireland. The stated objectives of the government in relation to equality and equity illustrate both the breadth and depth of its intent:

— to ensure that everyone enjoys equality of opportunity and equity of treatment;
— to increase the level of cross-community contact;
— to encourage greater mutual understanding and respect of the different cultures and traditions. (Department of Finance and Personnel and HM Treasury, 1992: 142)

This policy is operationalised via specific initiatives, examples of which include 'Targeting Social Need', schemes such as 'Making Belfast Work' and the 'Londonderry Initiative' – aimed at regenerating the heart of Belfast and Londonderry – and comprehensive fair employment legislation. Importantly, within the education sector, developments such as integrated education, Education for Mutual Understanding (EMU) and the cross-community contact scheme all represent a commitment on the part of the government to the objectives outlined. The government-sponsored programme of community relations is a key component of the equality and equity strategy.

Community relations re-emerged on the Northern Ireland policy agenda in 1987 when the then Secretary of State, Tom King, set up a Central Community Relations Unit (CCRU) to advise him on all aspects of relations between the two traditions. Previous attempts at improving community relations in the early seventies, by establishing an independent Community Relations Commission and a Ministry of Community Relations, had failed. The government recognised that it had a role to play in formulating and sponsoring policies which improved relations through the administration of public services. CCRU reports directly to the Head of the Northern Ireland Civil Service and is charged with formulating, reviewing and challenging policy *throughout* the government system with the aim of improving community relations. All Northern Ireland government departments are therefore required to scrutinise critically their policies and programmes to ensure that community relations issues have been taken into account in delivering key services such as education, health, housing and economic development. CCRU was also charged with developing new ideas which would improve relations and supporting ongoing efforts aimed at reducing prejudice. In short, community relations was propelled into the heart of the government's decision-making process within the civil service.

Several initiatives, supported by government funding, aimed at improving cross-community contacts followed. In September 1987 £250 000 was made available by the Department of Education to promote cross-community contact among young people under 19, and to provide new resources for groups already working in the field of peace and reconciliation. Activities seeking assistance under the schemes had to 'improve cross-community understanding, be in addition to existing activity, be purposeful, and wherever possible, result in ongoing contacts between young people from the two communities' (Northern Ireland Information Service, 1987). Overall the Department of Education had a budget of £750 000 for community relations to complement the work of the newly established CCRU. As part of education reform in Northern Ireland the minister also included education for mutual understanding (EMU) and cultural heritage as compulsory cross-curricular themes.

Such was the 'success' of the cross-community scheme, as measured by the number of applications for assistance and the subsequent involvement of some 400 schools (about one-third of all schools in Northern Ireland), that a wider ranging £2m initiative was launched in February 1989. This not only included an extra £250 000 to expand the existing cross-community scheme for young people but also the formation of a Cultural Traditions Group and the creation of a new charitable body (January 1990), the Northern Ireland Community Relations Council to provide a focal point and resource centre for all those working to improve community relations. The latter aimed to establish a forum for a range of ad hoc groups already involved in the field – the Churches Central Committee for Community Work, the Corrymeela Community, the Inter-Church Group on Faith and Politics, the Northern Consensus Group, Peace and Reconciliation – Derry, Quaker Peace and Service, and the Two Traditions Group. The Cultural Traditions Group, with a budget of £1m and under the leadership of the former NI Controller of the BBC, was charged with designing programmes in the arts, media, museums and education which would encourage a more constructive debate about the cultural traditions in Northern Ireland.

Finally, the government offered financial assistance to local councils if all constitutional parties agreed to initiate a community relations programme. The important condition of the offer was the fact that 'constitutional parties', which excluded Sinn Féin, had to 'agree' a programme, thereby pre-empting partisan wrangling.

LOCAL GOVERNMENT – THE ANTITHESIS OF EQUALITY AND EQUITY

Such a magnanimous gesture towards councils on the part of the government seemed somewhat at odds with its official stance on expanding their functions. Since the reorganisation of local government in 1973 discussions about its role have focused on whether major powers should be restored or not, with unionists in favour of devolution and nationalists opposed to it. Article 4 of the 1985 Anglo-Irish Agreement allows for the transfer of power to locally elected representatives but there is a marked reluctance on the part of government in regard to such moves. A former Minister of State at the Northern Ireland Office summarised the government's position:

If we are to give more power to local authorities, it must be done on the basis that is widely acceptable and ensures *fair and equitable* treatment for all the local council areas. It is clear that is not the case in all areas of the Province at present.... (Mawhinney, 1991a: 963; authors' emphasis)

Such remarks, by a minister, did not conjure up an image of local councils at the forefront of a government strategy to achieve greater equality and equity.

Of particular concern is the record of fair employment *within* councils, given their new role in community relations. Evidence of employment patterns in local councils emerged from investigations carried out under the Fair Employment Agency and latterly the Fair Employment Commission. The first round of employment monitoring returns from the 26 district councils revealed that they employed 8678 individuals, accounting for 6 per cent of Northern Ireland's public sector employees. The composition of the workforce by religion showed that 66.2 per cent were Protestant and 33.8 per cent Roman Catholic. This compared with a 'probable economically active community' comprising 62 per cent Protestant and 38 per cent Roman Catholic. Disaggregating the workforce by standard occupational classification (SOC) revealed in SOC1 (managers and administrators) that Protestant and Roman Catholic proportions were 75.1 per cent and 24.9 per cent respectively (Fair Employment Commission, 1991a: 33–5). The evidence, therefore, suggested an imbalance in representation at the general level, compared with the population profile, but more specifically an imbalance at the highest grades of employment. This was subsequently confirmed in a survey of the composition of *senior staff* throughout the public sector in Northern Ireland, undertaken by the Commission. The senior staff profile in district councils, defined in three bands (£16–25k, £23–25k and £35k+), revealed 78 per cent Protestant employees and 22 per cent Roman Catholic – the table summarises the information. This composite position obscured a high 81.6 per cent Protestant workforce in the middle band (£23–25k) compared with 18.4 per cent Roman Catholics (Fair Employment Commission, 1992: 26–7).

Table 4.1   Fair Employment Statistics – District Councils

	Protestant %	Roman Catholic %
Economically active persons	62.0	38.0
District Council employees	66.2	33.8
District Council employees in SOC1	75.1	24.9
Senior staff in District Councils	78.0	22.0

At the level of individual local authorities, fair employment tribu-
nals have handed down a series of verdicts finding discrimination
against Catholics. In 1992 alone, five councils (Belfast, North Down,
Ballymena, Limavady and Dungannon) have been found guilty of
unlawful discrimination. One case in particular illustrates the
excesses involved. Belfast City Council suspended its Catholic Senior
Community Services Officer for writing a newspaper article in
defence of people in Catholic west Belfast. The Commission found
that the decision to suspend the officer 'was influenced by political
considerations' (Fair Employment Commission, 1991b: 69). In
engaging a new employee for the post, a Protestant candidate was
appointed in competition with five Catholics. The Fair Employment
Tribunal found that, compared to the candidate appointed, all five
were better qualified educationally and had more relevant
experience (McKittrick, 1992).

It must, of course, be accepted that Belfast City Council is something of an aberration in local authority terms and its image has
proved a major drawback for progressive authorities committed to
cross-community consensus and the delivery of local services. Indeed
a number of councils have had remarkable achievements in areas
such as economic development, waste disposal, tourism and leisure
provision. That said, Dungannon District Council, a local authority
much praised for its exemplary 'responsibility sharing' (a euphemism
for power sharing) between political parties, recently paid compensation resulting from unlawful discrimination in a clerical appointment.

Why then has the government chosen to locate community relations as a function within the remit of local councils, given their
record in this regard? Local authorities would not seem to be a natural choice for government to further the cause of equality and equity.
Alternative arrangements could have applied, such as the direct
employment of community relations officers by the Community Relations Council, a well-respected independent voluntary body, or by
CCRU. Some clues to the policy background are evident from ministerial answers in Parliament. In commenting on the response of two
separate councils to the community relations initiative the minister
stressed the role and example of local politicians in cross-community
cooperation:

> Given the behaviour and some of the debates that have taken place
> in Belfast recently, community relations still have some way to go
> within the council chamber, never mind outside it.

> I was pleased that Magherafelt Council had unanimously voted to accept the [community relations] proposal. That is the best of all cross-community support (Mawhinney, 1991b: 991).

Vesting responsibility for community relations in local councils is, it seems, a way of promoting consensus at political level and in turn, by example, in the community. A small but significant momentum exists for power sharing at council level. The responsibility for community relations puts consensus firmly on the policy agenda of councils, which are symbolically important in making progress on the wider political front.

THE LOCAL GOVERNMENT COMMUNITY RELATIONS INITIATIVE

In 1989 CCRU invited district councils to submit proposals for action to improve community relations in their areas. Councils were offered 75 per cent grant aid from CCRU for the employment of community relations staff, the provision of financial support for appropriate cross-community activities and assistance with the development of local heritage and cultural activities. A budget of £279000 was provided for the programme by CCRU in 1990–1, increasing to £1m in 1991–2 and £1.3m in 1992–3. The specific conditions laid down for participation were:

— councils had to agree on a cross-party basis to participation in the scheme;
— councils had to draw up a community relations policy statement;
— the policy statement and individual projects undertaken had to be agreed on a cross-party basis;
— community relations officers had to be appointed to administer the scheme and their posts had to be advertised with that title;
— projects had to include the development of cross-community contact, the promotion of mutual understanding and increasing respect for cultural diversity.

The first council (Dungannon) joined the scheme in February 1990, and by the end of that year twelve councils had entered the programme. Eight further councils joined the scheme in 1991, three in 1992 and the final group (Cookstown, Carrickfergus and North

Down) in 1993. All 26 councils are now involved in the initiative which, at the outset, received funding for three years and has subsequently been extended by the same period. The Community Relations Council recently welcomed the fact that district councils were now involved in the initiative: 'This has been a very positive development, particularly since it has been preceded by the establishment of cross-community consensus among the elected representatives of the councils involved' (CRC, 1992). 'Cross-community consensus' was certainly a prerequisite for councils' involvement in the community relations programme. This is not to suggest, however, that council chambers are devoid of the occasional partisan fracas!

The political parties expressed mixed reactions to the principles underpinning the programme. The SDLP argued that the absence of trust was at the heart of Northern Ireland's problems and any improvement in community relations would come only when trust was restored. Sinn Féin had an ambivalent attitude in that it sought reconciliation through constructive dialogue and debate, but claimed that this could not take place until the unionist majority veto in the six counties was removed. The Alliance Party fully endorsed constructive community relations work designed to promote understanding and trust between the two communities. Responses from the two unionist parties ranged from qualified support in the case of the Ulster Unionist Party (UUP) to opposition on the part of the Democratic Unionist Party (DUP). Whilst the UUP supported schemes to encourage the affirmation and exploration of local regional identities, it claimed that an undue emphasis on commonalities could be as misleading as the picture of a culturally polarised community. The DUP saw the promotion of good community relations as no more than a political gimmick by government ministers, in which public money was squandered on over-rated reconciliation schemes. Good community relations for them was the elimination of terrorism (CRC, 1992). The unionist and government positions respectively are best described by a parliamentary question posed by an Ulster Unionist MP and the Minister's response:

> I pay tribute to the work that the Minister has done on community relations, and it is valuable work but does he agree with me that we must not fall into the trap of thinking that community relations programmes can solve the problems in Northern Ireland? ... Does

the Minister agree that the best thing that can be done to improve community relations is to defeat terrorism? (Trimble, 1991: 1076)

The Minister responded by agreeing with the premise of the first question:

There is no sense in which success in community relations terms alone will resolve the fundamental and deepseated problems that affect the community in Northern Ireland. There is also no doubt that the winning of the battle against terrorism will play a significant role in easing community tensions ... there is nonetheless, an important role for a community relations programme, and the programme is commanding greater and wider support in the Province with every passing year. (Mawhinney, 1991c: 1076)

IMPLEMENTING THE INITIATIVE AT DISTRICT COUNCIL LEVEL

Under existing council structures, community relations officers are located in community services departments or, in authorities where no such function exists, leisure services, recreation and tourism departments. While they are directly accountable to senior council officials representing their employers, they are also required to submit monthly returns and progress reports to CCRU who, on the basis of grant aiding the programme, have a responsibility for monitoring and evaluation.

The extent to which the programme is supported within each local authority tends to be contingent upon a number of variables, not least of which is the political complexion of the council. Because the programme is located within the remit of local government, it has assumed a certain political aura and provoked, among some councillors, a degree of suspicion. One community relations officer, describing the range of feelings towards the programme within her council, commented:

Democratic Unionists are opposed to the programme. They are suspicious of the Government's intention, especially after the Anglo-Irish Agreement, and they see it as a cosmetic exercise. Sinn Féin are tolerant of community relations, but are uncooperative because of Stormont's involvement. Some councillors, like the SDLP and the UUP are more supportive, they see it as a potential vehicle for

electioneering. But all councillors are aware of the financial benefits. (Interview with community relations officer, 1992)

Because of the programme's potential for confronting emotive political issues, community relations officers, in highly political councils,
are sometimes delegated 'non-threatening duties' such as community
arts or main events organiser. The contentious nature of the programme in some authorities has left community relations officers
feeling particularly vulnerable.

It only takes one individual somewhere along the hierarchical line
to object and the whole thing collapses. (Interview with community relations officer, 1992)

Community relations is like a disaster waiting to happen in this
council (Interview with community relations officer, 1992).

These fears are heightened by incidents in which inexperienced
officers, who inadvertently stray from 'acceptable' community relations, incur the vitriol of angry elected members at council meetings.
A community relations officer described one such experience:

Councillors were really angry because I was asking people their
religion so that I could fill in my monitoring forms. They were wor-
ried that information like that could be used against people. Now I
just make guesstimates. (Interview with community relations
officer, 1992)

As a result of such incidents, community relations officers now claim
to be more astute in the art of achieving a delicate balance between
the promotion and development of community relations, and accom-
modating political sensitivities within councils. As one officer put it:
'You swim with the tide and when no one's looking you jump out and
do something and then jump back in again quickly'(Interview with
community relations officer, 1992).

In spite of the occasional well-publicised controversial incident,
most community relations officers enjoy a degree of support within
council, at both official and member level. This support is most
clearly visible in those local authorities where previous initiatives
and examples of cooperation are tangible indicators of commitment
to community relations at council level. Some local authorities have
established sub-committees to help inform, direct and clarify the
specific role of the community relations programme. In one authority, for example, where there is 'responsibility sharing' between

unionists and nationalists, the council has approved a community
relations policy which insists that contact between the communities
'must be over and above that which exists already, and there should
be a community relations value-added element to programmes'
(interview with senior council official, July 1992). Similarly, in
another council, policy demands that priority is given to funding
applications 'where the potential and commitment exists to allow
proposed projects to extend towards actively sharing and addressing
issues of difference between communities' (local authority community relations policy document, 1992).

IMPLEMENTING THE INITIATIVE AT COMMUNITY LEVEL

The rationale for the introduction of the community relations programme points out:

> Northern Ireland remains a deeply divided society, within which
> exist two separate groups with different political aspirations, reli-
> gious beliefs, cultural traditions and social values. It is from this
> essential division that violence flares and political instability per-
> sists, with such heavy human and financial costs. Reducing these
> divisions, is therefore, a major part of Government policy. (CCRU,
> 1991: 2)

While most community relations officers accept this view, they argue
that it is often inconsistent with grass-roots perspectives on the conflict. In their experience most people in Northern Ireland attribute
the perpetuation of the conflict to a minority of extremists in both
communities who support violence as a legitimate means to an end.
Few people see the relevance of a programme aimed at addressing a
problem which is perceived to exist only in those districts where levels of violence have been consistently high. An attitude prevails,
most frequently encountered by community relations officers in
mixed communities, that Protestants and Catholics have coexisted
for years without any problems. In segregated communities it is also
argued that lack of contact means community relations has never
been an issue – people from opposite religions don't have to meet!
These views have led opponents of the initiative to question community relations officers on the merits of their programmes, when
funds could be more usefully spent on pressing community services

priorities. In the light of these attitudes, most community relations officers have found the public to be more acquiescent to approaches which aim to increase contact through activities that also provide an entertainment or mutual interest value. They have found that more focused projects, which are intended to address prejudiced, sectarian attitudes and other divisive issues, tend to appeal more to a minority of sympathetic and interested individuals.

Awareness of implementation issues at both council and community level influences the nature of projects promoted by community relations officers. There is, though, another element which may unconsciously determine the character of their programmes; community relations officers' own perceptions of what constitutes a community relations problem. Compare the following statements from two officers:

> In general community relations in 'X District Council' are good. That is not to say that they cannot be improved upon, but in assigning the work to be done in the field it is important to view 'X District Council' in isolation, and not to group it with other areas in Northern Ireland where community relations are poor and the problems are great, and therefore the potential level of community relations work to be done is greater than in 'X District Council'. ('X District Council' Community Relations Report, 1991)

> The 'Y Borough' area has had a lower incidence of actual visible sectarian strife than in many other areas in the Province. While this situation is extremely favourable for the successful implementation of a community relations programme, it is important not to be complacent. It is important that negative stereotypes and attitudes are addressed by targeting the programme at specific groups. ('Y District Council' Community Relations Report, 1991)

These extracts illustrate a divergence in how the community relations officers perceive their roles. In the former assessment, the absence of terrorist incidents is synonymous with good community relations. In the latter, even though such events are also rare, there is an acknowledgement of insidious and deep-rooted community divisions.

Other issues which have impinged upon the implementation of projects at community level are the difficulties in accessing Protestants, and in finding and resourcing 'neutral' venues. In accessing

Protestants, the intuitive judgement of most community relations officers is that fear of a hidden agenda and of making political concessions has caused Protestant reluctance to become involved in projects. Some community relations officers also suggest that the Protestant tradition, wherein social life is inseparable from specific institutional links (such as the church or the British Legion), may preclude participation in outside activity. Where the potential for contact and interaction does exist, community relations officers have found that both Protestant and Catholic community groups are often unwilling to meet in parish halls or community buildings which are synonymous with the 'other side'. This is particularly the case in polarised and segregated districts where traditional meeting places are usually church-affiliated. The problem is exacerbated by a scarcity of 'neutral' venues, and even where acceptable meeting places are available, community relations officers have some difficulty in arranging funding and transport. Recognising that capital resources are limited, and that the likelihood of funding for new venues or transport is slim, some community relations officers have established successful transport cooperatives with local voluntary agencies which have facilitated travel to non-contentious, central locations.

CROSS-COMMUNITY PROJECTS IN COUNCILS

Any attempt at classifying the diverse range of projects undertaken by community relations officers in councils is fraught with difficulties. In general, however, there are five broad types of projects as follows:

High-profile community relations. Projects under this category are generally one-off events aimed at promoting the community relations function through public relations. They tend to attract large numbers but are not part of a long-term developmental strategy. Examples include tea dances, intercommunity 'It's a Knockout' and the cavalcade of song – a collection of songs written for and performed by schoolchildren.

Inter/intra community development. Projects include both single identity and cross-community development work. Single identity projects recognise that polarised communities first need to address their own prejudices and misunderstandings prior to engaging in cross-community work. Inter-community development builds upon a network of established groups interested in pursuing common goals which straddle the sectarian divide (health, housing, roads, economic development). Good community relations is an important by-product of this process. An example is cross-community economic development committees.

Cultural traditions. Projects under this heading attempt to capitalise on the cross-community benefits which accrue to groups with a shared cultural interest in sport, music, dancing, drama and so on. The approach is to focus on what binds communities rather than what separates them. Examples of this type of project are cross-community drama groups, inter-district music twinning and heritage trails.

Focused community relations. By definition, projects under this heading are much more directed and aim to tackle, head-on, controversial community relations issues. The approach is premised on the idea that people adopt an avoidance strategy and steer clear of politics and religion, particularly in mixed (Protestant/Catholic) company. This approach suggests that such issues, if left unresolved, compound insidious sectarianism and bigotry. Examples of such projects include anti-sectarianism and prejudice reduction workshops.

Substitute funding. These are events which were running prior to the appointment of a community relations officer, and projects initiated by other council departments, but subsequently funded through the community relations programme. The focus and content of these events have changed during the course of the evaluation to include a community relations agenda. Examples of substitute funding are the Lord Mayor's show, Christmas lights and fireworks displays. In general inter/intra community development, cultural traditions and focused community relations projects are the most effective in pursuing the long-term objectives of 'promoting greater mutual understanding and increasing respect for cultural traditions'.

AN ASSESSMENT OF THE PROGRAMME

Notwithstanding some of the implementation problems, the achievements of the programme are significant and have been documented elsewhere (Knox et al., 1993). Some of the more important are:

a. the endorsement of the programme and its objectives across the political parties by all 26 local authorities;
b. the increasing enthusiasm with which councillors and officials embrace community relations as an important function of the local authority;
c. the range and effectiveness of projects undertaken by community relations officers which encourage contact, cooperation, mutual understanding and respect for different cultural traditions;
d. the growing confidence with which community relations officers undertake a sensitive task, sometimes in difficult circumstances, and their increasing credibility as professionals;
e. the improving community relations trend, evidenced in both data gathered as part of an evaluation of the programme and the annual Northern Ireland Social Attitudes surveys (Gallagher and Dunn, 1990; Gallagher, 1992).

Yet the community relations programme in councils must be put into perspective. The budget for this initiative is £1.3m or £0.83 per capita in 1992–3, out of a public expenditure budget in Northern Ireland of £7bn. The programme's objectives are long-term involving changes in attitudes and behaviour and can be influenced either positively (e.g. peace talks) or negatively (e.g. increased sectarian killings) by extraneous factors. It is not a 'quick fix' programme but a long-term developmental scheme. The most effective community relations work in councils has emerged through community development issues. Those councils with an established community services department and access to a network of local groups have benefited to a greater extent from the new community relations function. Collaboration between community development and community relations produces sustainable cross-community benefits through a twin-track approach.

Over and above the intrinsic merits of the individual projects the programme has a significant symbolic value. First, an important prerequisite for the successful reduction in prejudice is that 'contact should be endorsed by an "authority" and/or in a favourable social climate' (Amir, 1969). Establishing community relations as part of the remit of Northern Ireland's 26 councils is a major achievement by CCRU and an endorsement of the programme's objectives. Such an achievement is all the more significant when set within the context of the vitriolic political battles which have taken place in some councils over the presence of Sinn Féin councillors. Secondly, the initiative has forced community relations onto the policy agenda of local authorities. Being the only remaining democratic institution of government, since the demise of the Northern Ireland Assembly, dealing with community relations matters in councils creates a public awareness of its importance. Doing so in those local authorities whose track record of discrimination among their own workforce has been poor, is even more important. Thirdly, a number of councils have now engaged in *de facto* power sharing or 'responsibility sharing'. This involves rotating the post of chairperson or mayor between political parties and in some cases proportional representation on committees. Such a public expression of good cross-community relations between politicians is both an endorsement of the initiative's principles and an open display of 'leading from the front'. The benefits of cross-community example at the political level are not easy to measure but there is little doubt that they contribute to the 'favourable social climate' required for reducing prejudice. Finally, the community relations initiative cannot be evaluated in isolation. It is part of a broader commitment by government to tackle both the underlying divisions in Northern Ireland and its chronic social and economic problems. The community relations programme must be judged as one (important) element of a more comprehensive thrust by government to improve equality of opportunity and equity of treatment.

REFERENCES

Amir, Y. (1969) 'Contact Hypothesis in Ethnic Relations', *Psychological Bulletin*, 71, 319–42.

Central Community Relations Unit (1991) *Community Relations in Northern Ireland*. Belfast, CCRU.

Community Relations Council (1992) 'What the Local Parties Say on Community Relations', *Community Relations*, 8.

Connolly, M. and C. Knox (1988) 'Recent Political Difficulties of Northern Ireland Local Government', *Policy and Politics*, 16: 2, 89–97.

Department of Finance and Personnel and H.M. Treasury (1992) *Northern Ireland Expenditure Plans and Priorities 1992–93 to 1994–95*. Belfast, DFP.

Department of the Environment, Local Government Branch (1992) *District Rate Statistics 1992–93*. Belfast, DoE.

Fair Employment Commission (1991a) *A Profile of the Workforce in Northern Ireland – A Summary of the 1990 Monitoring Returns: Report No.1*, Belfast: Fair Employment Commission.

Fair Employment Commission (1991b) *Second Annual Report.* Belfast, Fair Employment Commission.

Fair Employment Commission (1992) *A Profile of Senior Staff in the Northern Ireland Public Sector – Survey of Employment Patterns.* Belfast, Fair Employment Commission.

Gallagher, A. M. (1992) 'Community Relations in Northern Ireland' in *British Social Attitudes: the 9th Report,* ed. by R. Jowell, L. Brook, G. Prior and B. Taylor. Aldershot, Dartmouth.

Gallagher, A. M. and S. Dunn (1990) 'Community Relations in Northern Ireland: Attitudes to Contact and Integration' in *Social Attitudes in Northern Ireland 1990–91,* ed. by P. Stringer and G. Robinson. Belfast, Blackstaff Press. 7–23.

Knox, C. (1990) 'Sinn Féin and Local Government Elections: the Government's Response in Northern Ireland', *Parliamentary Affairs,* 43: 4, 448–63.

Knox, C., J. Hughes et al. (1994) *Community Relations.* University of Ulster: Centre for the Study of Conflict.

McKittrick, D. (1992) 'Belfast Council Guilty of Religious Bias Over Job', *Independent,* 22 December.

Macrory, Sir P. (1970) *Report of the Review Body on Local Government in Northern Ireland.* Cmnd 546. Belfast, HMSO.

Mawhinney, B. (1991a) Oral Question on Community Relations. *Hansard,* 17 January.

Mawhinney, B. (1991b) Oral Question on Community Relations. *Hansard,* 14 February.

Mawhinney, B. (1991c) Oral Question on Community Relations. *Hansard,* 11 July.

Northern Ireland Information Service (1987) *Community Relations – Minister's Press Statement.* 14 September, p. 3.

O'Dowd, L., B. Rolston and M. Tomlinson (1980) *Northern Ireland: Between Civil Rights and Civil War.* London, CSE Books.

O'Leary, C., S. Elliott and R. Wilford (1988) *The Northern Ireland Assembly 1982–1986, A Constitutional Experiment.* London, Hurst.

Trimble, D. (1991) *Oral Question on Community Relations. Hansard,* 11 July.

5 Criminal Justice and Emergency Laws

Brice Dickson

EMERGENCY LAWS PRIOR TO DIRECT RULE[1]

Although the current spate of troubles in Northern Ireland began in 1968 the phenomenon of political violence is by no means a novel one in this part of the world. Ever since the invasion of Ireland by King Henry II's troops towards the end of the twelfth century the island's history has been dominated by the struggle of some of its inhabitants to break free from what they have perceived as British control. That control manifested itself in the laws passed by the Parliaments of England and (after the union of Scotland with England in 1707) Great Britain. Under Poynings' Law (1495) any legislation passed by a Parliament in Ireland was invalid unless approved in London.

In the seventeenth and eighteenth centuries the opposition to the British occupation of Ireland was so extensive that repressive legislation was frequently enacted in an attempt to quell it. The hardest-hitting Acts were the penal laws, passed mainly in the reigns of King William III and Queen Anne (1692–1714). These laws affected people's religious, political and social rights. Catholic bishops were banished from Ireland and were liable to be executed if they did not leave; Catholics were not permitted to vote for or sit in Parliament or town councils, or be members of a jury; nor could they practise as lawyers, or even as teachers; they could not buy land or take a lease for more than 31 years; when they died, the estate of Catholic landowners could not be passed to one son unless he became a Protestant – otherwise the estate was divided between all the Catholic sons. It should be noted, however, that similar restrictions applied to dissenting Protestants, such as the mainly Northern-based Presbyterians.

In the eighteenth century there was a lack of local officers willing and able to police Ireland, so the British army was increasingly used in a law enforcement and even an administrative capacity. The Irish Parliament conferred extraordinary powers on magistrates and troops in the so-called Whiteboy Acts, which were also employed against violent rural groups in the North known as Oakboys and Steelboys. At this time detention of suspects without trial, and trial by court-martial, were common. During the whole of the nineteenth century there was more or less constant agrarian violence and sporadic mass civil disobedience throughout Ireland but especially in the South. The United Irishmen, under the Protestant Wolfe Tone, rebelled in 1798 and there were further revolts in 1803 (led by Robert Emmett), 1848 (the 'Young Ireland' movement) and 1867 (the Fenian rising). Then in 1916 came the Easter Rebellion in Dublin. The British response to these events was a series of measures that were at times coercive and at times conciliatory. A police force was established along military lines and became the model on which many other police forces throughout the British Empire were based. The responsibility for taking prosecutions at assizes was given to Crown solicitors acting under the direction of the Attorney General. Between 1800 and 1921 no fewer than 105 Coercion Acts dealing with Ireland were enacted. By 1900 a law suspending the operation of *habeas corpus* (the judicial remedy which prevents detention without charge) had been introduced four times for periods totalling 11 years.

Whereas dissent in England was dealt with by the ordinary criminal law, in Ireland draconian legislation such as the Suppression of Local Disturbances Act 1833 was passed. This Act allowed offences to be tried by court-martial established under military procedures, supposedly to eliminate the possibility of intimidation in ordinary courts. The Peace Preservation Act 1870 empowered magistrates in Ireland to compel witnesses to testify during the investigation of a crime, prior to any trial. The Protection of Life and Property (Ireland) Act 1871 permitted arrest and detention without trial of persons reasonably suspected of being members of a secret society. The Prevention of Crimes (Ireland) Act 1882, passed just after the murder in Dublin of the new Chief Secretary of Ireland, Lord Cavendish, allowed the suspension of jury trial in cases such as murder but there was such an outcry over this that the power was never exercised; instead special juries consisting of the larger property owners were used or the powers of summary trial were extended. Coercive powers were further extended by the Criminal Law and Procedure (Ireland) Act 1887, which gave power to magistrates to interrogate witnesses in private, allowed associations to be declared unlawful, widened the definition of intimidation and enabled trials to be transferred to a different county if otherwise the trial would not be fair and impartial.

Ireland was partitioned by the government of Ireland Act 1920. As the North had a far from peaceful birth the new Parliament in Belfast, dominated by members of the Unionist Party, quickly took measures to safeguard its position against violent rebellion. One of the first of these measures was the Civil Authorities (Special Powers) Act (NI) 1922, a law which was renewed annually until given a five-year lifespan in 1928 and made permanent in 1933. The Special Powers Act conferred a wide regulation-making power on the Minister of Home Affairs for Northern Ireland and declared in section 1 that the Minister, or any officer of the local police to whom he had delegated the power, could 'take all such steps and issue all such orders as may be necessary for preserving the peace and maintaining order'. At various points in the period 1922 to 1968 the Act and the regulations made thereunder allowed for arrests without warrant and detention for up to 48 hours solely for the purpose of interrogation, internment without trial, entry without warrant by the police or army into any home believed to be used for any illegal purpose, prohibition of the publication of any printed matter, curfews, and a ban on inquests into sudden deaths (Walsh, 1984: 326–33).

An inquiry into the operation of the Special Powers Act conducted by the London-based National Council for Civil Liberties concluded as follows:

> the Northern Irish Government has used Special Powers towards securing the domination of one particular faction and, at the same time, towards curtailing the lawful activities of its opponents ... It is sad that in the guise of temporary and emergency legislation there should have been created under the shadow of the British Constitution a permanent machine of dictatorship – a standing temptation to whatever intolerant or bigoted section may attain power to abuse its authority at the expense of the people it rules. (NCCL, 1936: 39)

Not surprisingly, the repeal of the Act was one of the central demands of the civil rights campaigners who began to lobby for reform from the mid-1960s (Purdie, 1990). Such a call, however, was interpreted by the Unionist government as a further attack on Northern Ireland's very right to exist. In 1969 regiments of the British army were called in to assist the local police (the Royal Ulster Constabulary) in maintaining order and two years later internment without trial was activated. By no measure was internment a success. The level of violence in Northern Ireland increased and a rent and rates strike compelled the government to enact the Payments for Debt (Emergency Provisions) Act (NI) 1971, a law which enabled arrears of rent and rates for housing and other public services to be deducted directly from welfare benefits or from the salaries paid to public sector employees. This remained in force for the next 20 years even though the rent and rates strike was called off when internment ended in 1975.

EMERGENCY LAWS AFTER DIRECT RULE

In March 1972 the Belfast Parliament was suspended and 'direct rule' from Westminster was imposed. The level of violence soared (Dillon and Lehane, 1973). A Commission under the chairmanship of Lord Diplock was consequently appointed to consider:

> what arrangements for the administration of justice in Northern Ireland could be made in order to deal more effectively with terrorist organisations by bringing to book, otherwise than by internment by the Executive, individuals involved in terrorist activities. (Diplock, 1972: 1)

Despite the fact that the Commission's examination of the problem was quite cursory, not to mention its heavy dependence on the perspective of the British army (Greer and White, 1986), the bulk of its recommendations were quickly implemented by the Northern Ireland (Emergency Provisions) Act 1973 (the EPA 1973). The Act was to apply for one year but could be renewed.

The EPA 1973 repealed the Special Powers Act but re-enacted many of its provisions as well as establishing so-called Diplock Courts – courts where persons accused of 'scheduled' offences (those listed in a Schedule to the Act) could be tried in the absence of a jury and where statements could be admitted as evidence in circumstances where they would be excluded in ordinary courts. In 1974, within a week of the bombing of two pubs in Birmingham, further anti-terrorist police powers were introduced for the whole of the United Kingdom in the Prevention of Terrorism (Temporary Provisions) Act (the PTA 1974). This allowed detention for up to seven days (any period after the initial 48 hours being authorised not by a judge but by a government minister), the banning of named organisations and the issuing of exclusion orders preventing people from entering the United Kingdom or moving freely between one part of the UK and another; special powers of interrogation at airports and seaports were also part of the package. Again the Act was intended to endure for only one year but could be renewed.

Internment was phased out in 1975 but the EPA and the PTA have remained in force and their most recent incarnations contain a larger number of provisions than ever. There have been several 'independent' reviews of these emergency laws, some by judges, but all have been premised on the assumption that, given the political violence in Northern Ireland, some such laws are necessary, the only question being which ones. The EPA 1973 was first reviewed by the Gardiner Committee in 1975 (Gardiner, 1975) and then by the Baker Committee in 1984 (Baker, 1984). From 1988 to 1993 the annual renewal debate in Parliament was preceded and informed by a review of the operation of the Act conducted by a government-appointed official, Lord Colville, though only his review for 1989 was officially published (Colville, 1990). New versions of the EPA were enacted in 1978 and 1987, the one currently in place dating from 1991 (Dickson, 1992a). The PTA was examined in the Shackleton Report (Shackleton, 1978) and the Jellicoe Report (Jellicoe, 1983); since 1985 it too has been reviewed each year prior to the Parliamentary renewal debate, the first two of these reviews being conducted by Sir Cyril Philips and all subsequent ones by the same Lord Colville who has looked at the EPA. New PTAs were enacted in 1976 and 1984; the one in force at the moment was enacted in 1989 (Bonner, 1989). Unlike its predecessor and the EPA, the PTA 1989 does not require complete re-enactment after five years – it can simply be renewed each year indefinitely.

In the midst of the application of these emergency laws radical reforms were carried out to the 'ordinary' police powers in Northern Ireland, mirroring changes made in England some four years previously. The Police and Criminal Evidence (NI) Order 1989 (the PACE Order) came into force on 1 January 1990 (NILQ, 1989) and was accompanied by four Codes of Practice on matters such as the treatment of suspects and the exercise of search powers. A similar Code on the treatment of suspects under the EPA was approved by Parliament towards the end of 1993; in January 1994 it replaced the non-statutory *Guide to the Emergency Laws* issued in 1990. Northern Ireland has also had its law on the right to silence fundamentally altered, whether the criminal proceedings be terrorist-related or not (Jackson, 1991). This was achieved by the Criminal Evidence (NI) Order 1988, which allows inferences of guilt to be drawn from a person's refusal to answer questions put by police officers during an interrogation session or refusal to give evidence at a subsequent trial.

THE RATIONALE FOR THE PRESENT EMERGENCY LAWS

When the EPA and PTA are debated in Parliament each year the government takes the opportunity to state its reasons for supporting their renewal and, often, their strengthening. Whatever the anti-terrorist strategy may have been in the past (Hadden et al., 1990) the ostensible policy today is to counter terrorism within the rule of law by making as few alterations as possible to the ordinary criminal law. It is possible to argue, however, that the real reason for retaining the emergency laws is not that the ordinary criminal law is deficient in preventing, detecting or convicting terrorists (the PACE Order has put the ordinary law on to a much more powerful footing than that which existed in 1973) but that the general public believes this to be the case and expects some special measures to be taken by the government to make the law more effective. As intimated by Sir Patrick Mayhew, the Secretary of State, in a speech at Coleraine in December 1992, the government may also now view the emergency laws as a potential bargaining chip in any future negotiations with paramilitary organisations: by agreeing to repeal some of the laws (which, if the laws are not vital in the first place, will hardly lead to serious consequences) the government could be seen to be obtaining a significant *quid pro quo* – a cessation of violence. This was one of the carrots implicitly held out by the Downing Street Declaration in December 1993.

Taken at their face value the emergency laws are designed to achieve two major goals: the *prevention* of terrorism (largely the role of the PTA) and the *conviction* of terrorists (the role of the EPA). To assist in the former the PTA confers extensive arrest and detention powers. Under section 14 a police officer can arrest without warrant any person whom he or she has reasonable grounds for suspecting to be a member or supporter of a banned organisation, a contributor to acts of terrorism or to the resources of a banned organisation, a person who is assisting in the control of terrorist funds, a person who is failing to comply with an exclusion order banning him or her from a part of the United Kingdom or, most significantly, 'a person who is or has been concerned in the commission, preparation or instigation of acts of terrorism'. The terrorism in question must be connected with the affairs of Northern

Ireland or with any other affairs *except* the affairs of other parts of the United Kingdom (Welsh arsonists, Scottish nationalists and animal rights activists cannot therefore be treated as terrorists).

While it is a relatively straightforward exercise to examine how the emergency laws have operated in practice (Walsh, 1983) it is much more difficult to assess whether they have been effective or not. In the first place we have no way of knowing whether the level of politically motivated violence would have been any higher in the absence of such laws. We are entitled to assume, though, on the basis of the experience gained between 1971 and 1975, that the unrest would have been still greater if a more oppressive measure such as internment had been reintroduced, although supporters of that policy today claim that it could be implemented in a much more selective, and therefore more effective, manner than it was in the 1970s. We might also say that the unrest would have been greater if the prosecuting authorities had pressed charges of treason against terrorists or if the government had ensured that the death penalty was available to the courts when dealing with terrorists who commit murder: the experience of the period during and after the hunger strikes in 1981, when 10 republicans fasted to death, indicates that the martyrdom of politically motivated offenders is guaranteed to recruit more members to paramilitary organisations and to lead to an upsurge in sectarian violence (Beresford, 1987). Some would argue, of course, that while there has been no officially sanctioned death penalty an unofficial 'shoot-to-kill' policy has been operated by the police and army, especially during the 1980s. Between 1982 and 1992 some 75 persons were killed by the on-duty members of security forces (CAJ, 1992), yet to date only four of those concerned have been convicted of murder or manslaughter.

If we examine the statistics on arrest and charge it seems clear that the emergency laws in Northern Ireland are today being used as much to gather intelligence information about persons thought to be involved in terrorism as to bring terrorist suspects themselves to court. In the 1980s the police and prosecuting authorities vigorously pursued a policy of encouraging detainees to inform on their friends and associates in return for personal immunity from prosecution or some financial reward. On one assessment this 'supergrass' phenomenon led to approximately 500 persons being charged on the word of 27 informers between 1981 and 1988 (Bonner, 1988). However there was considerable public disquiet at the tactics being employed and the Court of Appeal eventually decided that most of the convictions were unsafe, thereby reducing the overall conviction rate in these cases to 24 per cent. Since then there has been only one case where an informer's evidence has been used against accomplices (the Brian Nelson case).

Table 5.1, which is based on statistics on the operation of the EPA and PTA issued by the Northern Ireland Office's Information Service and on the Office's annual *Commentary on Northern Ireland Crime Statistics*, demonstrates that about three-quarters of all persons arrested

Table 5.1 Persons arrested, charged and tried under the emergency laws, 1978–92

	Year	*(1)* Persons arrested under the EPA or PTA	*(2)* Persons charged after such arrests (%)	*(3)* Persons proceeded against in Diplock Courts	Column (2) as percentage of Column (3)
	1978	3843	384 (10)	956	40
	1979	2734	588 (22)	922	64
	1980	1851	435 (24)	585	74
	1981	2488	780 (31)	598	130
	1982	2116	361 (17)	793	46
Average	1978–82	2606	510 (19)	771	66
	1983	1651	197 (12)	638	31
	1984	1149	223 (19)	507	44
	1985	1080	202 (19)	698	29
	1986	1380	170 (12)	596	29
	1987	1951	392 (20)	713	55
Average	1983–87	1442	237 (16)	630	38
	1988	1782	384 (22)	515	75
	1989	1670	472 (28)	456	103
	1990	1614	433 (27)	470	92
	1991	1788	366 (20)	423	87
	1992	1846	549 (30)	413	133
Average	1988–92	1740	441 (25)	455	97

under the emergency laws are released without charge. One can only assume that the purpose of an arrest, in many cases, is to interrogate the detainee, there not being any real prospect of charges being laid. Conversely, Table 5.1 also shows that a high proportion of persons dealt with by the Diplock Courts have not been initially arrested under the emergency laws: even allowing for the fact that the persons tried in Diplock Courts in one year are rarely going to be the same persons as those arrested and charged in the same year (given that delays between arrest and trial are measurable in months rather than weeks), the totals for five-year periods show that a significant proportion of Diplock defendants must have been arrested under ordinary arrest powers, the figure for the entire 15-year period being 36 per cent. This suggests that the emergency arrest powers are not as vital to the fight against terrorism as the government would sometimes have us believe.

Needless to say, by no means all of the persons arrested under the EPA or PTA are detained in custody for the full seven-day maximum. The latest available figures, for the first quarter of 1993, indicate that of the 433 persons arrested 119 (27 per cent) were detained for longer than two days and 55 (13 per cent) were detained for longer than four days (the maximum under the PACE Order). A comparison with the same quarter's figures five years previously show little divergence: of the 411 persons arrested 105 (26 per cent) were detained for longer than two days and 62 (15 per cent) for longer than four days. Of the people charged after such arrests 14 per cent had been detained for longer than four days in the 1993 quarter but 41 per cent in the 1988 quarter. The percentage of long detentions does not seem to have diminished, lending some statistical support to the view that detention powers are used as an excuse for short-term internment. But as the proportion of charges gained out of these longer detentions seems to be increasing the security forces will naturally claim that they are 'productive'.

It is equally difficult to assess whether the emergency laws have been necessary to ensure that persons responsible for committing terrorist acts are convicted. We cannot judge how successful the ordinary criminal law would have been in bringing perpetrators of such violence to book, without examining each case individually and in great detail. The record of the emergency laws in this context, however, is not particularly impressive. Table 5.2, based on figures contained in the annual reports of the Chief Constable of the RUC and in the Northern Ireland Office's annual *Commentary on Northern*

Table 5.2   Terrorist incidents and convictions in Diplock Courts, 1978–92

Year	Terrorist incidents			Persons convicted in Diplock Courts	Persons given an immediate custodial sentence
	Deaths	Shootings	Bombings		
1978	81	755	748	837	559
1979	113	728	624	844	689
1980	76	642	402	550	354
1981	101	1142	578	562	381
1982	97	547	368	744	428
Average 1978–82	94	763	554	707	482
1983	77	424	410	612	365
1984	64	334	258	474	242
1985	54	237	251	657	310
1986	61	392	275	587	333
1987	93	674	393	689	343
Average 1983–87	70	412	317	604	319
1988	93	537	466	497	269
1989	62	566	427	424	238
1990	76	559	320	448	256
1991	94	499	604	392	273
1992	85	506	497	362	223
Average 1988–92	82	533	463	425	252
Totals	1227	8542	6621	8679	5263

Ireland Crime Statistics, sets side by side the annual figures for terrorist incidents in Northern Ireland and the annual figures for persons convicted and imprisoned after a trial in the Diplock Courts.

From these statistics the conclusion must be that while the frequency of terrorist incidents is increasing the number of convictions in the Diplock Courts is decreasing. Comparing the last five-year period with the previous five-year period, there has been a 17 per cent increase in deaths, a 29 per cent increase in shootings and a 46 per cent increase in bombings while there has been a 30 per cent drop in the number of persons convicted in the Diplock Courts and a 21 per cent drop in the number of persons given an immediate custodial sentence after a trial in the Diplock Courts. To that extent the emergency laws can be said to have been unsuccessful. Of course it is possible that in recent years many more persons have each been convicted of a raft of terrorist incidents: no research has yet been carried out to verify this and no official clear-up rate for terrorist incidents is made public.

PUBLIC OPINION

Given that the effectiveness of the emergency laws is not easy to observe in terms of reductions in terrorist incidents or increases in terrorist convictions, are there any other indicators of the impact of those laws? There are three which spring immediately to mind. The first is public opinion: how do the general public perceive the manner in which the emergency laws have been operating? The second is the influence of the emergency laws on the 'ordinary' laws of Northern Ireland: has the ordinary system been in any way 'infected' by the standards used in the emergency system? The third is the performance of the laws on the international scene: how do they measure up when set against the requirements contained in international human rights documents?

Such evidence as exists on public opinion is scant. To date the polls which have been conducted have not related directly to the impact of the emergency laws but to connected matters such as the image of the RUC or the need for a Bill of Rights. Brewer (1992) rightly observes that public attitudes towards the police in Northern Ireland are determined by the broader conflicts that characterise the society, although his analysis shows that the communities are not as polarised as is sometimes assumed. Nevertheless he finds that only 42 per cent of nationalists believe that the RUC is doing a good job in controlling sectarian crime while the figure for unionists is 88 per cent, even if unionists on low incomes, and those aged 18-24, are much less likely to give a positive assessment of the RUC's performance. Gallagher (1992) adds that there is a sharp differentiation between Catholics and Protestants in their attitudes towards the use of vehicle checkpoints, random searches of pedestrians and house searches. He finds as well that 73 per cent of Protestants feel that the courts treat Protestants and Catholics equally when processing conflict-related offences but that only 56 per cent of Catholics think this is the case.

All of these figures tell us little about whether people's perceptions of the police would change if the emergency laws they were operating also changed. Nor do they tell us whether people would like to see fewer or a greater number of emergency legal measures in place. The current Chief Constable, Sir Hugh Annesley, has left no one in doubt that he wishes the police to be given many more powers, for when he presented his Annual Report for 1992 he went out of his way to list a number of other measures which he felt should be introduced in order to make the fight against terrorism more effective. These included shifting the onus of proof on to the defendant, strengthening the incentives to a suspect to answer police questions and more readily making admissible as evidence information obtained from the bugging of private telephones or from informers.

More revealing is Gallagher's finding that only 21 per cent of Protestants are opposed to the current law on the right of silence in Northern Ireland, while the figure for Catholics is 62 per cent; surprisingly, however, as many as 53 per cent of Protestants think that the police should have to obtain a warrant before searching a suspect's home, the figure for Catholics being 79 per cent (Gallagher, 1992: 101). But if there appears to be a split along sectarian lines as regards the acceptability of some of the emergency laws, there is a much greater degree of agreement over the need for a Bill of Rights. While it is true that many people may wrongly perceive a Bill of Rights as aiming to achieve something which goes beyond protecting people against authoritarianism, the degree of support for such a document is still remarkably widespread. A survey conducted in the wake of the Opsahl Commission's recommendation in June 1993 that a Bill of Rights be urgently introduced indicated that 67 per cent of the people in Northern Ireland agreed with that recommendation and only 9 per cent disagreed, the remainder having no opinion either way (*Irish News*, 5 July 1993).

Emergency powers are relevant not just at the pre-trial stage but also at the trial stage, but assessing whether judges in Northern Ireland are satisfied with their operation at that stage is well-nigh impossible. Unlike their brethren in Great Britain and Ireland, they are not prone to making extra-judicial public pronouncements on controversial matters. A survey of their reported decisions indicates that on occasions they have acted to frustrate the apparent intention of Parliament by interpreting the emergency laws in a libertarian manner (e.g. to maintain the burden of proof on the prosecution and to preserve a judicial discretion to exclude a confession which is considered to have been obtained unfairly) (Dickson, 1992b). The judges in the Court of Appeal also effectively put an end to the prosecution's reliance upon supergrass evidence. While the judiciary has refused to be involved in authorising seven-day detentions, it is unclear whether this is because they consider four-day detentions to be long enough or because they do not wish to be implicated at all in the emergency detention system. With one or two notable exceptions, there is little to suggest that decisions by judges in Northern Ireland are any more pro-Establishment in their tone than decisions of judges in the rest of the United Kingdom.

THE IMPACT ON THE 'ORDINARY' CRIMINAL JUSTICE SYSTEM

The influence of emergency laws on the ordinary laws of Northern Ireland is a phenomenon which is probably invisible to non-lawyers but which nevertheless exists in practically all aspects of the criminal process (Greer, 1987). The RUC arrest people using emergency laws even when the arrest powers under the ordinary law would suffice; no doubt this is because the emergency laws can trigger a maximum detention period of seven days rather than just four (and even then only if the suspect has appeared at least twice before a magistrate). The army power of arrest extends to all offences, though in practice it is confined to terrorist-related offences, and the changes to the law on the right of silence apply to all persons arrested by the police regardless of the suspected offence, though of the 40 or so cases where the new law has been invoked (some 5 per cent of all scheduled cases since the end of 1988) none has been a non-terrorist case. No coroner or coroner's jury in Northern Ireland can issue any kind of verdict (only bland 'findings'), let alone a verdict of unlawful killing. All adult prisoners in Northern Ireland are held in maximum security prisons because of the distribution of terrorist offenders throughout the four prison locations.

Other features of the ordinary justice system are more a by-product of the troubles themselves than of the emergency laws. Examples would be the rise of 'informal' justice exercised against 'hoods' by paramilitary organisations in areas where there is little or no support for the RUC (Munck, 1988); delays in dealing with court cases, especially in civil matters, due to the log-jam created by the terrorist cases; the use of armed police, not otherwise the norm in the United Kingdom, and the lack of neighbourhood policing, even in relatively trouble-free areas, because of the danger of unprovoked attacks. On the credit side it is possible to argue that the justice system has experienced some positive side-effects arising out of the troubles: the RUC is one of the most accountable police forces in the United Kingdom, the Office of the DPP has been independent of the police since 1972, the prison system is generally acknowledged to be more humane, certainly less crowded, than in Great Britain and lawyers in Northern Ireland are much more aware than their colleagues elsewhere of the protections enshrined in the European Convention on Human Rights – indeed the cases which have emanated from Northern Ireland have contributed significantly to the developing jurisprudence on the interpretation of that Convention (Dickson, 1992c).

CONFORMITY WITH INTERNATIONAL HUMAN RIGHTS STANDARDS

When measured against the standards contained in international conventions on human rights the government's emergency laws have, on the whole, passed the test. The United Kingdom has had to defend its laws or practices on four separate occasions in the European Court of Human Rights. In *Ireland* v. *UK* (1978), still the only inter-state case ever to have reached the European Court, the Court held that five interrogation techniques employed against internees amounted to inhuman and degrading treatment, contrary to Article 3 of the Convention. The British government gave an undertaking that use of the five techniques had been discontinued, but no steps were taken to punish those who had administered them and compensation was paid to victims only years after the event. In *Brogan* v. *UK* (1988) the Court held that detention for periods of longer than four days and six hours was a breach of Article 5(3) of the Convention, which requires detainees to be brought promptly before a judge or other officer authorised to exercise judicial power. The government responded not by shortening the maximum seven-day detention period allowed under the PTA but by 'derogating' from the

Convention, i.e. opting out of Article 5(3). This was within the UK's power to do provided it complied with Article 15 of the Convention. Two later cases challenged the legitimacy of the derogation on the ground that the conditions specified in Article 15 were not fulfilled, namely, that there be a public emergency threatening the life of the nation and that the measures taken be strictly required by the exigencies of the situation. Both of these challenges failed (*McConnell* v. *UK*, 1989, and *Brannigan and McBride* v. *UK*, 1993), the Court declaring in the latter that 'there can be no doubt that such a public emergency existed' and that the non-involvement of judges was justified because '[i]n the context of Northern Ireland, where the judiciary is small and vulnerable to terrorist attacks, public confidence in the independence of the judiciary is understandably a matter to which the Government attach great importance'.

The European Court has upheld the British government's line on several other aspects of the emergency laws which have been challenged under the European Convention. In *Brogan* v. *UK* it accepted that arresting someone on the basis of a suspicion of his or her involvement in unspecified acts of terrorism was not a breach of the requirement in Article 5(1)(c) that arrests must take place only on suspicion of an offence; in the same case it rejected the argument that, because so few people are subsequently charged, arrests under the emergency laws are not for the purpose of bringing people before a court, also required by Article 5(1), but in order merely to gather information from them or to harass them. In *Fox, Campbell and Hartley* v. *UK* the Court held that persons arrested under the emergency laws did not have to be told at the time of their arrest why they were being arrested, despite the requirement along these lines in Article 5(2) of the European Convention; it was enough, said the Court, if the detainees were made aware of the reasons for their arrest through the nature of the questions subsequently put to them by their interrogators. That condition was satisfied in the *Fox* case itself but not in the later case of *Murray* v. *UK* (1993).

The European Commission of Human Rights (which must deal with all applications under the European Convention before they can be referred to the Court) has also supported the British government on most occasions. In *Farrell* v. *UK* (1984) it refused to condemn the standard enshrined in Northern Ireland's law on the use of force by members of the police and army ('such force as is reasonable in the circumstances [may be used] in the prevention of crime or in effecting or assisting in the lawful arrest of offenders or suspected offenders': Criminal Law Act (NI) 1967, section 3(1)), even though this standard appears on its face to be less demanding than the Convention's test of 'force which is no more than absolutely necessary'(Article 2(2)). In *Stewart* v. *UK* (1985) the Commission again failed to grasp the opportunity to require the law on lethal force to be tightened and did not condemn the use of plastic bullets as a riot control weapon. In *McVeigh et al.* v. *UK* (1979) it refused to condemn the powers applied at ports for the examination and detention of travellers. In *McFeeley et al.* v. *UK* (1980) the Commission held that the Convention did not oblige Britain to confer special status on prisoners convicted of politically motivated offences in Northern Ireland, while in *X* v. *UK* (1978) it saw no breach of privacy (under Article 8 of the Convention) in preventing an IRA prisoner from being visited by his wife without their conversation being listened to by prison officers. In *Murray* v. *UK* (1993) it accepted that the army's procedures for entering and searching homes under the EPA, and for photographing suspects, are not a breach of Article 8, nor is the power to detain people under 'house arrest' for up to eight hours while a search is being conducted a breach of Article 5 of the Convention on the right to liberty (*O'Neill and Kelly* v. *UK*, 1992).

There have been several other relevant applications adjudicated upon by the Commission but none has dented the government's emergency law policy. Many others are currently pending in Strasbourg, raising issues such as denying suspects access to a solicitor while in police custody, drawing inferences of guilt from the refusal of suspects to answer police questions, refusing to compel testimony from members of the security forces at inquests into civilian deaths, screening witnesses at a criminal trial and issuing 'public interest immunity certificates' to keep secret from the court the movements of and information available to security force personnel.

The other major international human rights instrument to which Britain is obliged to adhere is the United Nations' International Covenant on Civil and Political Rights, though, unlike the Republic of Ireland, Britain has not signed the Optional Protocol to the Covenant which would allow individuals to complain about their government's action before the UN's Human Rights Committee. While it is arguable that the emergency laws in Northern Ireland breach that Covenant in several respects (Hunt and Dickson, 1993), the absence of effective enforcement mechanisms in the Covenant means that the government can escape any serious challenges to its policies. Of late, however, substantial embarrassment has been caused to the government through the lobbying of UN bodies by various human rights NGOs (non-governmental organisations). These have been particularly vocal during sessions of the Human Rights Committee (which must consider quinquennial reports from UN members as to how they are complying with the Covenant), the Sub-Commission on the Prevention of Discrimination and Protection of Minorities and the Committee against Torture. The issue which has attracted most attention is whether the practices employed by the police during interrogation sessions in the three 'holding centres' in Northern Ireland amount to torture, cruelty or inhuman or degrading treatment. As well as reports issued by Amnesty International, Helsinki Watch, Liberty (formerly the National Council for Civil Liberties) and the Lawyers' Committee for Human Rights, much of the work in this field has been done by the Belfast-based Committee on the Administration of Justice (the CAJ). The CAJ believes that the EPA and PTA should be repealed in their present form. It claims, not without some justification, that the ordinary criminal law, properly applied and perhaps supplemented by one or two provisions, could adequately cope with the struggle against terrorism while at the same time better protecting basic civil liberties.

NOTE

1. The following summary of laws enacted prior to 1921 is based largely on pages 4–6 of the briefing paper on the Northern Ireland (Emergency Provisions) Bill prepared in 1991 by the Committee on the Administration of Justice, Belfast. In turn that briefing paper owes much to Molloy (1986).

REFERENCES

Baker, Sir G. (1984) *Review of the Operation of the EPA 1978*. HMSO, Cmnd 9222.

Beresford, D. (1987) *Ten Men Dead: the Story of the 1981 Irish Hunger Strike*. London, Grafton.

Bonner, D. (1988) 'Combating Terrorism: Supergrass Trials in Northern Ireland', *Modern Law Review*, 51, 23.

Bonner, D. (1989) 'Combating Terrorism in the 1990s: the Role of the PTA', *Public Law*, 440.

Brewer, J. (1992) 'The Public and the Police' in *Social Attitudes in Northern Ireland: the Second Report*, ed. by P. Stringer and G. Robinson. Belfast, Blackstaff Press.

Committee on the Administration of Justice (1992) *Inquests and Disputed Killings in Northern Ireland.* Belfast, CAJ.

Colville, Lord (1990) *Review of the Operation in 1989 of the EPAs 1978 and 1987.* HMSO, Cmnd 1115.

Dickson, B. (1992a) 'Northern Ireland's Emergency Legislation – the Wrong Medicine?', *Public Law,* 592–624.

Dickson, B. (1992b) 'Northern Ireland's Troubles and the Judges' in *Northern Ireland: Politics and the Constitution,* ed. by B. Hadfield. Milton Keynes, Open University Press.

Dickson, B. (1992c) 'The European Convention on Human Rights and Northern Ireland' in *Mélanges offerts á Jacques Vélu,* ed. by Bruylant Brussels. 1407–29.

Dillon, M. and D. Lehane (1973) *Political Murder in Northern Ireland.* Harmondsworth, Penguin.

Diplock, Lord (1972) *Report of the Commission to Consider Legal Procedures to Deal with Terrorist Activities in Northern Ireland.* HMSO, Cmnd 5185.

Gallagher, A. M. (1992) in *Social Attitudes in Northern Ireland: the Second Report.* ed. by P. Stringer and G. Robinson. Belfast, Blackstaff Press.

Gardiner, Lord (1975) *Report of a Committee to Consider, in the Context of Civil Liberties and Human Rights, Measures to deal with Terrorism in Northern Ireland.* HMSO, Cmnd 5847.

Greer, D. (1987) 'The Impact of the Troubles on the Law and Legal System of Northern Ireland' in *Northern Ireland: Living with the Crisis,* ed. by A. Ward. New York, Praeger.

Greer, S. and A. White (1986) *Abolishing the Diplock Courts.* London, Cobden Trust.

Hadden, T. et al. (1990) 'Emergency Law in Northern Ireland: the Context' in *Justice Under Fire: the Abuse of Civil Liberties in Northern Ireland* (2nd ed.), ed. by A. Jennings. London: Pluto Press.

Hunt, P. and B. Dickson (1993) 'Northern Ireland's Emergency Laws and International Human Rights', *Netherlands Quarterly of Human Rights,* 11, 173–84.

Jackson, J. (1991) 'Curtailing the Right of Silence: Lessons from Northern Ireland', *Criminal Law Review,* 404.

Jellicoe, Lord (1983) *Review of the Operation of the Prevention of Terrorism (Temporary Provisions) Act 1976.* HMSO, Cmnd 8803.

Molloy, E. (1986) *Dynasties of Coercion; Field Day Pamphlet, No. 10.* Derry, Field Day Theatre Co.

Munck, R. (1988) 'The Lads and the Hoods: Alternative Justice in an Irish Context' in *Whose Law and Order?* ed. by M. Tomlinson, T. Varley and C. McCullagh, Belfast, Sociological Association of Ireland.

National Council for Civil Liberties (1936) *The Special Powers Acts of Northern Ireland: Report of a Commission of Inquiry.* London, NCCL.

NILQ (1989) *Northern Ireland Legal Quarterly,* vol. 40, no. 4 (a collection of articles on the Police and Criminal Evidence (NI) Order 1989). Belfast, Faculty of Law, Queen's University, Belfast.

Purdie, B. (1990) *Politics in the Streets: the Origins of the Civil Rights Movement in Northern Ireland.* Belfast, Blackstaff Press.

Shackleton, Lord (1978) *Review of the Operation of the Prevention of Terrorism (Temporary Provisions) Act 1976.* HMSO, Cmnd 7324.

Walsh, D. (1983) *The Use and Abuse of Emergency Legislation in Northern Ireland.* London, Cobden Trust.
Walsh, D. (1984) 'Civil Liberties in Northern Ireland' in *Civil Liberties 1984,* ed. by P. Wallington. Oxford, Martin Robertson.

CASE REFERENCES

Brannigan and McBride v. *UK* Judgment of European Court of Human Rights 5/1992/350/423–4; 26 May 1993
Brogan v. *UK* (1988) 11 European Human Rights Reports (EHRR) 117
Farrell v. *UK* (1983) 5 EHRR 465
Fox, Campbell and Hartley v. *UK* (1991) 13 EHRR 157
Ireland v. *UK* (1979–80) 2 EHRR 25
McConnell v. *UK* Application no. 14671/89
McFeeley et al. v. *UK* (1981) 3 EHRR 161
McVeigh et al. v. *UK* (1983) 5 EHRR 71
Murray v. *UK* Application no.14310/88
O'Neill and Kelly v. *UK* Application nos. 17441/90 and 17711/91
Stewart v. *UK* (1985) 7 EHRR 453
X v. *UK* (1978) 14 Decisions and Reports 246

Part Three
Subgroups

6 Women and the Northern Ireland Conflict: Experiences and Responses

Valerie Morgan and Grace Fraser

INTRODUCTION

As localised conflict situations proliferate, and ethnic, tribal or religious groups in almost all parts of the world strive to establish their distinct 'national' identity, many social and political issues which initially appear to have only tenuous links with the specifics of violent conflict are being illuminated in new ways. Relationships which have either been unexamined or taken for granted are having to be analysed or re-analysed in the light of experiences generated in Bosnia or South Africa or Northern Ireland. Among these is the relationship between nationalism and feminism (Hamilton and Barrett, 1986).

The direct, often horrific, personal experiences of women in societies experiencing violent ethnic conflict, and the more indirect impact on women's lives of the upheavals in the economy, the labour market and the family which occur in such situations, both raise complex questions about the interaction of the nationalist and feminist agendas.

> women in former Yugoslavia have an ambivalent attitude towards nationalism ... recognising the social matrix of Nationalism is certainly not difficult for women ... they accept its elements of community and sentiment as traditionally female milieu ... or they reject the nationalist matrix as being nearly identical to the one which women have been able to escape. (Rener, 1993)

Generalisation is inevitably difficult since the specificity of each context produces a range of differing events and responses for women and men. In some of the countries which have emerged from the break-up of the former Soviet empire, many women define their reactions to the interaction of resurgent nationalism and feminism in terms of the changes that are increasing their exclusion from the labour market, destroying social and welfare benefits – such as child-care – and making their economic participation impossible. Where there is a strong religious element in the forging of new national identities, different problems arouse feminist concern: for example, in some areas the definition of nationality through Islamic codes can be experienced by women as a threat to their political and legal rights (Glavanis, 1993).

The experience of women in Northern Ireland over the last 25 years needs to be viewed within this more general frame. In addition any analysis has to take account both of theoretical debates about women and conflict, and of the specific context of the historical experience of women in Great Britain, the Republic of Ireland and Northern Ireland itself. In terms of gender relations all three regions could be categorised as essentially conservative. Great Britain has had gender equality legislation, covering aspects of employment and social and economic legislation, since the mid-1970s, but its impact has been limited; since the 1980s gender issues have had low priority in the formulation of government policy (Phillips, 1991). Indeed recent ministerial utterances about 'one-parent families' and 'traditional values' could be interpreted as an attack on the changing role of women. In Ireland, the position of women is deeply grounded in both religious and national identity. The reality of women's experience within both the Catholic and Protestant religious traditions, and in both the North and South jurisdictions, has been in the main one of marginalisation and exclusion from power; but this reality has been confounded by idealised models of women which have had significant influence on popular, especially nationalist and Catholic, thinking about politics and religion. Many years after the Easter Rising, Yeats was to comment in relation to the play which he wrote with Lady Gregory *Cathleen ni Houlihan,* (first performed in Dublin in 1904 with Maud Gonne, 'a divine being', as the Poor Old Woman, Ireland),

> Did that play of mine send out
> Certain men the English shot?

In the present period of the Northern Ireland troubles, the meek, submissive figure of Mary, the Virgin Mother, Queen of Ireland has combined in nationalist mythology with the noble female personification of Ireland, to provide a potent, ambiguous and complex symbol in the struggle against British imperialism. The overall effect is to reproduce a highly conservative, highly sentimental, even patriarchal, image of 'Mother Ireland', which is detached from the worlds of political activist and feminist alike (McWilliams, 1991). Interestingly, there appear to be no symbolic equivalents on the Protestant, unionist side, though Monica McWilliams also argues that in Protestant mythology while 'women become invisible' their 'prime role as homemakers' is emphasised in the same way as for women in the Catholic tradition. Thus Northern Ireland, in spite of violent political upheaval for over 25 years, has retained many features of a highly traditional social structure with strong rural roots, one in which the religious values of both the main communities still have considerable influence in defining the appropriate position of women in the home and in the family (Davies and McLaughlin, 1991; Edgerton, 1986).

THE INDIRECT EFFECTS ON WOMEN OF 'THE TROUBLES'

Twenty five years of violent conflict have inevitably had significant effects on the economic and social structure of Northern Irish society and this has had numerous repercussions for women. There has been no overt agenda to change women's lives, but the local situation, interacting with government policy in the United Kingdom as a whole and the shifts in the European and global economies, has had a considerable, if indirect, impact on women from both communities. The nature and implications of these changes can be illustrated with reference to employment, education and social policy.

There remains an ongoing debate about the impact of 'the troubles' on the Northern Ireland labour market and similarly their impact on the economic participation of women is not clear cut. Overall there has been a marked increase in the employment of women outside the home, from under 37 per cent of the female population in 1971 to over 47 per cent in 1991 (Montgomery, 1993) and in the proportion of married women, especially those with young children, in paid employment (Trewsdale and Toman, 1993). This change is clearly related to wider European trends, though local factors, such as high male unemployment and the decline of some of the traditional male areas of employment, may have played a part in encouraging women to remain in or return to the labour market. On the other hand the great majority of women still work in very traditional areas, the service industries, clerical work and education and health-related occupations (EOCNI, 1993). One specific feature of employment patterns in Northern Ireland is the very high proportion of the labour force employed either directly or indirectly by government in the civil service, central and local government agencies and the legal and security services. This pattern is partially a direct response to the political situation (i.e. the increased employment in the police, prison service, and so on) and partially a reflection of the narrow economic base and the decline in traditional industries. For women in paid employment this pattern has contributed to the development of a marked dichotomy between those in public sector posts who have relatively good wages and conditions of service and those in part-time and casual work where low pay and poor conditions are common (Trewsdale, 1987; McWilliams, 1991).

Developments in education have similarly had a tangential effect on girls and women. The segregated education system has been seen as a possible source of community division and there has been an implicit adoption, in government policy, of a reconstructionist model (Gallagher, 1989; Dunn, 1986). Amongst other initiatives, this has led to many studies of participation rates and achievement levels and to measures aimed at equalising the distribution of funding (Morgan, 1992b). While these have been primarily driven by a community relations agenda there has been a spin-off effect for gender equality. For instance, there is now clear awareness of the long-term implications of gender stereotyped subject choices, and attempts are made in the programmes of study of the new Northern Ireland Curriculum to ensure that girls continue to study science throughout the period of compulsory schooling. The limited provision for the teaching of science and technology in girls' schools has also been recognised and some concrete policies introduced to redress imbalances.

In the more general area of social policy it has been claimed that because the focus of so much of government policy has been on controlling violence, mitigating its impact and trying to establish more acceptable political structures, other issues have been given little attention. One such area of neglect has been gender equality. There is a Northern Ireland Equal Opportunities Commission which has campaigned on a wide range of women's issues, but government response to evidence about the difficulties women face has been slow and hesitant. In some instances, for example in relation to the provision of childcare, this reflects a general ambivalence about changes in the role of women which affects all parts of the United Kingdom (Taillon, 1992). In other cases, however, political violence affects the response as recent research into domestic violence illustrates. Direct reaction to incidents of violence is affected both by the security situation which makes it dangerous for the police to respond immediately to reports of attacks on women in some areas, and also by cultural responses which in some instances appear to accept and tolerate male violence against women as a response to stress (McWilliams and McKernan, 1993; Sharoni, 1992). The contested nature of the society puts a brake on shifts both in policy and legislation, but also has a profound effect on attitudes to women's issues, on both sides. On the nationalist side, even when there is agreement that women's issues are important and significant, there is concern that concentration on a feminist agenda at this point could provide a distraction from the central struggle about the nature of the state. On the unionist side any form of political or social protest, or proposed programme of change, poses difficulties because of the implied threat to the existing structures; in addition there is deep suspicion of any consideration of gender equality because of perceived links between feminism and nationalism.

THE RANGE OF WOMEN'S EXPERIENCES OF AND RESPONSES TO VIOLENCE

Commitment to unionism and nationalism

The actual impact of violence on individuals in Northern Ireland has varied immensely, from those who have lost their lives to those who have never heard a bomb explosion. This is as much true for women as men. Women and girls of all ages have been killed in bombings, shootings, fires and as a result of plastic bullets. A much larger number have been injured and more still have had members of their family or friends killed or injured. It is perhaps not unexpected that the great majority of those killed and injured as the result of violence have been men, since, in spite of the prominence of incidents which appear to be completely random sectarian attacks, the majority of killings have been targeted with the security forces and paramilitary groups the major targets. During the 25 years of the troubles over 3300 people have been killed and of these just over 200 were women. Women have, however, been among the victims of some of the most horrific and emotive incidents; five women were killed in the 'Poppy Day' bomb in Enniskillen in 1987; seven died in the fire-bombing of the La Mon House Hotel in 1978; and girls and women were among the victims of the Shankill Road bomb and Rising Sun Bar shooting in

Greysteel in October 1993. At the other extreme, many women in Northern Ireland have never had any greater contact with the troubles than being stopped at a security road check (Geary and Morison, 1992).

Similarly women's responses to violence run on a continuum which includes individuals who are deeply and exclusively committed to the ideals of one side or the other and become actively involved in politics or sectarian organisations (legal or illegal); those who express indifference or seek to 'shut out' what is going on; and women who are actively participating in peace-seeking and reconciliation. In relation to ethnic and political violence in Northern Ireland and in many other parts of the world, suggestions have been made that women react differently from men in that they are 'natural peacemakers' with views that are 'more moderate' than those of men (Goot and Reid, 1975; Stilanen and Stanworth, 1984). These views are usually expressed in the context of studies which take male behaviour as the norm and treat women's attitudes as a deviation. However, there is little concrete evidence to support such models and indeed what empirical material there is, for example from attitude surveys, suggests that the range of views expressed by women is little different from that put forward by men (O'Donnell, 1977). Women clearly do have an interest in safeguarding their families and particularly their children, and this is likely to impel them to seek an end to violence; but they also have a major role in transmitting culture and tradition between the generations and in the process may perpetuate and reinforce separation and hostility (Morgan, 1992a).

Clear commitment to the political ideals of unionism or nationalism manifests itself most obviously through involvement in the constitutional political parties. The formal participation of women in political life in Northern Ireland, however, remains very limited. None of the major parties has more than a handful of women members in official positions, and none of the Northern Ireland members of either the Westminster or European parliaments are women. Indeed very few women have ever represented any of the political parties in major initiatives; for example in inter-party negotiations over the constitutional future, they have rarely been active in discussions with the British government or the Northern Ireland government departments, and almost no women have acted as media spokespersons. Such a situation in Northern Ireland is perhaps not surprising since women are not well represented in national politics in either Great Britain or the Irish Republic. A greater level of involvement in local politics and local government might be expected, but in fact women constituted only 11.2 per cent of all elected local representatives on district councils in 1990. Of the 26 such councils in Northern Ireland women councillors exceeded 20 per cent of the total in only five cases and there were two councils which had no women members. Such limited participation is probably the result of the interaction of several forces. It seems likely that women perceive the political parties in Northern Ireland as antagonistic to their active participation, and certainly Northern Irish political life has a highly conservative and masculine image. It may also be that women have limited interest in structures which appear to achieve little and which at local government level have very limited powers and responsibilities. Certainly the 1990 Social Attitudes Survey data indicates that while nearly as many women (34 per cent) as men (38 per cent) stated that they supported a political party, considerably more of the non-aligned women (47 per cent) than the non-aligned men (38 per cent) maintained that they had no preference for any particular party (Morgan, 1992a).

Deep commitment to nationalism or unionism is, of course, also expressed through involvement with paramilitary groups, although here empirical data is difficult to collect. The number of women who sympathise with the objectives and methods of the groups who use violence is impossible to estimate, as is the ratio between male and female supporters. Information about convictions for involvement in terrorism is available but it is extremely difficult to get quantitative information about the actual number of either women or men who have been active in paramilitary groups. From what evidence is available it seems that only a very small number of women have been active members of either the Provisional IRA or the Protestant paramilitary groups. In 1992, for example, there were 22 women in Maghaberry prison who were classified by the republican movement as 'POWs', out of 3000 republican 'political' prisoners in jails worldwide. But, writing in *An Glór Gafa – The Captive Voice*, in the summer of 1990, the Women POWs in Maghaberry commented, 'Irish women are every bit as revolutionary as Irish men and their resistance is every bit as fierce, be they IRA Volunteers, Sinn Féin activists or campaign organisers and protesters'.

Branches of Cumann na mBan, the female auxiliary of the IRA, originally founded before the Easter Rising and dissolved around 1980, seem to be attached to companies and appear to have operated mainly in a supportive role to the military. Tasks included responsibility for the selection and stocking of 'safe houses', training and provision of first aid, 'cleaning and loading of guns, where practicable' (Buckley and Lonergan, 1983). Women taking a more prominent role have included Mairead Farrell, whose killing while on an IRA operation in Gibraltar in 1988 attracted huge media attention, proving that, in propaganda terms, the significance of women paramilitaries can far outweigh their numerical strength. However, at a more strategic level, the influence of women on the formation of policy within the paramilitary groups remains obscure. Within Sinn Féin itself the situation may be different – the party has had a women's department since 1980; but, in an interview with *The Guardian* newspaper in 1991, Rita O'Hare, then Sinn Féin's Director of Communications, admitted that women are under-represented in the party, as they are in all political movements in Ireland. At the same time she argued that their contribution to Irish republicanism had been crucial, especially during the H-block campaign of the 1970s when 'women were the driving force' (*The Guardian*, 1991). In February 1980, republican women prisoners in Armagh stepped up their 'no work' protest to a 'no wash' protest in response to the corresponding male campaign. The division of feminist opinion over how to respond to worsening conditions inside Armagh prison was important because it highlights the contradictions imposed upon feminists in Ireland by the continuing civil strife. Feminists were opposed to 'oppression' but in this case was the oppression self-inflicted? By supporting the Armagh women, were feminists in fact 'neglecting' the 'real' feminist issues in Ireland, such as the treatment of the victims of domestic violence, the situation of one-parent families and the legislation on divorce, contraception and divorce? (D'Arcy, 1981). Significantly, republican women, certainly those who are most committed to their political cause, see no contradiction between their political allegiance and feminist aspirations. Much of the summer 1990 issue of *An Glór Gafa* was devoted to highlighting 'the oppression of women', linking this oppression explicitly with the continued British presence in Ireland:

> Women in Ireland are forced into constant battle as members of Republican communities. The main source of our oppression is the British occupation and domination of our country. Until the British have been forced to withdraw, women will continue to bear the brunt of repressive policies and to fight oppression in all its forms. (*An Glór Gafa*, 1990)

This discussion of women's involvement in paramilitary groups has drawn its examples exclusively from the republican movement. This is not to imply that women are not involved on the loyalist side but it does reflect the almost total lack of evidence about loyalist women paramilitaries. Such lack of evidence makes it impossible to discuss their role and activities on any clear factual basis. The upsurge in loyalist violence which has occurred from about 1990 has not to date produced a literature similar to that on the republican side, in which at least the shadowy outlines of women's position can be discerned and in which the debate about the relationship between paramilitary and feminist goals is beginning to be articulated.

Commitment to Peace

There is, of course, no contradiction between active involvement in one of the constitutional political parties and membership of groups which campaign for peace, so there is an overlap between women whose links with the constitutional political parties were described above and those considered in this section. Throughout the period of the current troubles there have been groups who have organised around a commitment to peace. Some have been specifically concerned to campaign for the cessation of violence, from whatever source, while others have had a broader commitment to community relations, cross-community contact and reconciliation. These organisations have not of course had exclusively female membership, but most have had women in the majority. Specific 'peace' groups have frequently arisen as an immediate spontaneous response to a particularly horrific incident; the best-known example being the Peace People, formed in 1976 by a group of Belfast women when three children were killed by a car which ran out of control in the aftermath of a shooting incident. Such groups have been able to mobilise mass action and demonstrations for the cessation of violence over a brief period, but they have found it difficult to translate this into sustained political action. It appears to be possible to arouse intense public emotion in opposition to violence but much more difficult to focus the rather amorphous response which is generated in such contexts into a programme with political and social power.

On the other hand a considerable number of peace-related organisations operating with less publicity and on a much smaller scale have been active for many years. The Corrymeela Community, Protestant and Catholic Encounter and numerous locally based

community groups would fall into this category. Almost all have had
many, often a large majority of, women members. During the 1980s
many have become more focused and have set out to achieve specific
goals linked to local community provision. In this they have been
increasingly successful, but they remain outside the formal power
structures and have, until recently, had little support from official
government agencies, the political parties or the churches. This may
now be changing and organisations such as the Community Relations
Council and the Central Community Relations Unit have over the
last few years supported and funded a wider range of initiatives. This
in itself may occasionally pose problems if an activity becomes too
closely identified with a government agency or if accepting funds
from such sources is seen as problematic. Overall the involvement of
women in peace and reconciliation work presents a picture of energy,
commitment and solid achievement in specific contexts, but the
limits and frustrations which they have encountered also illustrate
the extent to which the traditional, almost exclusively male, power
structures can thwart, marginalise or even take over those who seek
to operate through new channels.

The Uncommitted and the Uncertain

In considering those women who identify clearly with unionist or
nationalist ideologies and those who actively work for community
reconciliation it has to be borne in mind that the actual numbers
directly involved are small. Going to vote at election time is as close as
the majority of women in Northern Ireland get to direct contact with
unionist or nationalist politics, and expressing a wish for peace in
conversation is likely to be as close as they have got to reconciliation.
This is not to claim that they are not concerned about political violence and community division, but is simply a reflection of the social
and economic conditions, role models and family responsibilities
which dominate most women's lives. Northern Ireland is still a traditional society where women's sphere frequently remains the home
and the family, where many live in small towns and rural areas and
the majority have limited resources and mobility. In such a context
many women have few opportunities for any active participation in
politics or peace-making.

Women do join organisations and groups but these are mainly
long-established bodies focusing on church activities, charity work or
what might be characterised as traditional women's interests and

issues. In most cases such groups do not deliberately turn their backs on what is happening in Northern Ireland, but they frequently do not see reaction to political violence or development of cross-community reconciliation as things which come within their remit. A recent study of the functioning of such organisations in rural and small town communities suggests that the whole process of choosing to join a group, becoming a member and participating in activities is closely bound up with family and friendship networks and also significantly affected by age and social class groupings (Morgan and Fraser, 1993). Thus, for example, the charity shops, selling a mixture of second-hand clothing and craft products from developing countries, which are a familiar feature of most small towns, are staffed almost exclusively by female volunteers and these are usually older women who have time available during the day. They are normally recruited informally through a friend or relative who already works in the shop and is of the same age and social group. In a society where kinship and friendship are usually contained within one's own ethnic community this inevitably leads to many groups being composed almost entirely of either Protestants or Catholics – not through deliberate exclusion or prejudice, but because many women know very few members of the 'other' community well enough to ask them to join a group. In this way a circle is established which is difficult to break, precisely because it is so natural and automatic.

If women's membership of local charity and leisure groups tends to run along intra-community lines as a result of informal networks, membership of church-related women's organisations is usually structurally divided. Yet from a community relations perspective these organisations are potentially very significant. Most of the major Protestant denominations have specific women's organisations: for example the Presbyterian Church in Ireland has the Presbyterian Women's Association, and in the Church of Ireland there is the Mother's Union. In the Catholic Church the pattern is less clear-cut since most of the organisations which serve similar purposes are parish-based, and although they have a predominantly female membership they are not exclusively single-sex. Most of the church-related women's groups have a similar set of functions and range of activities: they provide a forum for devotional meetings, meetings with a social, leisure or hobby focus, fund-raising work (frequently for overseas missionary work) and the organisation of catering services for church events. However, they are especially significant in the Northern Ireland context because, for a considerable number of women, especially in rural communities, they provide the only setting in which they experience regular attendance at structured meetings and have a chance to talk and work with women outside their circle of family or close friends. As such they provide a forum through which cross-community contact could possibly be developed. However, this path is fraught with difficulties.

While most of the major churches have a formal commitment to support the improvement of community relations there are a number of the Protestant groups which see inter-church contact as undesirable and spiritually dangerous, and they would be opposed to links with Catholic women in particular. Those churches which do not have such clear doctrinal prohibitions still face problems if they wish to develop contacts across the Protestant–Catholic divide, caused by suspicion, anxiety and unfamiliarity. Even when there is a direct statement in the objectives of the group which appears to point towards contact – as with the Presbyterian Women's Association, which has as one of its aims 'to provide a link with the women of the Church in Ireland and throughout the world' – this may be interpreted and operationalised in a particular way. So a PWA branch is likely to organise joint meetings and projects with other local branches, contacts with related churchwomen's groups in other countries, especially where there is a missionary link, and some meetings with other Protestant churches in Northern Ireland. But what it is not likely to do is equally significant.

This picture may appear negative and may suggest that women in the churches in Northern Ireland, even where they give tacit approval to efforts to improve community relations, do not carry this into action. This ignores the very real difficulties which face the women involved, which are often practical, even mundane. Thus, for example, Protestant women usually organise through specific designated bodies and there is very often a minister's wife who takes a lead and acts as a contact person. This structure is not parallelled in the Catholic church where women work through mixed-sex parish organisations and a number of different women may take the lead in different aspects of the activities. As a result even making contact to discuss the possibilities of joint activities can appear daunting. Without informal links of kinship and friendship, neither group is clear about procedures, and in a situation which is inevitably somewhat tense, anxieties are heightened by fears of 'getting it wrong' at the first step. For those in leadership positions there is often the particular concern as to how to bring all the members with them.

Protestant ministers' wives appear to feel constrained by their position so that, although they are expected to take the lead in any initiative, they are also circumscribed by expectations about their behaviour and the fear that anything they do will be seen as a reflection on their husband and could undermine his position. As a result many of the women's groups in the churches present a picture of detachment from aspects of the reality of life in Northern Ireland. This picture may often be as much a reflection of constraints they do not know how to break, as an indication of lack of commitment to better cross-community relations.

UNDERSTANDING WOMEN'S RESPONSES

These difficulties bring out clearly the need to analyse a little further the basis of the responses which women, across the whole political, religious and social spectrum, bring to the conflict. The limited political response in terms of involvement in national or local party politics has been noted, but recent research suggests that this is in part a reflection not of disengagement but of the way in which women define politics. It seems likely that women are active in political work but do not describe their involvement in these terms. Thus, over the last few years, there has been a considerable growth in the number and effectiveness of local community groups in which women have played very prominent roles. These groups have campaigned on a range of issues such as childcare provision and leisure facilities. In a number of cases groups based in unionist and nationalist areas have been able to work together over specific projects, especially in some of the working-class housing areas of Belfast. These are in a sense highly political actions, but the women who take part resist the label, suggesting that it is not that women are less interested than men in politics but that they are exploring different forms of political action possibly in response to the 'closed shop' operated by men and possibly also in an attempt to break out of the rigid forms of political debate in Northern Ireland.

While the labels Catholic and Protestant are routinely used to describe the two communities it is frequently emphasised that the conflict is not a religious conflict. Although it is probably true that social, economic and political issues are more central to the actual struggle between the communities than differences in religious beliefs, the conflict is deeply influenced by religious ideology. To an extent which would be quite unfamiliar in most other parts of Western Europe, attitudes, values and even language are affected by a theologically inspired view of the world which affects the thinking even of those who are not practising members of their churches. As in many other cultures women in Northern Ireland are more regular and committed churchgoers than men and so it is particularly true that their views cannot be understood without reference to religion. The relationship between faith and attitudes to the divisions in Northern Irish society is, however, far from simple. For some women their beliefs impel them to an active search for peace since they see reconciliation as central to the Christian message. For others their religious life is essentially apart from the political and social turmoil of the society and can provide a haven. For yet others salvation demands separation from those who are defined as doctrinally in error, and so cross-community links are potentially dangerous at a very fundamental level.

CONCLUSION

The picture of women's experiences which is emerging from recent research in Northern Ireland suggests that some common assumptions about women's experiences and attitudes in conflicted societies are oversimplified and in need of re-examination. The model of women as the peace-makers who always strive to eliminate violence does not reflect the range and subtlety of their responses. Women do wish to protect their families, and particularly their children, from the impact of violence, but this has to be taken in conjunction with evidence that they have firm views and commitments which span the whole range from active support for the use of violence as a way of achieving political objectives to equally firm support for integration of the two communities. The wish to protect the family from physical harm coexists with the desire to preserve culture and tradition, by physically violent means in some cases. Women's views may differ from those of men, but to describe that difference in terms of women being more moderate may be no more than a reflection of the way their views have been sought and analysed in studies which have been essentially male-centred. More interesting is the possibility that women in Northern Ireland display a complex and flexible range of responses to their social, economic and political situation which also challenges many of the existing political structures and raises again the issue of the relationship between nationalism and feminism with which the chapter began.

REFERENCES

An Glór Gafa – The Captive Voice (1990), 2: 2, Summer.

Buckley, S. and P. Lonergan (1983) 'Women and the Troubles, 1969–1980' in *Terrorism in Ireland*, ed. by Y. Alexander and A. O'Day. London, Croom Helm.

D'Arcy, M. (1981) 'Tell Them Everything', in C. Loughran, *Armagh and Feminist Strategy*. London, Pluto Press. (Quoted in C. Loughran, 'Campaigns around Republicanism – Women Prisoners in Armagh Jail', *Feminist Review* 1, 23, June, 59–79.)

Davies, C. and E. McLaughlin, eds (1991) *Women, Employment and Social Policy in Northern Ireland*. Belfast, Policy Research Institute.

Dunn, S. (1986) 'The Role of Education in the Northern Ireland Conflict', *Oxford Review of Education*, 12: 3, 233–42.

Edgerton, L. (1986) 'Public Protest, Domestic Acquiescence: Women in Northern Ireland' in *Caught up in Conflict: Women's Responses to Political Strife*, ed. by R. Ridd and H. Calloway. London, Macmillan.

Equal Opportunities Commission for Northern Ireland (1993) *Where do Women Figure?* 4th edn. Belfast, EOCNI.

Gallagher, A. M. (1989) *Majority Minority Review 1: Education and Religion in Northern Ireland*. Coleraine, Centre for the Study of Conflict, University of Ulster.

Geary, R. and J. Morison (1992) 'The Perception of Crime' in *Social Attitudes in Northern Ireland*: the Second Report, ed. by P. Stringer and G. Robinson. Belfast, Blackstaff Press.

Glavanis, K. (1993) 'The Women's Movement, Feminism and the National Struggle in Palestine: Unresolved Contradictions' in ESRC Seminar, *Women and Political and Economic Involvement*. University of Ulster, Jordanstown.

Goot, M. and E. Reid (1975) *Women and Voting Studies: Mindless Matrons or Sexist Scientism*. New York, Sage.

The Guardian (1991) 'Interview with Rita O'Hare'. London, 12 November.

Hamilton, R. and M. Barrett (1986) *The Politics of Diversity: Feminism, Marxism and Nationalism*. London, Verso.

MacCurtain, M. (1989) 'Fullness of Life: Defining Female Spirituality in Twentieth Century Ireland' in *Women Surviving – Studies in Irish Women's History in the Nineteenth and Twentieth Centuries*, ed. by M. Luddy and C. Murphy. Dublin, Poolbeg Press.

McEwen, A., C. Curry and J. Watson (1992) 'Subject Preferences at A–Level in Northern Ireland', *European Journal of Science Education*, 8: 1, 39–56.

McWilliams, M. (1991) 'Women's Paid Work and the Sexual Division of Labour' in *Women, Employment and Social Policy in Northern Ireland*, ed. by C. Davies and E. McLaughlin. Belfast, Policy Research Institute.

McWilliams, M. and J. McKernan (1993) *Bringing it Out into the Open –Domestic Violence in Northern Ireland*. Belfast, HMSO.

Montgomery, P. (1993) 'Paid and Unpaid Work' in *Women's Working Lives*, ed. by J. Kremer and P. Montgomery. Belfast, HMSO for Equal Opportunities Commission for Northern Ireland.

Morgan, V. (1992a) 'Bridging the Divide: Women and Political and Community Issues' in *Social Attitudes in Northern Ireland*: the Second Report, ed. by P. Stringer and G. Robinson. Belfast, Blackstaff Press.

Morgan, V. (1992b) *Common Curriculum, Equal Curriculum, Gender Issues and the New Northern Ireland Curriculum*. Belfast, Equal Opportunities Commission for Northern Ireland.

Morgan, V. and G. Fraser (1993) *Women, Community and Organisations*. Coleraine, Centre for the Study of Conflict and Centre for Research on Women, University of Ulster.

O'Donnell, E. E. (1977) *Irish Stereotypes*. Dublin, College of Business Studies.

Phillips, A. (1991) *Engendering Democracy*. Cambridge, Polity Press.

Rener, T. (1993) 'Nationalism and Gender in Postsocialist Societies – is Nationalism Female?' ESRC Seminar, *Women and Political and Economic Involvement*. Queen's University, Belfast.

Rooney, E. (1992) 'Women, Community and Politics in Northern Ireland – Isms in Action', *Journal of Gender Studies*, 1: 4, 475–91.

Sharoni, S. (1992) 'Every Woman is an Occupied Territory: the Politics of Militarism and Sexism and the Israeli–Palestinian Conflict', *Journal of Gender Studies*, 1: 4, 447–62.

Stilanen, J. and M. Stanworth, eds (1984) *Women and the Public Sphere*. London, Hutchinson.

Taillon, R. (1992) *Grant-aided ... or Taken for Granted? – a Study of Women's Voluntary Organisations in Northern Ireland*. Belfast, Women's Support Network.

Trewsdale, J. (1987) *Womanpower No. 4, the Aftermath of Recession, Changing Patterns of Employment and Unemployment in Northern Ireland*. Belfast, Equal Opportunities Commission for Northern Ireland.

Trewsdale, J. and A. Toman (1993) 'Employment' in *Women's Working Lives*, ed. by J. Kremer and P. Montgomery. Belfast, HMSO for Equal Opportunities Commission for Northern Ireland.

7 Children and Conflict: A Psychological Perspective
Ed Cairns and Tara Cairns

The arrival of troops on the streets of Northern Ireland had the effect of placing local children firmly in the world's spotlight. Twenty-five years later the words 'Children in Northern Ireland' can still conjure up the image of a very small child, stone in hand taking on the might of the British army on some dreary Belfast or Derry street. This image influenced what people thought in the early days of the 'troubles' would happen to children in Northern Ireland. And what they expected was that children in Northern Ireland, as a result of the strain of growing up against a background of continuous political violence, would become shell-shocked zombies flooding the psychiatric hospitals, or amoral juvenile delinquents totally out of adult control.

Certainly children in Northern Ireland have had widespread experience of the political violence. For example in an early survey (McKeown, 1973), of harassment on the way to school, involving all of the post-primary schools in the province, over half reported that a degree of harassment had occurred.

More recently indirect experiences of the violence have included having a friend or relative killed or injured or the occurrence of an incident close to home. For example, when McGrath and Wilson (1985) interviewed 522 ten- and eleven-year-old children almost 20 per cent of the children reported that they had been in or near a bomb explosion and 20.1 per cent reported that they had a relative or friend injured or killed because of the troubles. Overall 12 per cent said that they felt that the area where they lived was 'not safe to live in'. Even those children who live in parts of the province relatively untouched by the violence have not remained innocent of the turmoil in other areas. In this context television news has played an important role (Cairns et al., 1980; Cairns, 1984; Cairns, 1990).

It would appear, therefore, that children in Northern Ireland have had a substantial level of both direct and indirect experience with the political violence and its consequences. The remainder of this section will review the evidence in an attempt to decide if this experience has been associated with any particular psychological effects.

MORAL DEVELOPMENT

One of the first predictions made at the beginning of the present civil disturbances in Northern Ireland was that a new generation would emerge which would be morally scarred. This 'truncation of the development of moral judgment in a whole generation of children' (Fields, 1973), it was suggested, would take two principal forms. One would be the development of anti-authority attitudes (Fraser, 1974). The other would be, according to a major church report, a 'catastrophic and terrifying decline in respect for the sacredness of human life' (*Violence in Ireland*, 1976). Despite these gloomy predictions the empirical evidence suggests that Northern Ireland can still be characterised as a deeply religious and moral society which is notable for the absence of any marked generation gap.

One basic statistic which can be used to measure the overt religiosity of any society is the proportion of the population who are likely to attend church. Greer (1980) has reported two surveys of sixth-formers in Northern Ireland, carried out in 1968 and 1978. In 1968 76 per cent of girls and 65 per cent of boys claimed that they attended church at least monthly while ten years later the figures had dropped slightly to 68 per cent and 56 per cent respectively. Data from the Social Attitudes Survey (Cairns, 1991) have indicated that this behaviour is maintained into adulthood. For example, while some 50 per cent of those surveyed in Great Britain reported that they never attended church, the equivalent figure for Northern Ireland was 10 per cent.

There is, therefore, hard evidence that Northern Ireland is a church-going if not a religious society. But does this mean that it can be considered a moral society? In fact some patchy evidence suggests that compared to their peers in England or in the United States (but not in the Republic of Ireland) Northern Irish children and young people are more likely to perform badly on objective tests of moral reasoning. For example Breslin (1982) in a large study involving 17-year-olds claimed that only 28 per cent could be classified at the principled state of moral development. Similarly both Kahn (1982) using the *Defining Issues Test* and Cairns and Conlon (1985) using the *Sociomoral Reflection Objective Measure* found that Irish children on average scored at a lower level compared to their North American peers. In particular there is a suggestion that 'Northern Irish young people are not so aware of the complexity of moral problems' (Cairns, 1987).

Apparently contrary evidence comes from studies which have adopted a more straightforward approach. For example Greer (1990) has reported a series of virtually identical surveys of Protestant school pupils, in the last two years of secondary education, carried out in 1968, 1978 and 1988. Across this time span answers to the majority of questions probing moral attitudes and values either did not change, or indeed indicated a more orthodox belief. Only four out of more than twenty measures produced a trend which indicated the 'rejection of traditional practice or moral judgment'(Greer, 1990).

Based on this evidence, therefore, it would appear that political violence in Northern Ireland has had little or no impact on the general moral attitudes and values of the generations who have grown up during this period. In turn there is evidence that stringent moral standards in Northern Ireland are not just confined to pencil and paper tests. According to a government report (PPRU, 1984) when the Northern Ireland rate of offences known to the police per thousand population was compared in 1981 with 12 similar sized areas, seven in England and Wales and five in the USA, then Northern Ireland ranked tenth lowest. This then, some would say, is the good news about Northern Ireland. A society where the majority of young people, like their parent's generation, have at least doubts about gambling, drunkenness and pre-marital sexual intercourse and where the majority of young people keep on the right side of the law.

MENTAL HEALTH

Another major area of concern has been for the mental health of young people in Northern Ireland. Here the most detailed clinical picture has been provided by Fraser (1974) who was a child psychiatrist working in Belfast when the troubles began. He suggests that the typical child victim of this time fell into a narrow age-band of between eight and thirteen years, had been exposed to a particular violent incident, and that at the time this had led to such things as a fainting fit, an asthma attack or sleep disturbance. These problems tended to continue after the precipitating event and to become worse with the passage of time. Indeed the original phobic anxiety attack often generalised to other stimuli.

Harder evidence was provided by McCauley and Troy (1983) who examined the records of children referred to a Child Psychiatric Clinic in Belfast in the years 1968 (that is before the 'recent' outbreak of violence), 1972, 1976 and 1980. What this exercise revealed was that in three of the four years around 400 children were referred annually. However in 1972, the most violent year so far, only 229 children were referred. What the authors consider to be most surprising was that over the 12-year span they examined, few changes had occurred in the pattern of referrals. The one major change that they did note was that the number of referrals dropped by around 10 per cent in 1980. Further they note that 1972 references to the violence were most likely to be general references, while in 1976 and 1980 it was more likely that mention of the violence would be of a specific event such as a bombing or a shooting. Overall, therefore, these authors cautiously concluded that their research provided no evidence for a direct link between child psychiatric disorders (strictly defined) and the political violence.

Four community-based surveys have been carried out in order to explore the relationship between stress and political violence among children in Northern Ireland. The first two of these (Fee, 1980, 1983) involved the administration of a teacher-rating instrument the *Rutter Teacher Questionnaire* and involved 11-year-old children living in Belfast (5000 in the first survey in 1975 and 7000 in the second in 1981). In the first some 15 per cent of children scored above the cut-off point on the questionnaire and in the second this had fallen to almost 9 per cent. While the prevalence in Belfast fell between 1975 and 1981 it was substantially higher in both years than that found in other similar parts of the world. The Belfast figure was, however, much lower than that reported by Rutter et al. (1975) in Inner London (25 per cent).

The third survey carried out in this area is that reported by McWhirter (1983). This involved a non-random sample of 1000 children from 'troubled' and relatively 'peaceful' parts of Northern Ireland, who were compared to 210 children from the north of England. All the children completed two standard personality tests. The Northern Irish sample consisted of two age groups, 10-year-olds and 14-year-olds, whereas the English sample had only 14-year-olds. The results indicated that Northern Irish children did not score any higher on the trait anxiety scales compared to the British or American norms or indeed compared to the English sample. Nor were there any differences between Northern Irish children from peaceful and troubled areas in terms of trait anxiety.

McWhirter's data thus appear to indicate that these children from Northern Ireland were not experiencing high levels of stress compared to English children, nor were children from areas which have been exposed to more political violence under more stress than children from more peaceful areas. However a major problem with this conclusion is that the instruments used to measure anxiety actually measured trait neuroticism, a stable personality construct, rather than anxiety that arises from environmental stress. In addition, McWhirter's study simply compared mean levels of trait anxiety in different subgroups but did not measure the children's actual experience of political violence.

McGrath and Wilson (1985), however, have presented results, from a random sample survey of the general population of children in Northern Ireland, which did attempt to relate children's stress levels to their experiences with political violence. In this study, in broad agreement with Fee's results, the overall percentage of children who scored above the cutoff point on the Rutter scale was 11 per cent, again suggesting that Northern Ireland has a somewhat higher Rutter Scale score than similar populations. Also McGrath and Wilson's findings suggested, as did Fee's, that it is in the area of antisocial behaviour and conduct disorder that Northern Ireland children score higher. This result parallels McWhirter's (1983) observation that Northern Irish children score higher on the (so-called) 'psychoticism' subscale of the Junior Eysenck Personality Questionnaire (JEPQ) – a subscale which taps mainly antisocial behaviour and psychopathy. McGrath and Wilson (1985) also reported that children who had had a relative or friend injured in the troubles, and children who thought that their area was 'not safe to live in', tended to have higher Rutter scores. Again McWhirter (1983) reported a parallel finding, in that children from the more violence-prone areas in her study had a higher 'psychoticism' score on the JEPQ compared to children from the more peaceful areas.

The pattern of results from these community surveys are therefore in broad agreement and indicate that although a proportion of children in Northern Ireland have had personal experience with political violence, and some feel anxiety symptoms as a result, nevertheless most of these children seem to be able to cope, and do not suffer serious psychological impairment. However there are worrying indications that the political violence may be linked to variations in the level of certain aspects of antisocial and sociopathic behaviour. The way in which children cope with the violence remains, however, largely unresearched. Fraser (1974) did suggest that children who experienced a severe stress reaction are more likely to have shown 'an earlier tendency to nervous symptoms' which in turn was related to the child's own coping style and to the emotional climate in the home.

McWhirter (1984) has hypothesised that children in Northern Ireland cope with political violence because they become habituated to it. When she compared ratings of stressful life events made by children in Northern Ireland and the north of England she found that there were no differences between the two groups of children in the types of events which they reported that they would find the most stressful. Indeed, Northern Irish children rated events directly associated with the political violence as least stressful. Unfortunately it is not clear that these results provide a clear test of the habituation hypothesis, but this is an idea that merits further study.

POLITICAL SOCIALISATION

An important but relatively neglected area has been the impact that growing up in Northern Ireland has had on political socialisation. Only one study to date has made a serious attempt to investigate this area directly (Russell, 1974). In this Russell administered questionnaires to some 3000 elementary and secondary schoolboys during 1971 and 1972. Perhaps the most telling political attitude he focused on was the boys' attitude to political violence. To do this he asked Protestants such questions as 'Do you think that people have the right to fight in order to keep Ulster British? 'while Catholics were asked for example 'Do you think that people have a right to fight in order to bring about a United Ireland?' At both age levels 60 per cent of the Catholic respondents were willing to approve of violence while among the Protestants those in favour rose from 51 per cent at the younger age level to 68 per cent at the older age level. Russell (1974) claimed that his questions were not simply tapping general antisocial attitudes. He pointed out that many of the same boys who approved of violence for political ends also claimed that they disliked the riots (prevalent at that time). Others said that while they approved of political violence they would not necessarily join in a riot even if one broke out near their home.

Apart from this one large study little direct research of this nature has been reported in this area in the intervening years. No doubt this has something to do with the sensitivity of school authorities to allowing children to be questioned on such issues. What research there is, however, has suggested that it is unlikely that there has been any dramatic general political radicalisation of the young in Northern Ireland. For example Fields (1973) concluded that 'violence and terrorism do not politicise growing children'. Indeed Jenvey (1972) has suggested that 'one of the major effects of living with the troubles has been to direct the young away from rebellion against the adult world characteristic of their age group towards conformity with parents'.

Recently there have been suggestions that young people, in both communities, are becoming more involved in politics and in a more radical way (Bell, 1990; Smith and Chambers, 1991). On the other hand there have been some claims that signs of what may amount to 'war weariness' are appearing amongst Northern Ireland's young people. For example at least two studies have claimed that the majority of children and young people actually reject political violence (Hosin, 1983; McWhirter, 1981). And when McWhirter (1983) asked young people to rate a series of possible future scenarios for Northern Ireland 50 years from now peace emerged as clearly the most desirable future – if the least likely.

Does this mean that children in Northern Ireland who have grown up with the troubles are interested in politics? A study by Hosin and Cairns (1984) asked 9, 12 and 15-year-old boys and girls who lived in Northern Ireland, Southern Ireland, Jordan and Iraq (a total of almost 3000 children) to write an essay entitled 'My country'. The essays were then content-analysed using six categories, one of which was 'politics'. The results of this study revealed that at every age-level fewer Northern Irish children mentioned politics compared to the children from the other three countries.

However in 1985 a survey which involved 940 16–25-year-old young people in Northern Ireland (International Youth Bridge, 1985) reported that 17 per cent claimed to be interested in politics. In comparison a survey in 1982 involving nearly 4000 young people in different European countries reported that 19 per cent claimed they were 'really interested' in national politics. The evidence from these two surveys appears to contradict the conclusions reached by Hosin and Cairns (1984) noted above.

A study by Whyte (1983) contains some interesting observations which may shed light on this apparent contradiction. This involved a small group of 11-12-year-old Catholic children living in West Belfast who apparently revealed a lively interest in political matters as evidenced by their ability to answer questions about such things as the name of the Prime Minister of the United Kingdom, the President of the United States, the Prime Minister of the Irish Republic and the Secretary of State for Northern Ireland. However, what Whyte actually found was that the children performed best on questions relating to politics outside Northern Ireland. For example 87 per cent were able to name the President of the USA but only 38 per cent could name the Secretary of State for Northern Ireland and only 34 per cent the Prime Minister of the Republic of Ireland. It may be therefore that in future researchers will have to distinguish carefully between interest in politics in general and interest in local Northern Irish politics. What the research reviewed above may be suggesting is that the majority of Northern Irish young people possess a reasonable level of interest in the former but not in the latter.

Of course it could be argued that in the end the best measure of political interest is willingness to vote in elections. The IYB survey found that of those who were old enough to vote (18 years or over) 59 per cent reported that they had actually done so. This figure is quite close to what one might expect to find from a similar adult sample in Northern Ireland. This result has received some support from a study by Willis and Cairns (1986) where 67 per cent of the respondents – 92 young Catholics between the ages of 18 and 25 years old – indicated that they intended to vote at the next election. Again these are somewhat contradictory results. Interest in local politics among young people in Northern Ireland appears to be relatively low. However it would appear that political behaviour, as indexed either by actual voting behaviour or intentions to vote, remains at a high level.

One possible explanation for this is that for some sections of the population at least voting is not in fact a politically related behaviour. Rather is it an end in itself. This is a phenomenon which has been commented on by other researchers. For example Mercer and Bunting (1980), reviewing a series of studies which had examined the motivations of young political demonstrators in Northern Ireland concluded that involvement in civil disturbances may have been for these young people 'somewhat divorced from any political issue'.

This in turn echoes an earlier observation made by Rose (1971) who suggested that in Northern Ireland 'the act of voting is not seen as an instrument to change policies but as a duty or a means of expressing substantive loyalties'. The question of how these loyalties are transmitted to each succeeding generation is one that has attracted only a limited amount of research, mostly carried out under the stimulus of Tajfel's Social Identity Theory applied to the conflict in Northern Ireland (Cairns, 1982). Much of this work has centred on the concept of social categorisation or 'telling' and has examined the age at which children in Northern Ireland learn to use first names (Cairns, 1980; Houston et al, 1990) or faces (Stringer and Cairns, 1983) to categorise others as in-group or out-group members. Generally this work points to the fact that, on average, this ability is not acquired until about age 10–11 years. Parallel to this, McWhirter and Gamble (1982) have demonstrated that the majority of children in Northern Ireland are about 9–10 years old before they understand the terms 'Catholic' and 'Protestant'.

Reviewing this research in detail, Cairns (1989b: 122) concluded that 'the process of developing awareness of one's own social identity probably occurs in parallel with the development of the awareness of the existence of the two major social categories in Northern Ireland'. What still remains to be investigated is when this social identity becomes an important one in the young person's repertoire of social identities and what factors influence this process. It may be important, however, that there is limited research plus anecdotal evidence that Catholic and Protestant children form friendships more easily in 'mixed' settings up to the pre-teen age level (Trew, 1989).

EVALUATION RESEARCH

What the commentators in the early days of the violence did not envisage is that one day children would become pawns in the hands of peacemakers in Northern Ireland (Cairns, 1989a). Researchers have therefore begun to interest themselves in the impact that these attempts at reconciliation have had on children, although as Trew (1989) has noted in a recent review, there is surprisingly little work in this area. Initially this research was concerned with holiday schemes aimed at bringing together children from the two communities, often in the USA. One study which has reported an attempt to evaluate the impact of such a programme on the self and social perceptions of the Catholic and Protestant children who took part in a holiday scheme in the USA has been reported by Toner, Hagan et al. (1990). An examination of the children's rankings of their own names and those of their room-mates and travelling companions suggested that there was a positive impact on the children's self-perceptions but not on their social perceptions.

The movement to establish integrated schools, as a counter to the religiously segregated schools attended by most children in Northern Ireland, has also begun to attract attention. Research in this area is only now getting under way and is as yet mostly unpublished. For example, Irwin (1991), an anthropologist, carried out an intensive study of one planned integrated secondary level school in Northern Ireland. This study claimed that there was evidence that the school was being successful in establishing positive inter-community friend-ships among those attending the integrated school.

Recently a more ambitious programme of research has begun, aimed at understanding integrated education in Northern Ireland and evaluating its impact on children. The research consists of three linked projects. The first (Dunn, Morgan et al., 1990) looked at cur-riculum issues, while the second (Morgan, Dunn et al., 1991) exam-ined the role of parents and teachers in relation to integration. The final project (Cairns, Dunn et al., 1992) targeted the impact of inte-gration on children. To do this the final study compared Catholic and Protestant children attending a planned integrated school with children attending unplanned integrated schools where there was either a predominance of Catholics or of Protestants plus a minority of children from the other community, or where the schools were totally segregated. To date only preliminary results are available. However, already there is evidence that children in both the planned and unplanned integrated schools are making friends on a cross-community basis. This replicates Irwin's (1991) results and those of Davies and Turner (1984).

METHODOLOGICAL CONSIDERATIONS AND FUTURE RESEARCH

Undoubtedly, as Cairns and Toner (1993) have noted, the protracted nature of the troubles in Northern Ireland has provided those with interests in child development a setting in which to examine both the reactions of children to exceedingly unfortunate conditions and the changing role of developmental research in a society under stress. However, in trying to establish the impact of political violence on children growing up in Northern Ireland researchers have met with many methodological problems, several of which as yet remain unsolved. To begin with, psychological data gathered before the onset of the troubles simply does not exist. Before-and-after comparisons have therefore proved impossible. Even today, for ethical reasons (see below) questionnaires and interviews are often administered anonymously, ruling out the possibility of follow-up studies. Longitudinal research is therefore almost totally absent.

Deciding how to measure the dependent variable has also caused problems. Interviews, teacher ratings, and questionnaires have been most commonly used. However, each type of measurement brings with it its own difficulties. For example, Fraser (1974) interviewed children and concluded that some were very directly involved in the violence to the extent of, for example, making petrol bombs. However, no allowance was made for the great temptation faced by a child aged eleven to exaggerate (Cairns, 1987).

A second popular measure has been teacher ratings (Fee, 1983). Unfortunately in such studies no check was made to ensure that teachers were using the same criteria to rate the children or that local school-based norms were not influencing the teachers (Cairns, 1987). Questionnaires have also been frequently employed. However, once again a question mark hangs over their validity. In particular problems with social desirability are likely to have caused problems (McWhirter, 1983). McWhirter suggests that asking the children directly about themselves is a much less problematic approach to measuring psychological adjustment in children and one which she therefore employed. Also some investigators have asked older children to write essays about themselves or about 'My Country' and then have counted the number of words which are related to the violence, such as 'bomb', (Cairns et al., 1980). However, problems arise, this time with the evaluation or interpretation of such results.

As a result of ethical problems along with problems of cueing and social desirability, a number of studies have employed even more indirect measurement techniques. Instead of simply asking children directly about their knowledge, attitude or reaction to something, this type of measurement attempts to tap this information without the children realising the aim of the study. For example, vocabulary tests provided cover when McWhirter, Young et al. (1983) investigated Northern Irish children's knowledge about the cause of death.

This they did simply by adding the word death, or dead, to the end of a standard vocabulary test. Unfortunately, vocabulary tests (in common with essays) provide only a crude index of awareness rather than a measurement of direct knowledge. Thus interpretation and evaluation of such data often presents a problem.

Davies and Turner (1984) report the use of a sociometric technique involving Catholic/Protestant friendship choices. Their results suggest that there is virtually no evidence of a religious barrier in the classroom or in play at school. However, as Cairns (1987) points out we still do not know whether the children were conscious that the friends and playmates that they were choosing actually came from the other religious group. Generally therefore, indirect types of measurement have tended to leave the critic wondering what it was that the investigation was really measuring.

The most important independent variable in any study trying to establish the impact of political violence on children growing up in Northern Ireland is the violence itself. Too often this has been treated as a homogeneous phenomenon. Cairns (1987) however suggests that there are three important dimensions to violence which should be assessed, a spatial, a temporal and a qualitative dimension. Also other independent variables exist which are often ignored and as a result may be considered as confounding variables, for example, social class, gender, intelligence and education.

A further difficulty with which investigators have wrestled is the problem of avoiding cueing the child's response. In a study on awareness of violence Jahoda and Harrison (1975) presented Catholic and Protestant children with a model street with four cardboard figures positioned on it and were asked to whom they would give an apparently innocent package found on the street – possibly a bomb. One of the criticisms of this study is that the children's responses may have been cued because the figures in the street included a policeman and a soldier. Further they were told that the street was located in an area of Belfast that at that time was notorious for violence.

Yet another factor which has been virtually ignored is the religion of the investigator. It is possible that the children may treat the investigator differently, or indeed the investigator may treat the children differently, because of his or her preconceptions about the other's religious group. To avoid this Stringer and Cairns (1983) employed a Catholic investigator to interview the Catholic children and a Protestant for the Protestant children.

Children are particularly vulnerable in any type of study. They are much less likely to exercise or even to recognise their right to refuse to participate in research. Children must therefore be protected before researchers are given permission to use children. In an attempt to avoid such ethical problems researchers have adopted indirect methods of measurement in order to avoid sensitising children to various issues. However indirect methods, as noted above, have led to weaknesses in research.

A final criticism is that use of theoretical approaches to the psychological impact of the conflict on children in Northern Ireland has been limited. Trew (1992) points to two broad areas in the contemporary stage of psychological research. The first area developed from the early work (e.g. Fields, 1973; Fraser, 1974), and examines the effects of the conflict on individuals. This area may lay claim to Freudian origins, but today is mainly concerned with a more generalised search for evidence of stress and coping (e.g. Wilson and Cairns, 1992). The second area in the contemporary research concentrates on the group dynamics of the conflict largely under the influence of Social Identity Theory (Cairns, 1982). However most of the studies employed to establish the impact of the political violence on children have had no theoretical basis whatsoever. Obviously more research is needed which is firmly theoretically based if progress is to be made.

CONCLUSIONS

The general conclusion is that the prophets of doom of 1969 have largely been proved wrong where crime and mental health have been concerned. This is not to say that the troubles in Northern Ireland have not had a more subtle impact on the vast majority of the children there. In particular continuing high levels of unemployment, low wages and consequent child poverty has probably been the greatest legacy of decades of political conflict. The poverty and/or the troubles on their own have also contributed to a steadily growing brain drain which, if Northern Ireland's young people continue to vote with their feet about the society they wish to live in, will undoubtedly have long-term consequences for all aspects of society in Northern Ireland long after the last soldier has returned to barracks.

Many of these questions remain under-researched because of the rather slow realisation of the complexity involved in answering the question, how has the violence affected children in Northern Ireland? Only now are researchers moving from a concern with the unidimensional short-term consequences of political violence to more multidimensional concerns. As a result, there is much less research investigating, for example, stress and the immediate consequences of violent events. Instead concern with the need to implement ways of reconciling the two conflicting groups and in particular concern with evaluating such work has come to prominence. In addition there has been a realisation that a multi-disciplinary approach, to what may at first seem purely psychological problems, is essential. Psychologists have learnt that they must embrace knowledge from other disciplines and must also help to bring psychological knowledge to the attention of those researchers who espouse a non-psychological approach, and more especially to the attention of policymakers, if they are to make a lasting impact in their attempts to improve life for children caught up in political violence.

REFERENCES

Bell, D. (1990) *Acts of Union: Youth Culture and Sectarianism in Northern Ireland.* London, Macmillan.

Breslin, A. (1982) 'Tolerance and Moral Reasoning among Adolescents in Ireland', *Journal of Moral Education*, 11: 2, 112–27.

Cairns, E. (1980) 'The Development of Ethnic Discrimination in Young Children in Northern Ireland' in *Children and Young People in Northern Ireland: a Society Under Stress*, ed. by J. Harbison and J. Harbison. Wells, Open Books.

Cairns, E. (1982) 'Intergroup Conflict in Northern Ireland' in *Group Identity and Intergroup Attitudes*, ed. by H. Tajfel. Cambridge, Cambridge University Press.; Paris Éditions de la Maison des Sciences de l'Homme.

Cairns, E. (1984) 'Television News as a Source of Knowledge about the Violence for Children in Ireland, North and South: A Test of the Knowledge-gap Hypothesis', *Current Psychological Research and Reviews*, 3: 4, 32–8.

Cairns, E. (1987) *Caught in Crossfire: Children and Young People in Northern Ireland.* Belfast, Appletree Press; New York, Syracuse Press.

Cairns, E. (1989a) 'Society as Child Abuser: Northern Ireland' in *Child Abuse and Neglect: Facing the Challenge*, ed. by W. S. Rogers and D. and E. Hevey. London, Batsford and the Open University.

Cairns, E. (1989b) 'Social Identity and Intergroup Conflict in Northern Ireland' in *Growing Up in Northern Ireland*, ed. by J. Harbison. Belfast, Northern Ireland Learning Resources Unit, Stranmillis College.

Cairns, E. (1990) 'Impact of Television News Exposure on Children's Perceptions of Violence in Northern Ireland', *Journal of Social Psychology*, 130: 4, 447–52.

Cairns, E. (1991) 'Is Northern Ireland a Conservative Society?' in *Social Attitudes in Northern Ireland*, ed. by P. Stringer and G. Robinson. Belfast, Blackstaff Press.

Cairns, E. and L. Conlon (1985) *Children's Moral Reasoning and the Northern Irish Violence*. Unpublished paper, University of Ulster.

Cairns, E., et al. (1980) 'Young Children's Awareness of Violence in Northern Ireland: the Influence of Northern Irish Television in Scotland and Northern Ireland', *British Journal of Social and Clinical Psychology*, 19, 3–6.

Cairns, E. and N. Toner (1993) 'Children and Political Violence: from Riots to Reconciliation' in *Psychological Effects of War and Violence on Children*, ed. by L. A. Leavitt and N. Fox. New York, Lawrence Erlbaum.

Cairns, E., S. Dunn, V. Morgan and V. McClenaghan (1992) *The Impact of Integrated Schools in Northern Ireland on Cultural Values on Social Identity*. Final Report to the Economic and Social Research Council (UK).

Davies, J. and I. F. Turner (1984) 'Friendship Choices in an Integrated Primary School in Northern Ireland', *British Journal of Social Psychology*, 23: 2, 185–6.

Dunn, S., V. Morgan, E. Cairns and C. Bowring-Carr (1990) *Curriculum and Culture in Integrated Schools in Northern Ireland*. Final Report to the Leverhulme Trust. Coleraine, Centre for the Study of Conflict: University of Ulster.

Fee, F. (1980) 'Responses to a Behavioural Questionnaire of a Group of Belfast Children' in *Children and Young People in Northern Ireland: a Society Under Stress*, ed. by J. Harbison and J. Harbison. Wells, Open Books.

Fee, F. (1983) 'Education Change in Belfast School Children 1975–81' in *Children of the Troubles: Children in Northern Ireland*, ed. by J. Harbison. Belfast, NI Learning Resources Unit, Stranmillis College.

Fields, R. (1973) *A Society on the Run: a Psychology of Northern Ireland*. Harmondsworth, Penguin.

Fraser, M. (1974) *Children in Conflict*. Harmondsworth, Penguin.

Greer, J. (1980) 'The Persistence of Religion in Northern Ireland', *Character Potential*, 9, 139–49.

Greer, J. (1990) 'The Persistence of Religion: a Study of Sixth-form Pupils in Northern Ireland, 1968–1988', *Journal of Social Psychology*, 130: 5, 573–81.

Hosin, A. (1983) *The Impact of International Conflict on Children's and Adolescents' National Perceptions: a Cross-cultural Study in Political Socialisation*. D.Phil. thesis, New University of Ulster.

Hosin, A. and E. Cairns (1984) 'The Impact of Conflict on Children's Ideas About Their Country', *Journal of Social Psychology*, 118: 2, 161–8.

Houston, J. E., et al. (1990) 'The Assessment of Ethnic Sensitivity Among Northern Ireland Schoolchildren', *British Journal of Developmental Psychology*, 8, 419–22.

International Youth Bridge (1985) *Young Ideas in Northern Ireland: Christian Belief and Life Style Among Young Adults in Northern Ireland*. Belfast, City of Belfast YMCA.

Irwin, C. (1991) *Education and the Development of Social Integration in Divided Societies*. Unpublished paper, Queen's University, Belfast.

Jahoda, G. and S. Harrison (1975) 'Belfast Children: Some Effects of a Conflict Environment', *Irish Journal of Psychology*, 3: 1, 1–19.

Jenvey (1972) 'Sons and Haters: Youth in Conflict', *New Society*, 21: 512, 125–7.

Kahn, J. V. (1982) 'Moral Reasoning in Irish Children and Adolescents as Measured by the Defining Issues Test', *Irish Journal of Psychology*, 2, 96–108.

McCauley, R. and M. Troy (1983) 'The Impact of Urban Conflict and Violence on Children Referred to a Child Guidance Clinic', in J. Harbison, ed., *Children of the Troubles: Children in Northern Ireland*, Belfast, NI Learning Resources Unit, Stranmillis College.

McGrath, A. and R. Wilson (1985) 'Factors which Influence the Prevalence and Variation of Psychological Problems in Children in Northern Ireland'. Paper presented to the Annual Conference of the Developmental Section of the British Psychological Society, Belfast.

McKeown, M. (1973) 'Civil Unrest: Secondary School's Survey', *Northern Teacher*, Winter, 39–42.

McWhirter, I., V. Young et al. (1983) 'Belfast Children's Awareness of Violent Death', *British Journal of Social Psychology*, 22, 2. 81–92.

McWhirter, L. (1981) 'The Influence of Contact on the Development of Interpersonal Awareness in Northern Ireland Children'. Paper read to the Annual Conference of the Development Section of the British Psychological Society, Manchester.

McWhirter, L. (1983) 'Contact and Conflict: the Question of Integrated Education', *Irish Journal of Psychology*, 6, 13–27.

McWhirter, L. (1984) 'Is Getting Caught in a Riot More Stressful than Seeing a Scary Film or Moving to a New School?' Paper presented to the Annual Conference of the Northern Ireland Branch of the Psychological Society, Portballintrae.

McWhirter, L. and R. Gamble (1982) 'Development of Ethnic Awareness in the Absence of Physical Cues', *Irish Journal of Psychology*, 5, 109–27.

Mercer, G. W. and B. Bunting (1980) 'Some Motivations of Adolescent Demonstrators in the Northern Ireland Civil Disturbances' in *Children and Young People in Northern Ireland: a Society Under Stress*, ed. by J. Harbison and J. Harbison. Wells, Open Books.

Morgan, V., S. Dunn, E. Cairns and G. Fraser (1991) *Parents and Teachers in Integrated Schools in Northern Ireland*. Final Report to the Economic and Social Research Council (UK).

PPRU (1984) *Commentary on Northern Ireland Crime Statistics, 1969–1982*, PPRU Occasional Paper 5. Belfast, Social Research Division, Policy Planning and Research Unit, Department of Finance and Personnel.

Rose, R. (1971) *Governing Without Consensus: an Irish Perspective*. London, Faber & Faber.

Russell, J. (1974) *Socialisation and Conflict*. PhD thesis, University of Strathclyde.

Rutter, M., A. Cox, C. Tupping, M. Berger and W. Yule (1975), 'Attainment and Adjustment in Two Geographical Areas: 1, the Prevalence of Psychiatric Disorder' *British Journal of Psychiatry*, 126, 520–33.

Smith, D. J. and G. Chambers (1991) *Inequality in Northern Ireland*. Oxford, Clarendon Press.

Stringer, M. and E. Cairns (1983) 'Catholic and Protestant Young People's Rating of Stereotyped Protestant and Catholic Faces', *British Journal of Social Psychology*, 22, 241–6.

Toner, I. J., M. S. Hagan et al. (1990) 'The Effects of Temporary Intervention of the Self and Social Perceptions of Children Experiencing Ongoing Stress'. Paper presented at the Biennial Conference on Human Development, Richmond, Virginia, March.

Trew, K. (1989) 'Evaluating the Impact of Contact Schemes for Catholic and Protestant Children' in *Growing up in Northern Ireland*, ed. by J. Harbison.

Trew K. (1992) 'Social Psychological Research on the Conflict', *The Psychologist*, 15: 8, 342–4.

Belfast, NI Learning Resources Unit, Stranmillis College.

Violence in Ireland: a Report to the Churches (1976) Belfast, Christian Journals.

Whyte, J. (1983) 'Control and Supervision of Urban Twelve-year-olds Within and Outside Northern Ireland: a Pilot Study', *Irish Journal of Psychology*, 6, 37–45.

Willis, P. and E. Cairns (1986) 'Attitudes towards Voting among Young People in Northern Ireland'. Unpublished paper, University of Ulster, Coleraine.

Wilson, R. and E. Cairns (1992) 'Psychosocial Stress and the Northern Ireland Troubles', *The Psychologist*, 5: 8, 347–50.

8 Paramilitaries, Republicans and Loyalists

Adrian Guelke

The term paramilitary organisation is used to describe groups in Northern Ireland such as the Provisional Irish Republican Army (IRA) and the Ulster Defence Association (UDA), which employ violence or the threat of violence for political ends. Outside of Northern Ireland, where the term paramilitary tends to be used to describe the character of security forces rather than those operating outside the law, they are more commonly referred to as terrorists. The media and politicians in Northern Ireland use both terms. However, academic analysts of the conflict have generally preferred to describe groups engaged in political violence, including bombings and the random killings of civilians, as paramilitary organisations. The term terrorism does not even appear in the index of John Whyte's magisterial survey of the literature on the conflict (Whyte, 1990). The reason for this is not sympathy among analysts of the conflict for the proponents of violence in either community in Northern Ireland. Rather it is principally because few academic analysts of the conflict would accept the assumptions that use of the term terrorism tends to imply, in particular, that a legitimate political order exists that is being challenged by the violence of a tiny minority of extremists on the fringe of society. The weakness of such a characterisation of the violence in Northern Ireland is that it underestimates the gravity of the conflict and the extent to which the violence is embedded in the deep sectarian divisions of the society. It also underestimates the historical roots of the use of violence by elements within each of the two main communities in Northern Ireland.

Thus, republicans are able to point to a physical force tradition in Irish nationalism stretching back over two centuries, while loyalists point to the role that the threat of violence played in the successful resistance of Protestants to Home Rule. Indeed, both can plausibly claim that the Republic of Ireland and Northern Ireland owe their very existence to acts or threats of violence. The IRA was born amidst the 1916 Easter Rising in Dublin. In particular, when the leader of the Rising, Pádraic Pearse, surrendered to British forces, he did so as Commandant General of the Irish Republican Army of the newly proclaimed Irish Republic. By presenting themselves as the descendants of the martyrs of 1916, the leaders of the Provisional IRA seek to secure legitimacy from history for their current campaign.

The historical counterpart to the IRA on the Protestant side was the Ulster Volunteer Force (UVF), established in 1912 to fight Home Rule. A small group of loyalists in Belfast engaged in acts of violence against Catholics in 1966 revived the name UVF to give legitimacy to their actions. However, their claim to such historical legitimacy was less plausible than that of the Provisional IRA for the simple reason that the IRA in one form or another has been in continuous existence since 1916, even though it has lost the adherence of most Irish nationalists in the years since the establishment of the Irish Free State. No such continuity existed on the loyalist side because outside of periods of crisis, unionists have been content to rely on the official security forces to uphold their position. But on both sides the paramilitary organisations' perceptions of the lessons of history have influenced their expectations of the effectiveness of their own violence. At the same time, the changes that have taken place in paramilitary strategies during the course of the current troubles show that their perceptions are not immutable and therein perhaps lies the best prospect for an end to the violence.

It is also important not to exaggerate the role that paramilitary organisations have actually played in the history of Ireland. In particular, they played little part in the onset of the current troubles in Northern Ireland. They were its products rather than creators. Thus the two paramilitary organisations which have been responsible for most of the violence that has occurred in Northern Ireland since 1968, the Provisional IRA and the UDA, were established after the start of the troubles. From its creation as an autonomous political entity within the United Kingdom in 1920 to the early 1960s, Northern Ireland was ruled by the Unionist Party on the self-fulfilling basis that only Protestants could be trusted to support the link with Britain. Catholic subordination was underlined by emergency legislation exclusively directed against that community and retained through long periods of tranquillity.

This system remained unchanged until the 1960s when deteriorating economic conditions in the province provided the impetus for reform during the premiership of Terence O'Neill. Politically, reform acted as a stimulus to Catholic demands for equality of treatment within Northern Ireland that was reflected in the emergence of the civil rights movement. It also prompted a backlash among Protestants who blamed reform for the ending of Catholic acquiescence in their subordination. Hardline loyalists regarded the civil rights movement as a plot to bring about a united Ireland, the traditional aim of Irish republicans. Their fears were also aroused by the social and economic trends of the period, particularly the erosion of residential segregation between the communities, which they saw as a threat to Protestant dominance. Disorder grew out of the conflict between Catholic hopes and Protestant fears. Violent clashes between the police and civil rights demonstrators who defied a government order banning them from marching through Northern Ireland's second city, Londonderry, in October 1968, are generally taken to mark the start of the current troubles. Another watershed occurred in August 1969 when British troops were dispatched to the province to aid the civil power after prolonged rioting in Londonderry and Belfast had exhausted the resources of the local security forces. Initially, Catholics welcomed the arrival of British troops, not merely because they protected Catholic housing estates from attacks by loyalist mobs, but because their presence enhanced the British government's responsibility for how Northern Ireland was governed. At the same time, the international attention that the situation in Northern Ireland was attracting raised Catholic expectations of far-reaching reform.

However, at the outset, the British government attempted to limit the scope of its involvement to reform of the security system. In particular, it wished to maintain the existing Unionist government's political autonomy. A major weakness of the policy was that from the perspective of the Catholic minority, it looked like a programme for the restoration of the *status quo ante*. Disappointment at the narrow scope of British policy provided the context for a radicalisation of Catholic opinion, especially in areas where conflicts with the British army over such sensitive issues as the routes of Orange Order marches provided an additional source of alienation from the British authorities. The enthusiasm with which Catholics had greeted the arrival of the troops gradually gave way to disillusionment. Events in Northern Ireland took the republican movement by surprise. In 1956, the IRA had launched a border campaign in support of a united Ireland, but in 1962 it had been forced to call off its campaign, in which 11 of its own members and six police officers were killed, due to lack of support from the Catholic minority in Northern Ireland. In the 1960s the republican movement came under the influence of left-wing intellectuals who blamed the failure of the movement in the past on its political isolation and its elitist militarism and persuaded it to concentrate its energies on campaigning on social and economic issues. The violent turn of events in Northern Ireland in 1968 and 1969 was a contingency for which the leadership of the republican movement was manifestly unprepared.

The republican movement split, leading to the formation at the end of 1969 of Provisional IRA and shortly afterwards of (Provisional) Sinn Féin. The Provisionals embodied a revival of the creed of physical force republicanism and quickly attracted support among Northern Ireland Catholics, especially in areas where there had been sectarian clashes. The Provisionals' paper, *An Phoblacht/ Republican News*, described the movement's aims as being:

> to end foreign rule in Ireland, to establish a 32-county Democratic Socialist Republic, based on the proclamation of 1916, to restore the Irish language and culture to a position of strength, and to promote a social order based on justice and Christian principles which will give everyone a just share of the nation's wealth. (*An Phoblacht*, 1970)

The fact that the Provisionals presented the conflict as a classical anti-colonial liberation struggle in which the enemy was British imperialism tied in with the disposition of much of the world to see Northern Ireland as a remnant of empire, a colonial problem in a post-colonial age.

Initial operations of the Provisional IRA were justified in terms of defending the Catholic ghettos. This applied even to the bombing of commercial premises in the city centre of Belfast which began in 1970, because, as one of the provisional leaders, Joe Cahill, explained, it stopped the army from concentrating its resources on the ghettos. The other justification the Provisionals advanced for the bombing campaign was that it added to the economic burden of British occupation as the cost of compensating businesses fell on the British taxpayer. The resort to the tactic of bombing reflected the ready availability of industrial explosives, such as gelignite, in contrast to a shortage of other weapons. As relations between the army and the Catholic community deteriorated, the stance taken by the Provisionals became increasingly aggressive. At the beginning of 1971, the Provisional IRA Army Council approved offensive operations against the British army. In February a soldier was killed in a gun battle with a Provisional IRA unit. He was the first army fatality of the current troubles. The bombing campaign was also stepped up, leading to a rising toll of civilian casualties as a result of bungled warnings, or even no warnings at all. In 1970 there were 153 explosions in Northern Ireland; in 1971 1022 (Flackes and Elliott, 1989: 415).

In response to the escalation of the Provisional IRA operations, the Unionist government introduced internment (providing for detention without trial) on 9 August 1971. It produced an explosion of Catholic anger and resentment, resulting in a massive increase in support for the Provisional IRA in the ghettos and a sharp jump in the level of violence. At the time of the introduction of internment, 34 people had died in political violence in the course of 1971. A further 139 people had died by the end of the year (Farrell, 1980: 287). The reaction of the Catholic community to internment contributed to a Protestant backlash, reflected in the establishment in September 1971 of the Ulster Defence Association (UDA), which brought together local loyalist vigilante organisations that had grown up in a number of working-class Protestant estates. The spiral of violence was given further impetus by 'Bloody Sunday', 30 January 1972, when 13 unarmed demonstrators were shot dead by British troops after an illegal civil rights march in Londonderry. 'Bloody Sunday' also triggered off anti-British violence in the Republic of Ireland during which the British embassy in Dublin was burnt down. A change in the direction of British policy followed. On 24 March 1972 the British government imposed direct rule on Northern Ireland, taking charge from the local Unionist administration and suspending Northern Ireland's parliament at Stormont.

The imposition of direct rule prompted Protestant protest on a scale that matched Catholic reaction to the introduction of internment. At the time most Protestants regarded the existence of a local administration and parliament at Stormont as their guarantee that they would not be forced into a united Ireland against their will. Inevitably, therefore, there was widespread suspicion among Protestants that direct rule had been imposed in order to pave the way for Irish unification. But if many Protestants saw the downfall of Stormont as a betrayal, most Catholics remained too suspicious of British intentions to celebrate the event as their victory, though it was welcomed by the main nationalist party, the Social Democratic and Labour Party (SDLP), in a statement which appealed to 'those engaged in the campaign of violence to cease immediately' (*Fortnight*, 1972). The call was ignored by the Provisionals, who presented their own proposals for a ceasefire linked to British withdrawal and the establishment of a federal Ireland. They had already dubbed 1972 'the year of victory' (*An Phoblacht*, 1972). The SDLP's hopes of an early end to internment to defuse the situation were also dashed. Catholic fury over internment and 'Bloody Sunday' and Protestant fears of a sellout by Britain in response to what they saw as rebellion formed an extremely potent mixture. In the course of 1972, there were 467 fatalities in political violence, the highest number of deaths in any year of the troubles (see Table 8.1).

A significant factor in the high level of civilian fatalities in the course of 1972 and the four subsequent years was a campaign of random sectarian assassinations carried out by members of loyalist paramilitary organisations, principally the UDA. It resulted in the deaths of hundreds of Catholic civilians. The practice of the loyalist paramilitaries was to let the killings speak for themselves and at the beginning of the campaign, claims of responsibility for particular murders were rarely made, providing the tenuous basis of the police's initial description of the killings as motiveless. However, the Catholic community had little difficulty in discerning the intimidatory intent behind the campaign and the killings strongly reinforced the trend towards residential segregation as Catholics fled to the safety of their own ghettos. Occasionally, republican paramilitaries responded in kind to the loyalist campaign. However, publicly, the Provisionals in particular disdained sectarian warfare, emphasising that their campaign was directed against British imperialism and not Protestants as such. In fact, the Provisionals' view of the conflict disposed them to suspect British involvement in the loyalist campaign. In its publications, the UDA proclaimed that a state of war existed in Northern Ireland, and described Catholics as being, virtually without exception, 'on the side of murder, terrorism, intimidation, and the total destruction of all loyalists' (UDA, 1971). From the perspective of the UDA, Protestants were a community under siege, entirely reliant on their own resources for survival. A forceful statement of this viewpoint was given in a 1973 UDA press statement:

We are betrayed, maligned and our families live in constant fear and misery. We are a nuisance to our so-called allies and have no friends anywhere. Once more in the history of our people, we have our backs to the wall, facing extinction by one way or another. This is the moment to beware, for Ulstermen in this position fight mercilessly till they or their enemies are dead. (Dillon and Lehane, 1973: 282)

Table 8.1 Deaths in Northern Ireland arising out of the security situation 1969–92

Year	RUC[1]	RUCR[2]	Army	UDR/RIR[3]	Civilians[4]	Total
1969	1	–	–	–	12	13
1970	2	–	–	–	23	25
1971	11	–	43	5	115	174
1972	14	3	103	26	321	467
1973	10	3	58	8	171	250
1974	12	3	28	7	166	216
1975	7	4	14	6	216	247
1976	13	10	14	15	245	297
1977	8	6	15	14	69	112
1978	4	6	14	7	50	81
1979	9	5	38	10	51	113
1980	3	6	8	9	50	76
1981	13	8	10	13	57	101
1982	8	4	21	7	57	97
1983	9	9	5	10	44	77
1984	7	2	9	10	36	64
1985	14	9	2	4	25	54
1986	10	2	4	8	37	61
1987	9	7	3	8	66	93
1988	4	2	21	12	54	93
1989	7	2	12	2	39	62
1990	7	5	7	8	49	76
1991	5	1	5	8	75	94
1992	2	1	4	2	76	85
Totals	189	98	438	199	2104	3028

[1] Royal Ulster Constabulary.
[2] Royal Ulster Constabulary Reserve.
[3] Ulster Defence Regiment and Royal Irish Regiment. The Royal Irish Regiment was formed out of amalgamation of the Ulster Defence Regiment and the Royal Irish Rangers on 1 July 1992.
[4] Including members of paramilitary organisations.
Source: Chief Constable's *Annual Report 1992.* Royal Ulster Constabulary, Belfast 1993, 82.

At its peak, the UDA had 'about 25,000 dues-paying members' (Nelson, 1984: 104). For most, membership meant taking part in patrols guarding Protestant neighbourhoods and participation in military parades that the organisation staged to demonstrate the force at its disposal. In 1974 the mass membership of the UDA played a key role in the success of the Ulster Workers Council strike by setting up road blocks, building barricades, and otherwise physically discouraging people from going to work. The strike brought down the power-sharing Executive, the heart of an ambitious British effort to achieve a settlement of the Northern Ireland problem through political accommodation between unionists and nationalists. Loyalist hostility towards the settlement focused on the provision for the establishment of a Council of Ireland, which many Protestants feared might become a stepping-stone to a united Ireland. The failure of the power-sharing experiment was a devastating blow both to British policy and to the middle ground of political opinion in Northern Ireland. In its wake the British government briefly considered the option of withdrawal before deciding on a further effort to promote political accommodation through the election of a Constitutional Convention charged with reaching agreement across the sectarian divide on a new political dispensation. After the failure of the Convention, the British government gave up for the time being its attempts to devolve power to Northern Ireland and adopted direct rule as a long-term policy, promoting it as the form of government which was the least unacceptable to both communities.

The policy of direct rule was accompanied by significant changes in security policy. Internment was ended, so too was the privilege of special category status for prisoners whose crimes were politically motivated. The government also closed down the incident centres which had provided a channel of communication between the authorities and the Provisional IRA during the latter's 1975 ceasefire. It became the fixed policy of the government that it would not negotiate with 'terrorists' in future. What the changes amounted to was a policy of criminalising political violence and playing down the notion that Northern Ireland was in a state of civil war that urgently required a political solution. At the same time, primary responsibility for security was shifted to the police and reliance on troops from Great Britain was reduced. Initially, the new approach was quite successful. It met a widespread desire in both communities for a return to normality and a lessening of the extreme political tension that the violence had given rise to. Protestants in particular felt reassured that they would not be forced into a united Ireland against their will. That fear had been a significant element in the perceptions of the loyalist paramilitaries. Another element in the perceptions of loyalist paramilitaries was the assumption that Catholics as a community

supported the Provisional IRA. This perception also began to
change, in large part due to the rise in 1976 of the Peace People, a
mass movement demanding an end to political violence that for a
time attracted a wide measure of support in the working-class ghettos of both communities.

The changes in Protestant perceptions were reflected in a sharp
fall in the level of loyalist paramilitary violence. Whereas loyalist paramilitaries were responsible for 40 per cent of the 924 fatalities
between 13 July 1973 and 12 July 1977, they accounted for 12 per
cent of the fatalities in the following quadrennium between 13 July
1977 and 12 July 1981 (McKeown, 1989: 41–3). The level of
republican violence also fell, though not as sharply. That too
reflected changes in republican perceptions in response to the
change in the British government's approach. The Provisionals'
expectation of imminent British withdrawal evaporated. As a consequence there was a change in the strategy of the Provisional IRA's
campaign, which an internal staff report explained as follows: 'We
must gear ourselves to Long Term Armed Struggle based on putting
unknown men and new recruits into a cell structure' (Coogan, 1980:
579). This implied a radical reorganisation of the Provisional IRA
from its existing quasi-military structure of territorially based bri-
gades and battalions. In practice, the switch to a cell structure was not
fully achieved. Preoccupation with sustaining the campaign on a
long-term basis led to efforts to conserve resources. The number of
actual operations declined very sharply. Careful planning went into
the operations that took place so as to maximise fatalities among
those the Provisionals considered legitimate targets, though the concept of a legitimate target itself came to encompass an ever wider category of people, wide enough to justify attacks on off-duty or even
retired members of the security forces, unionist politicians as well as
British ministers, prison officers, judges, and even commercial con-
tractors supplying services to the security services. However, the
somewhat greater selectivity of both the loyalist and the republican
campaigns of violence led to a fall in the proportion of civilian fatalities among total deaths as a result of the troubles.

At the same time, the Provisional IRA and the UDA both began to
place greater emphasis on political activity. In the case of the UDA,
disillusionment with loyalist politicians, particularly after the failed
1977 strike against British security policy, resulted in a decision by the
leadership that the organisation should develop its own distinctive
political position on the conflict. To this end, the New Ulster Political

Research Group was set up in January 1976. In March 1979 it published *Beyond the Religious Divide*, arguing the case for an independent Northern Ireland as a context in which the sectarian divisions of the society could be overcome and as 'the only proposal which does not have a victor or a loser' (New Ulster Political Research Group, 1979). However, the UDA leadership found little support for this message of political accommodation either among loyalists in general or even among rank and file members. Despite this, politicisation was a restraining influence on the violent activities of the UDA throughout the 1980s. In the case of the Provisional IRA, the failure of the organisation to gain anything from its 1975 ceasefire led to the displacement of the Southern leadership of the Provisionals by Northerners. The change in leadership was reflected in three trends within the movement after 1976: secularisation, radicalisation, and politicisation. An early indication of the change in the Provisionals' approach was a speech by Jimmy Drumm at Bodenstown in June 1977 in which he warned of the danger of 'the isolation of socialist republicans around the armed struggle' (Bishop and Mallie, 1987: 264).

A major drawback of the policy of direct rule was that internationally it made Northern Ireland look like a colony, a perception that worked to the advantage of the Provisionals, while the continuation of the Provisional IRA's campaign of violence blighted hopes within Northern Ireland of a return to normality. The lobbying of the SDLP and the Irish government also generated international pressure, particularly from the United States, for a change of policy. It came shortly after the election of the Conservative government in May 1979. The government launched a fresh political initiative aimed at establishing a devolved administration in Northern Ireland. It failed. To add to the government's woes, it faced a crisis in the prisons. As part of the policy of criminalisation, special category status for prisoners convicted of politically motivated crimes had been abolished. This had led to protests in the prisons. In 1980 a number of republican prisoners went on hunger strike in support of five demands, including the right to wear their own clothes and the right to free association within the prison. Their campaign was supported by mass protests on the streets in Catholic areas, underlining the failure of criminalisation to achieve its objective of the political isolation of those resorting to violence.

The government's difficulties prompted a further change of direction. In December 1980 at a summit between the British and Irish Prime Ministers, the two governments agreed to enter into dialogue on 'the totality of relationships' within the British Isles. However, the initiation of the Anglo-Irish process did not solve the prisons crisis in Northern Ireland. There was a further hunger strike by republican prisoners in 1981, in the course of which ten hunger-striking prisoners died. The prisoners' campaign attracted mass support from Catholics in Northern Ireland, its breadth underlined by the victory of Bobby Sands, the first of the hunger-striking prisoners, in a by-election in a parliamentary constituency with a narrow Catholic majority. Two prisoners were also elected to the Dáil in a general election in the Republic in June 1981. However, while the impact of the hunger strikes on opinion in the Republic of Ireland turned out to be temporary, the effect on Catholic opinion in Northern Ireland proved to be longer lasting.

The electoral success of the campaign on behalf of republican prisoners persuaded the Provisionals that the impact of the campaign of violence could be enhanced through the participation in elections of Sinn Féin, the movement's political wing. A fresh British initiative involving the election of a Northern Ireland Assembly in October 1982 gave the Provisionals an early opportunity to put its now policy into practice. With 10.1 per cent of the first preference vote, Sinn Féin achieved an immediate breakthrough, celebrated by the Provisionals as the 'ballot bomb' (*Iris*, 1982: 3). In the UK general election in June 1983, Sinn Féin did even better with 13.4 per cent of the votes in Northern Ireland, prompting speculation that at a future election Sinn Féin might overtake the SDLP. However, in elections in 1984 and 1985 there was a slight decline in the Sinn Féin vote compared to 1983. None the less, the challenge that Sinn Féin posed to constitutional nationalism in the form of the SDLP gave a significant impetus to the Anglo-Irish problem, helping to pave the way to the Anglo-Irish Agreement of November 1985. This enabled the Irish government to put forward views and proposals in relation to the government of Northern Ireland through the mechanism of an intergovernmental council. Following the Agreement there was a further swing of Catholic opinion towards the SDLP and away from Sinn Féin.

However, virtually the entire Protestant community was opposed to the Agreement and this was reflected in a pact between the two main unionist parties to cooperate to bring down the Agreement. Unionist protests against the Agreement took the form of mass demonstrations, civil disobedience, and shows of strength, both on the streets and through the ballot box. The crisis in the prisons in 1980 and

1981, the electoral rise of Sinn Féin, and the Anglo-Irish Agreement helped to revive loyalist suspicion both of Catholics and of the British Government. The consequence was a recurrence of assassinations by loyalist paramilitaries. These had virtually ceased during the late 1970s. Despite the polarisation of the two communities, the leadership of the UDA maintained its commitment to political accommodation, while justifying the assassination campaign of the Ulster Freedom Fighters (UFF), a *nom de guerre* used by the UDA, on the grounds that it was directed against republicans and not Catholics as such. In practice, the UFF's notion of a legitimate target, like that of the Provisional IRA, encompassed a very wide category of people. Furthermore, UFF claims that their victims had republican paramilitary connections were frequently disputed by the police.

However, the level of loyalist paramilitary violence remained low compared to what it had been in the mid-1970s. The UDA in particular devoted much of its energies to preparation for a 'doomsday' situation, while placing the onus squarely on the leaders of the two main unionist parties to make it clear when the moment for civil war had arrived. At the same time, the UDA's lack of confidence in unionist political leadership was forcefully expressed by one of the UDA's leading figures, John McMichael, who declared: 'If some of the present unionist leadership had been in power in 1912, Northern Ireland would never have come into existence' (*Fortnight*, 1986). The failure of the unionist campaign to bring down the Anglo-Irish Agreement through protests in the streets forced the two main unionist parties to change their strategy to one of seeking to secure the abrogation of the Agreement through negotiation. To be credible, the new policy required a willingness on the part of the unionist parties themselves to make concessions. The point was readily embraced by the leadership of the UDA as vindicating its advocacy of political accommodation. In January 1987 the UDA's 'Ulster Political Research Group' published proposals for the establishment of a Northern Ireland administration, which accepted what the two unionist parties had hitherto rejected, power-sharing with the SDLP (Ulster Political Research Group, 1987). A task force appointed by the two unionist party leaders to examine unionist options followed the UDA's lead and reported that many unionists would be willing to contemplate SDLP participation in government provided the link with Dublin was severed (*Fortnight*, 1987).

From a very different perspective, Sinn Féin published a discussion paper, entitled 'A Scenario for Peace', in May 1987 (*An Phoblacht*,

1987). It advocated elections to an all-Ireland Constitutional Conference in the context of a declaration of intent by Britain to withdraw. The paper argued that partition was a violation of the right of self-determination as laid down in the United Nations' 1966 International Covenant on Civil and Political Rights. This initiative was followed by an exchange of views between Sinn Féin and the SDLP during 1988. However, the summer of 1988 was marked by a recurrence of the Provisional IRA's campaign, fuelled by large arms and explosives shipments from Libya dating back to August 1985. On 20 August eight soldiers died in a bomb attack on a bus at Ballygawley in County Tyrone, prompting a wide-ranging review of the government's security policy.

In October, the Home Secretary, Douglas Hurd, announced a ban on the broadcasting of direct statements by spokespersons for, inter alia, Sinn Féin or the UDA. However, the broadcasters could still report the words of the spokespersons and the effectiveness of the ban was reduced further by the employment of actors to speak the words of interviewees, as they talked on film. Nevertheless, the broadcasting ban did have an inhibiting effect on the media's coverage of the political views of Sinn Féin and the UDA. This was most apparent in the case of the UDA. The murder of John McMichael in December 1987 and Andy Tyrie's resignation in March 1988 had already deprived the UDA of its two most articulate spokesmen. The ban added to the UDA's political marginalisation. While a candidate of the political party closely linked to the UDA, the Ulster Democratic Party (UDP), won election to the Derry City Council, the UDP otherwise fared poorly, securing few votes and little attention.

Sinn Féin also lost ground politically. For example, in elections to the European Parliament in 1989 its candidate's share of first preference votes fell below 10 per cent. At the other end of the political spectrum, there was a decline in the level of support for Ian Paisley and the Democratic Unionist Party. The shift in the political mood was reflected in a narrowing of the differences among the political parties that encouraged the Secretary of State for Northern Ireland, Peter Brooke, to launch a fresh political initiative in January 1990. Its basis was that three sets of relationships needed to be addressed in any negotiations: the relationship between the communities in Northern Ireland; relations between Northern Ireland and the Republic of Ireland; and the links between the United Kingdom as a whole and the Republic of Ireland.

However, it took the Secretary of State over a year to get agreement on the terms for negotiations. He eventually succeeded in arranging that negotiations among the parties would take place in a gap of 11 weeks between meetings of the intergovernmental council from the end of April to mid-July 1991. The prospect of talks among all the constitutional parties raised expectations of an end to 20 years of stalemate. The breakthrough elicited from a new umbrella organisation for loyalist paramilitaries, the Combined Loyalist Military Command, a commitment to maintain a ceasefire during the duration of the negotiations. In the event, little progress was made and talks hailed as historic failed to live up to their billing. Disagreement among the parties on procedural questions held up discussion on the substantive issues and by the intergovernmental council there had been precious little engagement among the parties on any questions of substance. The failure of the talks among the constitutional parties was followed by an upsurge in loyalist paramilitary violence. In the whole of 1991, 40 of the 93 deaths as a result of political violence were attributed to loyalist paramilitaries, far and away the highest level of loyalist violence since the mid-1970s (*Irish Times*, 1992). The escalation in loyalist paramilitary violence continued through 1992 and 1993.

A large part of the explanation was the emergence of a younger and more militant set of leaders in the UDA. The murder of McMichael and the ousting of Tyrie was followed by further changes in the membership of the UDA's Inner Council, partly as a result of a backlash against corruption within the organisation and partly as a result of the exposure of an agent for Military Intelligence in a key position in the organisation. The new leadership was determined to demonstrate its effectiveness in comparison with the old guard. Its measure of effectiveness was its capacity to match the violence of the Provisional IRA blow for blow. A large arms shipment from South Africa at the beginning of 1988 provided the loyalist paramilitaries with the means. While McMichael continued to be revered, it was as a military figure rather than as an advocate for political accommodation. In August 1992 the British government responded to the organisation's new militancy by banning it. That made the UDA an illegal organisation like the Provisional IRA.

While in practice a considerable number of the victims of loyalist violence continued to be Catholics with no known associations with republican paramilitaries, the fact that the loyalists targeted prominent members of Sinn Féin and others with republican paramilitary connections of one kind or another elicited a 'tit for tat' response from republican paramilitaries, which targeted Protestants they accused of involvement in the loyalist campaign. However, on a number of occasions, civilian bystanders were killed in such operations, most notably in the case of the Shankill Road bombing in October 1993, which was followed in the same month by an indiscriminate attack by loyalists on a pub in Greysteel in the west of the province. One consequence of the war between the paramilitaries has been a sharp fall in the deaths of members of the security forces (see Table 8.1). In the areas that have been most affected by the paramilitary war, such as Belfast, there has been a return to the levels of fear that existed during the random sectarian killings of the mid-1970s.

The political impact of these developments has been contradictory. Sinn Féin suffered a major electoral blow in April 1992, when Gerry Adams lost West Belfast in the UK general election. However, in local elections in May 1993, Sinn Féin increased both its number of councillors and its share of the poll. Further, two bombs planted by the Provisional IRA in the City of London in April 1992 and April 1993, each of which caused damage of approximately one billion pounds, demonstrated the potency of the threat the Provisionals' campaign posed to the UK economy. Notwithstanding such acts, doubts have grown within the republican movement as to the political effectiveness of the Provisional IRA's campaign of violence. These were made explicit in an interview given by a member of the Provisional IRA as far back as 1990 (*An Phoblacht*, 1990). Such doubts have been accompanied by a greater readiness to acknowledge unionist opinion as a force in its own right, existing independently of support from the British government.

These apparent shifts in republican perceptions have provided encouragement to negotiations between the republican movement and both the SDLP and the British government. The talks between the Sinn Féin president, Gerry Adams, and the leader of the SDLP, John Hume, resulted in a joint statement by the two leaders in April 1993. That was followed by the presentation of joint proposals to the Irish government. These were centred on the notion of the acceptance of the principle of self-determination for the people of Ireland as a whole, though this was tempered by recognition of the need to secure the agreement of the different traditions in Ireland to a settlement. While the British and Irish governments did not explicitly repudiate Hume's efforts to seek a basis for a cessation of the Provisional IRA's campaign of violence, these were sidelined by the two governments' own attempt to take the initiative in the wake of the Shankill and Greysteel atrocities. Their attempt in turn ran into difficulty when it was revealed in November 1993 that the British government had itself been engaged in an ongoing dialogue with the Provisional IRA over the possibility of a ceasefire, contrary to the government's stance of not negotiating with 'terrorists' and without the knowledge of the Irish government.

Such a development might have been expected to produce widespread fears among Protestants of a British Government sell-out. However, the response of unionists was surprisingly muted. That partly reflected the confidence of the Ulster Unionists that their pivotal role in shoring up the government's small overall majority in Westminster gave them the leverage over the British government to prevent any outcome contrary to their interests. Yet without concessions to nationalists, there seems little likelihood of the Irish government's securing the package deal it considers necessary to justify asking its electorate to approve amendments to the Irish constitution that would turn the controversial claim to Northern Ireland embodied in Articles 2 and 3 of the constitution from an aspiration into a reality. The likelihood of an overall settlement to end the conflict therefore seems small. At the same time, there is a considerable danger that the current negotiations will feed loyalist apprehensions of betrayal by the British government, and fuel violence by loyalist paramilitaries. That danger has been enhanced by loyalist perceptions of the Hume–Adams talks as the creation of a pan-nationalist front to achieve Irish unity.

Despite this danger, hopes of political progress are not entirely without foundation. There has been a measure of convergence in the positions of unionists and nationalists, as was evident during the second 1992 round of talks among the constitutional parties, even if a considerable gap between the two sides remains. There has also been evolution in the political attitudes of the paramilitaries, for the most part, in the direction of greater realism. It can at least be said that there is a greater prospect of an end to the violence than existed when the Provisional IRA and the UDA came into existence in the early years of the troubles. However, an appreciation of that prospect is not helped by trite comparisons of the situation in Northern Ireland with the transition to democracy in South Africa or the peace process in the Middle East. In contrast to South Africa and Israel/Palestine, the Cold War was not a significant factor in the dynamics of the Northern Ireland conflict. Consequently the end of the Cold War is less relevant to the prospects of peace in Northern Ireland than it

130   *Adrian Guelke*

has proved to be in the case of other regional conflicts exacerbated by East–West rivalry. An Irish miracle is not inevitable.

REFERENCES

Bishop, P. and E. Mallie (1987) *The Provisional IRA*. London, Heinemann.
Coogan, T. P. (1980) *The IRA*. London, Fontana.
Dillon, M. and D. Lehane (1973) *Political Murders in Northern Ireland*. Harmondsworth, Penguin.
Farrell, M. (1980) *Northern Ireland: the Orange State*. London, Pluto Press.
Flackes, W. D. and S. Elliott (1989) *Northern Ireland: a Political Directory 1968–88*. Belfast, Blackstaff Press.
Fortnight (1972), Belfast, 13 April.
Fortnight (1985/1986), Belfast, 16 December, 26 January, 231.
Fortnight (1987), Belfast, September, 254.
Iris (1982) Dublin, November,
Irish Times (1992), 1 and 2 January.
McKeown, M. (1989) *Two Seven Six Three*. Lucan, Murlough Press.
Nelson, S. (1984) *Ulster's Uncertain Defenders: Protestant Political Paramilitary and Community Groups and the Northern Ireland Conflict*. Belfast, Appletree Press.
New Ulster Political Research Group (1979) *Beyond the Religious Divide*, Belfast.
An Phoblacht/Republican News (1972), 2 January.
An Phoblacht/Republican News (1987), 7 May.
An Phoblacht/Republican News (1990), 28 June.
An Phoblacht/Republican News (1970), March.
UDA (1971), 19 October, 1, 2.
Ulster Political Research Group (1987) *Common Sense: Northern Ireland – An Agreed Process*. Belfast.
Whyte, J. (1990) *Interpreting Northern Ireland*. Oxford, Clarendon Press.

9 Majority–Minority Differentials: Unemployment, Housing and Health

Martin Melaugh

INTRODUCTION

> Inequality between Protestants and Catholics in Ireland originates
> from the policy of English and Scottish settlement carried through
> by the British Government in the sixteenth and seventeenth cen-
> turies to consolidate its earlier military conquest of the Gaelic and
> Catholic population. Over most of the period of four centuries
> since that 'plantation' began, inequality between planter and Gael
> was created and sustained by deliberate acts of policy. (Smith and
> Chambers 1991: 1)

In addition to the effects of the plantation and acts of government
policy other events had differing outcomes for the two peoples of the
north of Ireland. The advent of the industrial revolution in Ireland
and the formation of the Northern Ireland state both helped to
cement the difference in the relative social and economic standing of
the two main religious groups. The industrial revolution initially had
the greatest impact in the north-east of the island and Protestants
benefited disproportionately from the employment that it created.
The Northern Ireland state was formed at a time of turmoil in the
whole of Ireland and those who were 'loyal' to the new state and the
union were rewarded with jobs in the civil service, public employment and the security services. The relative Protestant advantage in
wealth and income brought about by these events has persisted to the
present day and is likely to do so for some time to come.

The Unionist Party enjoyed 50 years of control in Northern
Ireland without intervention from Westminster. During that time
many aspects of the operation of the state continued to benefit
Protestants more than Catholics. An element of this was a number of

forms of direct and indirect discrimination. Whyte (1983) produced a list of fields where discrimination was practised and ranked them from the greatest level of discrimination to the least. These were, electoral practices, public employment, policing, private employment, public housing, and regional policy. While the extent of direct discrimination in these fields was, and remains, the subject of debate (Hewitt, 1981, 1983, 1985; O'Hearn, 1983, 1985; and Kingsley, 1989) most researchers and commentators accept that this type of discrimination was practised mainly against Catholics over an extended period of time. Perhaps the most important consequence of this was the creation of a perception among the total Catholic population of a more widespread and systematic form of direct discrimination than the currently available evidence would support. Nevertheless, the Catholic allegations of discrimination by a number of local government districts, predominantly in the south and west of the region, were substantiated in many respects by later investigations (Cameron Report, 1969). There is also evidence that Catholics, in a few areas where they were in control of a local authority, discriminated against Protestants. As Catholics were less likely to be in a position to exercise such discrimination there was less of it; this is not in any way to excuse that discrimination which was carried out.

The Civil Rights movement focused British and wider public opinion on the relatively poorer circumstances of the Catholic minority in Northern Ireland. Under pressure from Westminster the Stormont government began to introduce a number of reforms in the late 1960s and early 1970s. Some reforms required little more than political will and the introduction of new legislation, and so were implemented fairly quickly. Other difficulties, in particular the relative economic disadvantage of the Catholic community, have proved more problematic. Reforms in this area have taken longer to implement and appear to have had less impact on the situation. At the heart of the problem is a cycle of disadvantage which, while affecting the poorest sections in both communities, is particularly pervasive in the Catholic community. This cycle involves a number of interrelated elements including education, employment, income, housing, wealth, social class, and health.

Issues related to education are considered elsewhere in this book (see Chapter 11) but it is worth noting here that an important effect of the segregated education system is the marked difference in the educational attainment of Catholics and Protestants (Gallagher, 1989). According to Northern Ireland Continuous Household Survey (CHS) estimates, based on samples of the population taken during 1988 to 1991, 52 per cent of Catholics had no formal education qualifications compared to 46 per cent of Protestants (Policy Planning and Research Unit (PPRU) 1993). While differences in educational attainment do not fully explain community differentials in employment opportunities (Eversley, 1989) they are an important factor in the job prospects of each individual.

EMPLOYMENT AND UNEMPLOYMENT

An assessment of the 1971 Census data showed that Catholics were two and a half times as likely as Protestants to be unemployed and Catholics in employment were over-represented in the semi-skilled and unskilled categories (Aunger, 1975). The 1971 Census provided data for a period when the Civil Rights movement was at its height and when allegations of discrimination in employment were widespread (Campaign for Social Justice, 1972). However, although the 1971 data showed that the occupational and industrial profiles of the two communities may have contributed to the differentials in unemployment, the data could not provide definitive answers to allegations of discrimination. Whyte's (1983) reassessment of the extent of discrimination during the Stormont years, while highlighting the likely impact of other potential explanations, did indicate that direct discrimination was an important element in the under-representation of Catholics in the workforce. In the case of public employment Whyte produced a list of demerit, with the most discriminatory first, consisting of local authorities under marginal unionist control in the west of the region, other local authorities, the Northern Ireland civil service, and the Imperial (Westminster-controlled) civil service. In the case of private employment Whyte was of the opinion that, 'in the past, discrimination caused a larger share of Catholic disadvantage than appears true today' (Whyte, 1983: 18).

In the field of employment there have been a number of policy and legislative initiatives introduced during the last 20 years. Some of the details of these changes are discussed in Chapter 3. The main statutory initiatives have been the introduction of fair employment legislation. However, the impression given by the delay in the introduction of some of the legislation is that it has been forced on a Westminster Parliament reluctant, or at best simply slow, to act. In his review of the issues involved in employment and religion in Northern Ireland,

Gallagher (1991) identified three main sources of pressure on the Westminster Parliament during the 1980s. The first came as a result of evidence which showed that, in spite of the 1976 Fair Employment Act, the unemployment gap remained between Catholics and Protestants. Secondly the Standing Advisory Commission on Human Rights was recommending additional legislation after carrying out a review of the 1976 Act. Finally, pressure from America and the MacBride Principles campaign was seen by the British as a potential threat to US investment in Northern Ireland.

The eventual response was the Fair Employment (Northern Ireland) Act 1989 which introduced a number of significant changes from the previous 1976 Act. The Fair Employment Agency was replaced by the Fair Employment Commission which had more powers and resources and a Fair Employment Tribunal was set up to deal with cases of alleged discrimination. Other important changes included a requirement for employers with more than 25 employees to register with the Commission and to monitor the religious composition of their workforces; it became illegal to discriminate indirectly; and limited affirmative action policies to redress imbalances in religious composition were to be permitted.

Part of the importance of tackling employment differentials, and especially those that occur as a result of discriminatory practices, lies in the wider economic and social repercussions that arise. As will be seen below, a number of these differences remain evident to this day. While there are some differences between the two communities in terms of economic activity rates the main difference is in the proportion which are unemployed. The Catholic population has consistently suffered from higher levels of unemployment. The differences in male unemployment have been, and are, particularly pronounced. The 1991 Census found that Catholic male unemployment was 28.4 per cent compared to 13.9 per cent for Protestants and other categories. In the case of females the equivalent rates were 14.5 per cent for Catholics and 8.8 per cent for Protestants. Evidence from other sources has shown similar results. In the 1992 Northern Ireland Labour Force Survey the unemployment level among economically Catholic males was 24 per cent compared with a figure of 10 per cent for Protestant males (PPRU, 1993). This relative level of difference in male unemployment has remained almost constant over the past two decades. Smith and Chambers, for example, concluded that during the period 1971 to 1985 'Catholic men were about two and a half times as likely as Protestant men to be unemployed' (1991: 195).

Data from the 1983–84 Continuous Household Survey (PPRU, 1985) show that, while the overall rate of unemployment was higher than at present, the relative standing of Catholic men 35 per cent and Protestant men 15 per cent, was roughly similar to that found earlier by Smith and Chambers and also similar to the most recently available data.

In addition to differences in the access to employment, there are also differences in the type of employment undertaken by the two Communities. The 1991 Census provides details of the major occupation groups by religion. According to the data, Catholics form 31.1 per cent of the total employed population aged 16–64 years. This figure can be used as the base for examining over- or under-representation in various occupation groups. In the case of professional occupations, craft and related occupations, plant and machine operatives, and also those on an employment or training scheme, Catholics are over-represented. In all other occupation groups, for example managers and administrators, clerical and secretarial, personal and protective, sales, and 'other' occupations, Protestants are over-represented.

Average income levels in Northern Ireland tend to be lower than in Britain. For example, in 1990 the average gross weekly household income in Northern Ireland was £256.59 compared to £335.67 in the UK as a whole (PPRU, 1992). Part of the explanation is due to higher unemployment rates in Northern Ireland, but wage rates for manual employment also tend to be lower in the region than for comparable work in Britain.

Given that Catholics tend to experience higher levels of unemployment it is not surprising to find that they are more likely to be dependent on state benefits. A survey based on data collected during the years 1988–91 found that 30 per cent of Catholic families were in receipt of Income Support compared to 16 per cent of Protestant families (PPRU, 1993). Partly as a result of this, and partly because of the less skilled occupations that Catholics tend to be employed in, income levels in Catholic households are lower on average than in Protestant households. Table 9.1 provides details from the Northern Ireland Continuous Household Survey of total gross household income by religion. Although the information covers only the period of the late 1980s and early 1990s it is clear that there has been a narrowing of the gap between Catholic and Protestant households. Nevertheless, differences in income levels remain a feature of Northern Ireland society. It should also be noted that because of

Table 9.1 Total gross household income from all sources, 1986–87 and 1988–91, by religion

| | CHS 1986–87 | | CHS 1988–91 | |
	Catholic	Protestant	Catholic	Protestant
Total gross income	%	%	%	%
Less than £2000	8	6	4	3
£2000–£3999	31	24	26	24
£4000–£5999	20	17	19	15
£6000–£9999	21	20	20	19
£10 000–£14 999	12	18	14	16
£15 000 and over	9	16	17	23

Source: Policy Planning and Research Unit (1993).

religious and cultural reasons the average family size of Catholic households is larger than Protestant households so the lower household income has to cover the expenditure of more household members.

Also of note are the area differences in household income across Northern Ireland. In 1987, for example, the average gross weekly household income in the east of the region was £235.09 while in the west the equivalent figure was £174.52. By 1990 there had been a considerable change in the figures, which for that year were £265.63 and £257.17 respectively (PPRU, 1992).

The differing average income levels between the two main religious groups also mean differing levels of expenditure. In 1989 the average weekly household expenditure among a sample of Catholic households was £186.69 compared to a figure of £208.01 in Protestant households (PPRU, 1992). According to the survey details Catholic households spent more on average than Protestant households on food; clothing and footwear; fuel, light and power; household services; alcoholic drink; and tobacco. In Protestant households more money was spent on motoring expenditure; housing; leisure goods; household goods; leisure services; and fares and other travel costs. The patterns of household income and expenditure are also reflected in ownership of consumer durables. Table 9.2 provides details from the CHS of the ownership of the main consumer durables by religion for the years 1983–84 and 1988–91 (PPRU, 1985, 1993). With the exception of the three most commonly owned items, namely a televi-

Table 9.2 Household ownership of consumer durables, 1983–84 and 1988–91, by religion

| | CHS 1983–84 | | CHS 1988–91 | |
	Catholic	Protestant	Catholic	Protestant
Consumer durable	%	%	%	%
Colour television	80	80	96	97
Refrigerator	84	92	96	97
Washing machine	70	75	82	84
Telephone	59	74	70	81
Central heating	53	56	77	78
Car or van	52	60	54	64
Freezer	15	22	53	64
Dishwasher	3	7	7	11

Source: Policy Planning and Research Unit (1985, 1993).

sion, a refrigerator, and a washing machine, there are significant differences between the two main religions with Catholics being less likely to own each of the items on the list. Given the lower level of income and the larger average household size, Catholic households spend a larger proportion of their disposable income on items such as food and clothing. This inevitably reduces the amount that can be spent on durable goods.

Secure and well-paid employment is important to people for a variety of reasons including such non-financial ones as self-fulfilment and self-esteem. However, an adequate income is desirable not only because of the lifestyle it allows but also because of the opportunity it brings for wealth creation and asset acquisition. The single most important asset that a majority of people are likely to possess is their home. The decision on whether to purchase or rent a dwelling depends on economic, personal and cultural factors. Households that are unable to afford to purchase a dwelling, or who do not wish to rent in the private sector, will look for accommodation within the public rented sector. In general, housing in Northern Ireland has suffered from problems of insufficient supply, poor quality, and unfit condition for much of this century. In the 1960s allegations of discrimination in the allocation of new and existing public sector housing were at their height. The issue of public sector housing proved to be very controversial in the 1960s and early 1970s and was one of the factors that led to broad support for the Civil Rights movement among the Catholic community.

HOUSING

Many historians and commentators view 5 October 1968 as the beginning of the current troubles in Northern Ireland. On the afternoon of that day the Royal Ulster Constabulary (RUC) moved to break up a civil rights demonstration in the Waterside area of Derry. The resulting violence had the effect of directing media attention to a situation which had largely gone unreported for decades and in addition it also increased the support for the civil rights movement.

Derry in 1968 was a city where a Catholic nationalist majority were subject to decisions taken by a local authority which was in control of the Protestant unionist minority. The city had a history of high unemployment, a housing shortage coupled with poor conditions, and a lack of regional investment in the area by the Stormont government. While the whole of Derry was suffering from a relatively poor economic situation in relation to the rest of Northern Ireland, there were also differentials between the Catholic and Protestant populations of the city.

The Derry Housing Action Committee (DHAC) was one of a number of groups organised to campaign on single issues. While these groups focused on matters of concern to the total population of the city, the question of discrimination against the Catholic majority in the city was also a factor in the actions of the groups. It was the DHAC which approached the Northern Ireland Civil Rights Association (NICRA) and persuaded it to give its support to a march planned for 5 October (Purdie, 1990). So it was the issue of housing in Derry that provided one of the sparks that began the present round of troubles. Indeed it was allegations of housing discrimination in Dungannon that had earlier given rise to the Campaign for Social Justice which in turn lead to the formation of the NICRA (McCluskey, 1989).

Some of the characteristics of housing in Northern Ireland are distinct from those in Britain. An important aspect of this is the high level of religious segregation in the region (Boal, 1982). The extent of residential segregation has not been constant but has increased during periods of political and civil unrest. Some of the largest population movements of recent times were a result of riots and intimidation in

Belfast during the summers of 1969 and 1971 (Darby and Morris, 1974). The result has been that much of the urban working-class population of Northern Ireland lives in areas surrounded by their 'own kind'.

As housing is relatively durable the size and condition of the housing stock in the late 1960s and early 1970s was determined by the cumulative effect of decisions and actions taken since the turn of the century. While other cities in the United Kingdom had undertaken schemes, before the First World War, to clear the worst of their slums, many of the housing authorities in Northern Ireland were slower to act (Brett, 1986). With the partition of the island in 1920 the Stormont parliament came into being but local authorities retained control of many housing functions. The period 1919–39 saw a marked increase in house-building activity in Britain; however there was no corresponding housing boom in Northern Ireland. In addition to the relatively small number built, the quality of those dwellings which were completed was also lower than in Britain. Many of the houses were built to a smaller size, lacked one or more basic amenities and, if situated in a rural area, they often lacked mains services of water, electricity and sewerage. The destruction and damage of domestic property during the Second World War added to housing shortages in the region and a number of housing initiatives were introduced. The main one was the 1945 Housing Act which provided for the establishment of the Northern Ireland Housing Trust (NIHT) as a public housing authority funded by government. The Act also increased the level of subsidies to local authorities to try and encourage more new housing. Despite these initiatives the level of new building was not sufficient to meet the demand, which was increasing due to obsolete stock and changes in population structure.

As the private rented sector declined, due mainly to declining profits and slum clearance in the urban areas, the public rented sector began to account for a larger share of the total housing stock. The public rented sector was divided between the local council housing and the housing built by the NIHT. The fact that there were a large number of local housing authorities during this period may even have had an adverse effect on the overall provision of public housing. In 1971 there were 61 housing authorities in Northern Ireland a system of provision which had a number of defects:

> There are far too many small councils. Twenty-seven local authority areas have a population of under 10,000, only five,

including Londonderry have a population of over 40,000. The consequences of this for housing provision and for other services are fairly clear in terms of insufficient population size, low rate receipts, inability to employ professional staffs, limited planning and development schemes, few economies of scale, and resultant inequality in standards between councils. (Birrell et al., 1971: 10)

It was in the early 1970s that comprehensive evidence started to become available on the overall condition of the housing stock and also information on the housing characteristics of Catholic and Protestant households. There have been and remain a number of marked tenure differences between the two religious communities. The 1971 Census showed that Catholics were less likely than Protestants to be owner occupiers or private renters and more likely to be in public rented accommodation. Even though there have been a number of important changes in the overall tenure mix, the most significant being the decline in the level of the private rented sector, there remain important tenure differences between the two religious groups. Catholics continue to be less likely to be owner occupiers and more likely to be public renters than Protestants.

Catholic households are on average larger than Protestant households reflecting larger family sizes among Catholics, which in turn are a result of cultural and religious factors. The larger household size is also reflected in the level of overcrowding which tends to be higher in Catholic households. Although Catholics tended to have larger families they were more likely, on average, to live in dwellings with fewer rooms than Protestants (Northern Ireland General Register Office, 1975); in more recent years this differential has declined (Registrar General Northern Ireland, 1993).

In addition to differentials in tenure and overcrowding there is evidence to suggest that the quality of dwellings inhabited by Catholic households were of lower quality than those of Protestant households (Northern Ireland General Register Office, 1975). The 1971 Census provided details of the level of amenities (hot water supply, fixed bath or shower, and inside toilet) broken down by religion. The data show that there were important differences in the level of amenities in the dwellings of the two communities in 1971. In each case the availability of exclusive use of amenities in Catholic households was substantially lower than in Protestant households. For example, 63.6 per cent of Catholic dwellings had exclusive use of all three amenities while the figure for Protestant dwellings was 72.0 per cent. Data at a district council area level was also available in the 1971 Census reports, but a breakdown by district and religion was not published. However, there were strong associations between the level of amenities in each of the 26 district councils and the proportion of Catholics living in those areas. Although highly suggestive of the fact that at an area level Catholic households were more likely to lack basic amenities, this type of association is not conclusive.

Unpublished data from the 1971 Census on amenity provision by district council and by religion were made available to the author.[1] A summary of part of this information is presented in Figure 9.1. The proportion of Catholic and Protestant households that had exclusive use of all three basic amenities was calculated for each of the 26 district councils. These data were then graphed on the basis of a ranking from the highest Protestant district council to the lowest. The first thing that is clear from the figure is the large difference in amenity provision in dwellings in the Greater Belfast area and those in the rest of the region, particularly in the west and south. Among Protestant households there was a 40 per cent difference between the district council area with the highest level of amenity provision and that with the lowest. Among Catholic households this difference was 60 per cent. So the main differential in amenity provision was an area one. However, it is also clear from the figure that in all but four of the district council areas, Catholic households were more likely than Protestant households to live in dwellings lacking amenities. It is worth noting that a number of those areas where the provision and condition of housing were poorest, were the same areas where the Civil Rights movement had active support.

At the time of the 1971 Census there was a close association between the provision of amenities in a dwelling and its physical condition. The differentials in amenity provision shown in Figure 9.1 therefore give an indication of associated differentials in housing conditions at that time. While the NIHE has carried out House Condition Surveys in 1974, 1979, 1984, 1987 and 1991, it was only the most recent one which included the religion of the household as a variable. Information on religion and house condition is scheduled to be published in the second report of the 1991 HCS which is due out in 1994.

Faced with evidence of serious housing shortages and a housing stock which was in a very poor condition, the Westminster

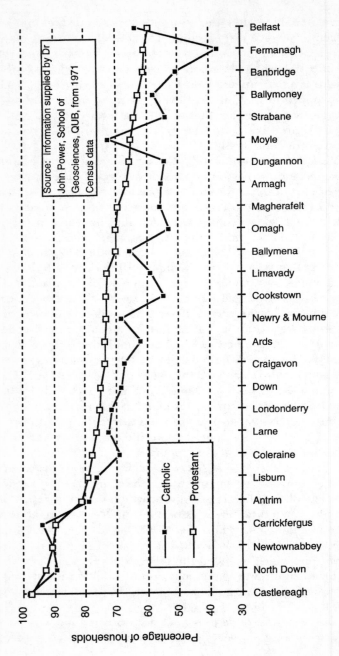

Figure 9.1 Percentage of Catholic and Protestant households with exclusive use of hot water, fixed bath and inside toilet, district council areas, 1971

government initially pressured Stormont to introduce a number of housing reforms and later took direct control of them in 1972. One of the most important measures taken was the establishment of the Northern Ireland Housing Executive (NIHE). In addition to taking on responsibility for the entire public sector housing stock the NIHE was to be the conduit by which problems in the other housing sectors were addressed. The very fact that decisions regarding the allocation of public rented accommodation were taken out of the hands of local councillors helped to reduce the extent of allegations of discrimination. In addition a points system based on housing need was introduced and, after a period of rationalisation, a standard system of rents was implemented across the entire stock. Both measures helped increase confidence in the fairness of the NIHE. The essential ingredient was the financial commitment given to the various housing programmes that were introduced in the 1970s and 1980s. For much of this period per capita government expenditure on housing in Northern Ireland has been substantially greater than that provided in Britain (Singleton, 1986).

The second report of the Standing Advisory Commission on Human Rights (SACHR) included an assessment of the impact of public housing provision on the two communities (SACHR, 1990). This assessment was based on a report into public housing in the region carried out by the Policy Studies Institute (PSI) (Smith and Chambers, 1989). The first of the main findings of the report was that there was no evidence of direct or indirect discrimination by NIHE against applicants or tenants. A number of differences did appear in the analysis of the data and the first of these was the fact that those on the waiting list expressing a preference to live on a Catholic estate had a lower chance of being rehoused than those wishing to live on a Protestant estate. The report also noted a number of distinct differences in the state of repair and dwelling standard of Catholic and Protestant estates. In some areas Catholic households were worse off, in others it was Protestant households.

As indicated above there are a number of remaining housing issues which have a differential impact on the two communities. There remains for example an unfitness problem among private sector housing in the rural areas of the west of the region. As there is a higher proportion of Catholics living in these areas unfitness is likely to have a disproportionate effect on them. Other problems include general disrepair among the housing stock, a number of problem estates, and housing shortages in key areas such as West Belfast.

HEALTH

Investigations into differences in health between groups of people in Britain have tended, in the past, to look for explanations based on social class, lifestyle and diet (Townsend and Davidson, 1982). In more recent years there has been more concentration on specific aspects of deprivation as measured by indicators such as unemployment, access to a car, and so on (Townsend Phillimore and Beattie, 1988). Although the whole issue of health is very complex and dependent on the interaction of many variables, it is clear that there is an important association between health and aspects of deprivation. Evidence considered earlier points to the fact that Catholics have, in general, been in an inferior economic position in comparison to Protestants, and that this has been true for some considerable time. Given this information, and the evidence on the relationship between deprivation and health, it would be reasonable to assume that the overall of the Catholic community is likely to be less good than that of the Protestant community.

While not explicitly including religion as a variable there has been one report on deprivation and health in Northern Ireland. This report was commissioned by the Department of Health and Social Services (DHSS) which asked the Policy Research Institute (PRI) and the Northern Ireland Regional Research Laboratory (NIRRL) to replicate the Townsend, Phillimore and Beattie (1988) study on deprivation and health. The Northern Ireland report was submitted to the DHSS in 1990 (PRI and NIRRL, 1990). The report looked at associations between a number of indicators of health and deprivation at ward level in the region. As in the Townsend study, a strong significant association was found between deprivation and health. A cursory inspection of those wards with the highest level of ill health shows that they include many inner city rural areas in Belfast and Derry. Even though a religion variable was absent from the study it would appear that Catholic wards are over-represented among those with the highest levels of ill health. This is only a tentative assertion and would require the inclusion of ward level information on religion.

Campbell (1993) points out that while research in the other areas of inequality in Northern Ireland, such as unemployment, has been the subject of numerous reports, the topic of health has received less attention. In an attempt to redress this research imbalance Campbell and Stevenson (1993) prepared a report for the DHSS (NI) based on a secondary analysis of CHS data and data from the Northern Ireland

Social Attitudes Survey. The study concluded that: 'In all aspects of lifestyle investigated Catholics were found to be more likely to engage in behaviour which could adversely affect their health' (Campbell and Stevenson, 1993). This included aspects such as smoking, drinking, diet and exercise. The study found few differences in the level of self-reported health status.

It is often difficult to disentangle the numerous variables which have an influence on the health of a particular group of people. For the Catholic community, issues of social class, income, and deprivation are all important factors in explaining differentials in health. Also of importance are issues related to lifestyle such as diet, exercise, smoking and drinking. These factors are often considered individualistic in nature. However, strong cultural and group pressures probably account for some of the observed differences in, for example, smoking and drinking habits.

FINAL COMMENTS

Perhaps the greatest period of Catholic disadvantage occurred in Ireland as a result of the 'penal laws' which spanned a period of 134 years. When the Northern Ireland state was established Catholics in the region were already at an economic and social disadvantage in comparison to Protestants. While the whole population of Northern Ireland benefited from the improving standard of living that was occurring in industrialised countries, the 50 years of Stormont rule did little to improve the relative standing of Catholics.

In the last two decades efforts have been made to address some of the causes of disadvantage and these initiatives have met with some success. However, it is clear from recent evidence considered above that a number of economic and social differentials remain. Perhaps the central area of concern is the persistent differences in employment and unemployment. Given the general nature of the Northern Ireland economy it would require a huge government-sponsored programme of private and public investment to achieve economic parity with Britain. For many reasons, not least the current difficulties facing the UK economy, this is not going to occur. In the absence of major investment or an unprecedented upturn in the economy, unemployment levels will remain high and Catholics are likely to remain disproportionately affected. Positive discrimination has been ruled out as a potential approach to this problem. However, it would seem that affirmative action is not sufficiently strong enough in the present circumstances to achieve the desired outcome.

This chapter has dealt solely with the differences that exist in the material and social conditions of the Catholic and Protestant communities. It should be remembered that in Northern Ireland there are other differentials which cut across religious denomination. Among these are economic and social differentials between men and women, the upper and the lower social classes, the young and the old, and those in good physical and mental health and those in poor health.

NOTE

1.   The author would like to acknowledge the assistance of Dr John Power, School of Geosciences, The Queen's University of Belfast, in providing tables of the breakdown of dwelling amenities by household religion and by district council area.

REFERENCES

Aunger, E. A. (1975) 'Religion and Occupational Class in Northern Ireland', *Economic and Social Review,* 7: 1, 1–18.

Birrell, W. D., P. A. R. Hillyard et al. (1971) *Housing in Northern Ireland.* London, Centre for Environmental Studies.

Boal, F. W. (1982) 'Segregating and Mixing: Space and Residence in Belfast' in *Integration and Division. Geographical Perspectives on the Northern Ireland Problem,* ed. by F. W. Boal and J. N. H. Douglas. London, Academic Press.

Brett, C. E. B. (1986) *Housing a Divided Community.* Dublin, Institute of Public Administration; Belfast, Institute of Irish Studies, Queen's University Belfast.

Cameron Report (1969) Disturbances in Northern Ireland. Belfast, HMSO, Cmnd 532.

Campaign for Social Justice (1972) *Northern Ireland – the Plain Truth,* 2nd edn. Dungannon, Campaign for Social Justice.

Campbell, R. (1993) 'Research into Inequalities in Health in Northern Ireland: What Research?', *Critical Public Health,* 4: 2, 2–8.

Campbell, R. and G. Stevenson (1993) *Community Differentials in Health in Northern Ireland.* Belfast, Queen's University Belfast.

Darby, J. and G. Morris (1974) *Intimidation in Housing.* Belfast, Northern Ireland Community Relations Commission.

Department of the Environment Northern Ireland (1992) *Housing Statistics 91: Northern Ireland Housing Statistics to December 1991.* Belfast, HMSO.

Eversley, D. (1989) *Religion and Employment in Northern Ireland.* London, Sage.

Gallagher, A. M. (1989) *Majority Minority Review 1: Education and Religion in Northern Ireland.* Coleraine, Centre for the Study of Conflict, University of Ulster.

Gallagher, A. M. (1991) *Majority Minority Review 2: Employment, Unemployment and Religion in Northern Ireland.* Coleraine, Centre for the Study of Conflict, University of Ulster.

Hewitt, C. (1981) 'Catholic Grievances, Catholic Nationalism and Violence in Northern Ireland During the Civil Rights Period: a Reconsideration', *British Journal of Sociology*, 32, 3, 362–80.

Hewitt, C. (1983) 'Discrimination in Northern Ireland: a Rejoinder', *British Journal of Sociology*, 34, 3, 446–51.

Hewitt, C. (1985) 'Catholic Grievances and Violence in Northern Ireland', *British Journal of Sociology*, 36, 1, 102–5.

Kingsley, P. (1989) *Londonderry Revisited: a Loyalist Analysis of the Civil Rights Controversy.* Belfast, Belfast Publications.

McCluskey, C. (1989) *Up off Their Knees.* Galway, Conn McCluskey and Associates.

Northern Ireland Expenditure Plans and Priorities: the Government's Expenditure Plans 1992–93 to 1994–95, vol. 2 (1992), London, HMSO, Cmnd 1917.

Northern Ireland General Register Office, Department of Health and Social Services (1975) *Census of Population 1971 Religion Tables Northern Ireland.* Belfast, HMSO.

O'Hearn, D. (1983) 'Catholic Grievances, Catholic Nationalism: a Comment', *British Journal of Sociology*, 34: 3, 438–45.

O'Hearn, D. (1985) 'Again on Discrimination in the North of Ireland: a Reply to the Rejoinder', *British Journal of Sociology*, 36: 1, 94–101.

Policy Planning and Research Unit (1985) *Continuous Household Survey – Religion. No. 2/85.* Belfast, Department of Finance and Personnel.

Policy Planning and Research Unit (1989) *Continuous Household Survey – Religion. No. 1/89.* Belfast, Department of Finance and Personnel.

Policy Planning and Research Unit (1992) *Family Expenditure Survey Report for 1987–1990. No. 2/92.* Belfast, Department of Finance and Personnel.

Policy Planning and Research Unit (1993) *Continuous Household Survey – Religion 1988–1990/91. No. 1/93.* Belfast, Department of Finance and Personnel.

Policy Research Institute and Northern Ireland Regional Research Laboratory (1990) *Spatial and Social Variations in the Distribution of Health Indicators in Northern Ireland.* Queen's University Belfast and University of Ulster.

Purdie, B. (1990) *Politics in the Streets.* Belfast, Blackstaff Press.

Registrar General Northern Ireland, Department of Health and Social Services (1993) *The Northern Ireland Census 1991 Religion Report.* Belfast, HMSO.

Singleton, D. (1986) 'Northern Ireland Housing: Number One Priority but for How Much Longer?' in *Aspects of Housing Policy and Practice in Northern Ireland 1984–1986,* ed. by D. Singleton. Belfast, Department of Town and Country Planning, Queen's University Belfast.

Smith, D. J. and G. Chambers (1989) *Equality and Inequality in Northern Ireland 4: Public Housing.* Policy Studies Institute Occasional Paper 47. London, Policy Studies Institute.

Smith, D. J. and G. Chambers (1991) *Inequality in Northern Ireland.* Oxford, Clarendon Press.

Standing Advisory Commission on Human Rights (1990) *Religious and Political Discrimination and Equality of Opportunity in Northern Ireland, Second Report.* London, HMSO, Cmnd 1107.

Townsend, P. and N. Davidson, eds (1982) *Inequalities in Health: The Black Report.* Harmondsworth, Penguin.

Townsend, P., P. Phillimore and A. Beattie (1988) *Health and Deprivation: Inequality and the North.* London, Croom Helm.

Whyte, J. (1983) 'How Much Discrimination was there under the Unionist Regime, 1921–1968?' in *Contemporary Irish Studies,* ed. by T. Gallagher and J. O'Connell. Manchester, Manchester University Press.

Part Four
Institutions

10 Church and Religion in the Ulster Crisis

Duncan Morrow

INTRODUCTION

Religion, or at least religious labels, are hard to avoid in Northern Ireland. Indeed in the age of the mass media, conflict in Northern Ireland has become synonymous with religious divisions in many parts of the world. Even domestically, labels such as 'Protestant' and 'Catholic' remain the most commonly used shorthand in describing different social groups and even specific political positions. The impression lingers that conflict in Northern Ireland is between two groups divided by religious confession or tradition.

Nevertheless, even the most cursory glance at the relationship of religion and politics indicates that their interconnection is not a simple one. On the one hand, Northern Irish people remain comparatively loyal to their churches. Repeated surveys have shown them to be among the most regular churchgoers in Western Europe (Cairns, 1991). The physical landscape of the province is marked by numerous church buildings, by religious symbols and slogans, by evangelical propaganda and by traffic jams before and after church services. In all of these senses, Northern Ireland conveys a markedly 'religious' impression. And it is in this observant and pious society, where political allegiances have largely followed the lines of Catholic–Protestant divisions, that conflict has appeared endemic. Clearly, there is some connection between religion and politics.

At the same time, the most fervent church-loyalists are seldom those most active in violence. There is little evidence that terrorists or paramilitaries in Northern Ireland are directly concerned by doctrinal or spiritual questions. Many church members argue that violence is something outside the churches. Indeed, it is the churches who have most consistently condemned violence and who have held their own members back from seeking revenge for the atrocities perpetrated on them. In this light, the churches are primarily crucial bulwarks against further chaos and destruction.

The question of the involvement of the churches in conflict, and their responsibility for it, cannot therefore receive a single answer. The Church, and religion generally, is a complex cultural reality whose relationship to contemporary politics has numerous dimensions. Understanding the role of the churches in Northern Ireland means examining more precisely the nature and importance of religion in political life.

Discussion about the churches is riddled with imprecise language which sometimes obscures important distinctions. Churches are not simple institutions with a single social science meaning and purpose, like political parties or pressure groups. Primarily, this stems from a claim to loyalty in the faith which goes beyond any state institution. As such churches are, firstly, communities of believers, whose actions singly and together make up the totality of each church. As such, the Church is those whose primary loyalty is following Jesus. On the other hand, churches are often identified most closely with the clergy and leadership of the institutions. Nevertheless, the entirety of any church is always more complex and even apparently contradictory than an institutional description allows.

This distinction has been important in theology for generations. In social science, however, the decline of religious observance in the West has increasingly reduced the Church to a private social institution. Inevitably, the political profile of 'the Church' has become largely its institutional role. The great modern exception to this was the persecution of individual Christians in Eastern Europe. There is therefore a sharp tendency to regard actions or positions taken by a church-leadership as synonymous with the whole Church, no matter how 'Christian' or otherwise. Likewise Christian acts carried out personally, without institutional blessing are lost on measurable scales. While we will clearly not avoid this trap, it remains important to acknowledge its existence.

Linguistic confusion also bedevils the term 'religion'. The French-American literacy critic and anthropologist, René Girard, has suggested that religion is the crucial mechanism by which all human cultures have coped with conflict and violence. Endemic conflict between human beings is solved by directing the violence onto one victim or group, a scapegoat. Peace is established between the members of the remaining group in relation to this scapegoat. The phenomenon that peace emerges from unity found in driving out the scapegoat is attributed to the special powers of the scapegoat, who is elevated to a special position for the group, having both the power to destroy and unify the group. From this experience stem the entire structure of the group, its laws, rituals and values. Religion is the ritual repetition of the original expulsion, recreating unity in the group. Religion is the alternative to chaos. Culture only exists with and because of religion. Central to religion is not so much the rationalistic expression of doctrine, as the action of recreating the expulsion, finding unity together (Girard, 1973). As such, those who leave the Church, even calling themselves atheist, but seek to bring peace by the expulsion of those held to be to blame, the scapegoats, are more, not less, religious. Much of the violence in Northern Ireland seems to adopt this pattern.

In Girard's work, the Christian gospel, and the life of Jesus, are held to expose this expulsion mechanism, by showing its operation from the viewpoint of the victim rather than the victimisers (Girard, 1987). To distinguish this reality from the others, Girard speaks of faith rather than religion. It is clear that the Christian churches have nevertheless participated in the ongoing scapegoating mechanism, seeking to impose their values and authority by force, and ritually re-enacting the process of expulsion. As such they too have often been religious institutions, not communities of faith. In a context of 'religious' churches and 'religious' groups seeking to expel their scapegoats, the possibility that the one would infect the other is great. Thus Christian religion can come to justify secular violence in the name of God, while secular violence can shape Christian religion. Both of these phenomena can be observed in Northern Ireland.

ASPECTS OF THE HISTORICAL BACKGROUND

Religion, and conflict surrounding religion, has played a role in Irish and specifically Northern Irish affairs since the Reformation. In this Ireland is not different to most of continental Europe. However, the specific conditions of political and religious movements in the north of Ireland resulted in ingrained communal divisions, where the lines of religious division ran almost parallel to political divisions.

Following the defeat of the Ulster Gaelic chieftains at Kinsale in 1601 a decision was taken actively to settle confiscated lands in mid- and west Ulster with settlers from Scotland and England whose loyalty to the crown could be taken for granted. Lands were assigned to a variety of new landowners who were put under obligation to settle them with armed Scottish and English families in segregated areas.

Very quickly it became clear that these conditions were impractical, and many landlords rented out their land to the previous inhabitants, especially in areas with poorer soils where it proved difficult to attract new immigrants. As a result, two groups, each with very different experiences of the same political and social upheavals lived in close proximity to one another.

This settlement, known as the Plantation of Ulster, was complemented with more successful migrations and plantations of largely Scottish groups in the east of the province, particularly in East Antrim and North Down. Eastern Ulster had long shared a close economic and social connection with the western seaboard of Scotland, and the more fertile soils and less hostile political environment proved attractive to considerable numbers (Bardon, 1992; Foster, 1988). Significantly for our purposes, the result was to import settlers not only of a different geographical origin and political loyalty but to introduce, for the first time on a large scale, Anglicans and Presbyterians into the north of Ireland. The native population, under threat from now-Protestant England, remained loyal to the religious authority of the papacy.

The 'reformation' in Ireland was not, in the main, a question of the mass indigenous conversion of natives but of the influx of large numbers of Protestants into Ireland. Furthermore, the importance of their Protestantism for the state was the guarantee that it provided of loyalty to crown institutions. Religion and power politics have therefore long been close in Northern Ireland. Presbyterian settlers, dominant in Scotland, were at times ambivalent in their loyalty to what was in effect an Anglican ascendancy. This was especially true during the eighteenth century when large numbers of Presbyterians emigrated to the United States. In some Presbyterian areas of Ulster there was considerable sympathy for the ideals of the American republicans in 1776 and after. Nevertheless, in those areas of Ulster where Presbyterians and Catholics came into regular direct contact, Presbyterians tended to ally themselves with Anglicans (Millar, 1980; Stewart, 1984). After the 1830s, with the spread of the railways and industrialisation, there were ever fewer areas in the north of Ireland where this was not the case.

It is not possible here to describe in detail the history of religious and political interrelationships. Suffice to say that at many of the crucial turning points in Irish history, whether in the 1641 revolt, Cromwell's campaigns or the Williamite Wars of 1689–91, local religious divisions were central in understanding political loyalties. The application of harsh social, economic and political restrictions to the Roman Catholic Church and to individual Catholics, known as the penal laws, bound together the social and economic destiny of church and people. Significantly, the emergence in the nineteenth century of a recognisably modern Irish nationalist movement focused in the first instance on Catholic emancipation. With the exception of the late eighteenth century, the recurrent theme was the close association between religious denomination and attitudes towards the political power of the crown in Ireland.

Frank Wright shows that Northern Ireland has always been on the frontier of the British metropolis (Wright, 1987). Although attached, it has always had a distance from the political centre, a fact of fundamental significance for the nature of the society. The destruction of native political and cultural institutions was never forgotten, and left the church as the only conceivable central rallying point until the democratic emancipation of Catholics through the nineteenth century. Likewise, Protestants on the frontier felt permanently vulnerable and unsure of the reliability of British support for their predicament. The result was an inevitable reliance on indigenous institutions. By far the most important permanent indigenous cultural institutions were the churches. By the late eighteenth and into the nineteenth centuries, different Protestant communities united by fear of Catholic resurgence emerged as a political unity.

Although some individual Protestants became notable Irish nationalists, the trend throughout the nineteenth century was towards the consolidation of political divisions on the basis of religious tradition, a tendency which has stretched into the present day. When Protestants opposed home rule for Ireland, the slogan 'Home Rule is Rome Rule' encapsulated the close association of religious and political identities and fears. When partition of Ireland was agreed, unionist politicians spoke of the creation of a 'Protestant parliament for a Protestant people'. From the outset, then, controversy over religion in Northern Ireland was directly linked to political loyalties.

DEMOGRAPHY AND DENOMINATION

The largest denominations in Northern Ireland today remain the descendants of the churches existent in Ireland after the plantation. In the interim, numerous other groups have emerged, all of which are usually classified as broadly Protestant. Numerically, the two most significant have been Methodists and Baptists (Registrar General Northern Ireland, 1993).

In statistical terms, churches in Northern Ireland remain relatively strong. In the 1991 Census for Northern Ireland, 89 per cent of people identified themselves as belonging to a specific Christian denomination. Of the total, 38.4 per cent declared themselves Roman Catholics, while 50.6 per cent belonged to a number of different Protestant churches. Nevertheless, raw statistics hide a number of important features.

Although Presbyterians and Anglicans (Church of Ireland) account for over 75 per cent of all Protestants, there are more than 45 separate denominations with more than 100 members in a population of less than 800000. This contrasts sharply with the Catholic population, unified into one institutional body. As we shall see, this contrast has had political as well as religious significance, as institutional unity of Catholicism has sometimes been seen as threatening by Protestants who contrast it with the fragmentary nature of Protestantism.

Naturally, the proportions in the population are not static and there have been important changes of denominational proportions since Northern Ireland was established in 1921. Immediately after the partition of Ireland, Catholics made up 34 per cent of the population in the north and Protestants 65 per cent. For many years, a higher Catholic birthrate was balanced by a higher emigration rate among Catholics. As a result, the relative proportions in the population changed little. There is some evidence, particularly in relation to migration, that these patterns had begun to change in the 1970s and 1980s. Significantly, interest in changes in denominational proportions is regarded as profoundly important for secular politics.

Changes in proportions can also be accounted for by the rise in the number of those refusing to answer the Census question on religion and those claiming no religion, who together accounted for 11 per cent of the population by 1991. Furthermore, there has been a sharp decline in the size of the two largest Protestant denominations. Between 1921 and 1991, the percentage of Presbyterians in the population fell from 31 per cent to 21 per cent. The corresponding figures for the Church of Ireland were 27 per cent and 18 per cent. This has only been partly offset by the rise in the number of those attached to smaller Protestant groups, who now make up 8 per cent of the population.

Although Northern Ireland is theoretically and statistically a mixed community in terms of religious denomination, there is increasing evidence that overall mixing masks increasing separation at local level. The 1991 Census revealed that within the Belfast Urban Area, over half the population lived in wards which were more than 90 per cent Catholic or Protestant. Furthermore, throughout Northern Ireland there was evidence that Protestants were moving from the west of the province and leaving Belfast City into areas of more concentrated population. Crucially, these marked religious cleavages, and changes within and between them have a significance beyond the level of faith or religious adherence. They continue to be used to provide important sociological indicators of political change.

Lastly, although attendance and membership remains high, especially when compared with other parts of Western Europe, there is evidence of a drift towards secularisation. Statistics indicate that, especially in the Belfast area, attendance in all denominations is declining. One survey of Presbyterians indicated that only half of those who left Belfast for the suburbs joined a church in their new home areas (Irish Inter-Church Meeting, 1991).

The churches in Northern Ireland remain numerically large institutions, but the changes within and between groups may be very important in forecasting future trends.

DENOMINATIONS IN NORTHERN IRELAND: POLITICS AND IDEOLOGY

The largest single denomination in Northern Ireland is the Roman Catholic Church. Nevertheless, in relation to all other churches combined, it remains a minority within Northern Ireland. Combined with the 95 per cent of the population of the Republic of Ireland who are, at least nominally, Catholic, the Church is by far the largest on the island of Ireland, taken as a whole.

The Catholic Church has long been the largest and most publicly prominent institution within the nationalist community. Sharing the suffering of the Catholic people of Ireland during the penal laws period, the history of the Church was always closely bound to that of the people. The Church was the one established institution able to claim the loyalty of the majority in Ireland. In Ireland, the British needed political partners who commanded sufficient support among the Irish population to be regarded as legitimate representatives and who could, at the same time, deliver public order. The Catholic Church was always the only conceivable institution which could combine both aspects. As a result, the clergy gained a politically pivotal position, between a threatened and sometimes hostile community and the British authorities.

The resulting high profile of the clergy confirmed for many Protestants, however, that the Church was the most important institution in the Catholic community. On the other side, the Church authorities came under attack from more radical republicans who accused the Church of leniency towards the British or Northern Irish authorities. Thus the Catholic Church has long been simultaneously accused of being the main organiser of republicanism and an agent of British imperialism.

For most Catholics, including clergy, religion itself is not the central feature of conflict in Northern Ireland (McElroy, 1991; Wilson, 1986). Religion is here defined narrowly to mean issues of doctrine and practice. Catholics have tended to regard political and economic inequity and injustice as the root of the Northern Irish problem. This is confirmed in the experiential pattern of the Church. The church authorities have always been aware of the material and political complaints of their parishioners. It is on these social and economic issues that they have negotiated with various governments, British or Northern Irish. Theology has seldom been at issue. At the same time, the very fact that it is the Church which negotiates or that the Church manages schools, social facilities and economic initiatives has raised the public profile of the Church in public affairs and confirmed some Protestants in their view that the church is the controlling influence in Catholic society. Perception, as much as substance, has been politically crucial.

The Irish Roman Catholic hierarchy has been one of the most loyal and conservative in the Catholic world. This has had important effects in Ireland, especially during the late nineteenth and early twentieth centuries. In reaction to the rise of secular liberalism in continental Europe, especially in Italy, the papacy became increasingly conservative in doctrine. The infallible authority of the Pope in certain situations was underlined, the veneration of the Virgin Mary was encouraged and in the *Ne temere* decree of 1909, the conversion of partners in mixed marriages was stipulated, together with the requirement that all children should be raised as Catholics. Protestant churches were confirmed as churches 'in error', and, in a famous phrase, 'error has no rights'. All of these had an impact on the relationship of Catholicism to Protestants in Ireland, strengthening Protestant concerns about the implications of a Catholic Ireland. The fact that the Irish Free State, later the Republic, was overwhelmingly Catholic, meant that more than in most states, the law reflected Catholic concerns and attitudes.

Likewise, changes in the 1960s and later also had significant implications for social relationships in Northern Ireland. The Second Vatican Council enabled more open relations between the churches. Many of the harsher aspects of the Roman Catholic Church were softened. Although inter-communion remained impossible, Protestant churches were declared to be 'separated brethren' and church unity to be a desirable goal. The resultant increase in ecumenical contact with Protestant churches and church-people in Ireland caused serious difficulties especially for Protestants, who remain split about the nature of the Catholic Church between those who regard it as fundamentally evil and unchristian and those who seek meeting and ongoing interchange.

The Catholic clergy are thus central figures in the social life of the Catholic community in Ulster. Many of the Northern Ireland's community assets such as schools, church buildings, youth clubs and social facilities are divided along religious lines with the connivance of clergy, politicians and popular support on all sides. After much controversy in the late 1920s, Protestant and Catholic clergy together with unionist and nationalist politicians agreed to the parallel education systems which, despite the growth of integrated schools, remain largely in place today. Once more, the clergy were the only group in the Catholic community who commanded sufficient confidence from both their parishioners and the Northern Ireland government to be given effective control. Most Catholic schools were therefore directly managed by local parishes. Recent changes in school management systems have altered this to some extent, but the influence remains strong.

When in 1980 a government report recommended the merger of all teacher-training colleges on one site, the Catholic clergy were supported by normally anti-clerical republicans in their campaign against such a move. Republicans did not object to the replacement of clerical control with secular control, but they saw the proposed merger as a political move by British imperialists to subvert Irish education in the North (Chilver Report, 1980; *Andersonstown News*, 1980/81: various). In effect, although both clerical and anti-clerical groups deny any identification, nationalism and Catholicism find themselves in the same political lobby for different reasons. Nothing could better demonstrate why outsiders identify the two together while insiders see recurrent differences.

In the 1980s, clergy also became involved in the management of a number of employment and training schemes. In the mid-1980s, under pressure from unionist politicians, the government announced that resources for some similar schemes run by non-church groups were to be withdrawn because of suspicions of close links between them and the IRA. At the same time, resources for church-linked schemes were stepped up, leading to further accusations from many republicans that the Church was doing the government's bidding.

The Catholic clergy have in general opposed political violence in Northern Ireland. Among many nationalists they are regarded as the strongest 'internal' opponents of the IRA. This too has underlined accusations from republicans that the Church is an agent for unionism. In fact, a recent survey of clergy showed that over 90 per cent supported constitutional nationalism as represented by the Social Democratic and Labour Party (SDLP) (McElroy, 1991). Paradoxically, the opposition of the clergy to republican violence within the catholic community has resulted in an even higher political and socioeconomic profile for the clergy providing further evidence for external critics, if any is needed, that the church dominates Catholic society yet does nothing to stop terrorism.

The term 'Protestantism' is often used in Northern Ireland as the counterpart of Catholicism. This has a certain political and social validity but is misleading when referring to the churches. There is no single Protestant church institution unifying the community. The community's institutional unity is political, although theological anti-catholicism has been important in giving ideological coherence to this unity. Institutional unity, in as far as it exists at all, is provided by political and cultural groups such as the unionist parties and the Orange Order, none of which are churches but in all of which church history and doctrine have played important parts.

Presbyterianism, the largest Protestant denomination, is rooted in Scottish Calvinism, strongly influenced in the nineteenth century by the evangelical revival. Traditionally, the Church has had both a liberal wing, which has been at times ecumenical and socially radical, and a conservative wing, marked by biblical fundamentalism and active hostility towards Catholicism. Although technically an all-Ireland church, Presbyterians are geographically concentrated in Counties Antrim and Down.

The Church of Ireland, once the established church of the whole island, is hierarchical in structure. It retains a stronger sense of an all-

Ireland purpose, stemming from the close political relationship between the Church and the Protestant ascendancy. Anglicanism in other countries has been strongly marked by Catholicism, but Anglicanism in Ireland has tended to be predominantly Protestant, evangelical or low-church. However, unlike Presbyterians, most Anglican opposition to Catholicism has been political rather than purely theological.

Ulster Methodists, who are the third largest Protestant denomination, also have had strong evangelical roots and a traditional interest in social reform. As the church most removed from political power, they have sometimes appeared less clearly identified in political terms.

Church attendance among Ulster Protestants is considerably lower than among Catholics. One survey in the 1980s found that 39 per cent of Protestants in Northern Ireland attended church weekly (Moxon-Browne, 1983). In working-class areas of Belfast attendance was much lower (Irish Inter-Church Meeting, 1991). Nevertheless, the churches have not been replaced by any other popular organisations. Trade unions and political parties remain small. The Orange Order no longer commands the support of previous years and membership of paramilitary groups is concentrated in geographical pockets. With different churches remaining the largest social institutions, the Protestant community is marked by subdivision and variation, contrasting sharply with the institutional monolith of Catholicism.

The absence of a single Protestant church means that the churches are not single institutional cultural focuses. Those Protestant clergy who have been prominent in public affairs have generally become so by virtue of their election to secular office rather than through their church position. Furthermore, the very fact of division means that secular power in the Protestant community has not been accumulated in one clerical centre. Even where resources have been placed under church management, such as employment schemes, the perceived effect is different under Protestant conditions.

Perhaps more importantly, Protestants have overwhelmingly supported the union with Great Britain. As a result, while the union has been maintained the Protestant clergy in Ulster have not had to mediate between their communities and authorities perceived to be closer to another community. They have thus been able to draw a clearer public distinction between the state and their churches' public activities. For example, once the Northern Ireland government had made certain guarantees about religious education and church representation on boards of management, the Protestant churches transferred most of their schools into full state control. Interestingly, Protestant clergy in the Irish Republic have sometimes acted in a protective manner for their values and communities similar to the role adopted by the Catholic clergy in the North, notably in the fields of education and health.

However, it is usually Protestants who ascribe a religious dimension to communal divisions. Clearly this is largely due to the public profile of the Roman Catholic Church, on both sides of the Irish border. In the face of this, Protestants have often fallen back on their religious differences as the most important aspect of their culture which needs protection in Ireland. Protestantism has therefore been a secular political identity in Northern Ireland.

Until 1920, most Protestants in Ireland spoke of themselves as Irish *and* British, in contrast to nationalist claims to be Irish *not* British. After partition, nationalists in Northern Ireland proclaimed themselves Irish, an identity seldom, if ever, denied them by the Irish south of the border. In this context, some unionists now preferred to describe themselves as British *not* Irish, only to find that, except during and immediately after World War II, this met little echo in England, Scotland and Wales. Unionists who were opposed to nationalism but who felt insecure about their continuing Britishness, therefore had to seek other self-descriptions and tended and tend to fall back on labels such as Northern Irish or, more usually, Protestant. It is therefore possible that a person in Northern Ireland who seldom goes to church might describe themselves as Protestant. Republicans who deny that unionists in Ireland are British thereby reinforce their identity as Protestants. Thus, ironically, those who deny most forcefully that religion is important in the context of Northern Ireland, contribute to the ongoing importance of religious identity in Ireland.

The divide between Protestantism as a statement of faith and as a political identity is therefore wafer-thin. Radical anti-catholic religious Protestants have always been overtly hostile to Catholicism. In a context of unionist insecurity about Britain's will to support their position, many have found the radical anti-catholic commitment of fundamentalist church leaders appealing. In this way, for example, the Reverend Ian Paisley, a minister in the small fundamentalist and anti-catholic Free Presbyterian Church, has had a strong appeal for working-class, and largely non-church, Protestants (Wright, 1973; Bruce, 1986).

There is an asymmetry in the way in which the churches relate to the communities which sometimes bear their names. The Catholic Church has had a high institutional profile, controlling community assets and without any rival within the community. The repeated experience of both clergy and people is that the substantial negotiations with the authorities are about social, economic and political questions. Simultaneously, the Protestant experience is that the Catholic Church is the main political operator within the community from which their enemies come. Protestant churches have been less important as social organisers, but Protestantism, and the anti-catholic dimension of Protestantism has been crucial to the political shape and ideology of unionism at various times and to the sustenance of a credible ideological basis for opposing republicanism once British nationalism fails. The Catholic experience of Protestantism is therefore that unionists raise religious objections to nationalism which tend to be regarded as diversions or unimportant by Catholics themselves.

THE CHURCHES, CONFLICT AND INTER-COMMUNITY RELATIONSHIPS

Churches are part of the historic fabric of Northern Irish society. With the partial exception of Methodism in the nineteenth century and of ongoing intermarriage, there is little history of conversion between the groups, of large numbers of Protestants becoming Catholic or vice versa. As such, the churches have been relatively stable human communities, living side by side, but with little trade in membership.

This stability has contributed to the historical importance of churches as the most continuous indigenous cultural institutions in Northern Ireland. Churches have become the most continuous vehicles for community memories, myths and histories. Given the circumstances of Catholics and Protestants in the north of Ireland, they have ministered not only to communities of faith but to communities with much shared secular communal experience. As such, each church has overwhelmingly ministered within and to one political tradition, each of which has at times felt threatened by the other. At least at the level of secular political life, the range of experience in each church is not substantially greater than the experience of one side of a political divide. The predominance of unionism within Protestant churches and nationalism within the Catholic church is not absolute, but it is overwhelming. As a result, the equation of nationalist/Irish/Catholic and unionist/British/Protestant has never been successfully or convincingly repudiated.

At one level, the preference of Protestants for a nominally Protestant state and of Catholics for a majority-Catholic state is not surprising. However, the capacity of Catholics in England to coexist within a Protestant state and of Protestants in many Catholic countries to exist happily in the twentieth century suggests that doctrine is insufficient reason for the continuing equation of the political and the confessional. The substantial issue of difference, of course, is ongoing political violence along this cleft. Given the fact that the Catholic Church institutionalises one community whose experiences are of historical violence by the state and its supporters, the fear and experience which unites church and community is one of violence coming primarily from the same traditional quarter. Likewise, the Protestant churches have given institutional and ideological shape to their community, and now minister to the experiences and fears of that community, where violence is seen as coming from the opposite quarter.

In the Northern Irish situation, the churches find themselves reflecting the secular experiences of their members. They may be deeply unhappy with violence stemming from their own communities, but they do not experience the grief, anger and bitterness of this violence as they do when they have to minister to a political death or injury in their own community. Unless the churches can fully admit the absolute partiality of their perspective, they will always be themselves partial. The churches' claims to the transcendent authority of God can either enable them to see their own partial humanity or it can become a way to universalise a partial experience, thus raising a partial experience to a transcendent and divinely sanctioned cause.

In communities who regard one another with suspicion or hostility, in which the fact of being a Protestant or being a Catholic in certain contexts is grounds for apprehension or fear, avoidance of situations of fear, which may mean the avoidance of one another, is a matter of common sense. Northern Ireland's past and present provides innumerable examples of good reasons for such suspicion. In a mixed and violent society the fears are easily generated and ultimately hard to avoid completely. Often people in mixed Catholic-Protestant groups are anxious to avoid raising questions whose impact might be so controversial as to break up the group.

Churches are not mixed. Churches provide a refuge and comfort. As a result, inter-community work, even the sharing of violent experience from different angles can seldom happen within a single church, but can only happen between them. Given their own historical antagonism to one another, and strong resistance to treating one another as equal, churches have not been quick to lower their defensive ramparts against one another. Therefore, churches have remained largely bastions of single-community experience, implicitly, or sometimes explicitly, sure that God is on their side. The churches may not be opposed in theory to changed community relations, but to participate actively in it means jumping over deeply felt historical and doctrinal differences.

Churches are places of intimacy, where birth, marriage and death are celebrated publicly, and where the violent death of a member of the community is felt by all. Inevitably, Protestant churches experience the fear and murder of their members more deeply than the fears and murders of those outside. The same is true for the Catholic church. If such atrocities repeatedly seem to come from the other community, the sense of fear or hostility can easily grow. The experience of violence can therefore reinforce the sense of isolation from one another in the churches.

The churches in Northern Ireland have therefore mirrored the divisions of secular society and, often unwittingly, they have given them an institutional shape and an ideological validity. Although the reasons given are different to those of secular society, the unwillingness of churches to treat one another as real equals has the same result as the refusal of other groups in secular society. The churches' actions or lack of them give credence to the religious labels loosely attached to whole groups. In effect, church actions towards one another are sufficiently analogous to the actions of secular groups for the attachment of the terms 'Protestant' and 'Catholic' to be used without successful contradiction. The boundary between a refusal to deal with one another equally on grounds of doctrine or grounds of political enmity remains very blurred.

CONCLUSIONS

While it is certainly true that secularisation has begun in Northern Ireland, the churches remain central cultural institutions especially in social organisation, in chaplaincy and sustenance of those under pressure, in public and private moral and political ideology and in formal and community politics. Churches are the largest voluntary institutions in Northern Ireland, often the focus of important social networks, sometimes invisible except in close inter-personal ties. They also fulfil important tasks even for those with no regular worshipping attachment. Church buildings are important community resources for many groups. In rural areas, church halls are gathering points for cultural and political activities whether services or campaigns against the closure of healthcare facilities. This network provides a substantial part of the social and community infrastructure in Northern Ireland (Morrow, 1991).

Churches are large voluntary economies both in terms of money collected and distributed and in terms of unpaid time committed. Numerous charities have benefited. Highly paid professionals and tradespeople give freely of their time which is nowhere accounted or audited. Many Credit Unions, now widespread in Northern Ireland, had clerical and parish involvement from the outset.

Although churches play different political roles for nationalists than for unionists, the generic labels 'Catholic' and 'Protestant' have continued to be used as shorthand to describe the conflict in Northern Ireland. They are likely to continue to do so. Despite the fact that Christian doctrine seldom provides the grounds for those in conflict, the issues in conflict are inevitably underpinned by their central institutions in a country which has sustained such a conflict for more than 25 years. At the very least, the churches have been unable to put effective distance between themselves and particular political causes. Clergy, drawn from their respective experiences and positions, have tended to share the suffering of their laity rather than transform it. No church has yet been able to break the identification of church and political position.

Religion and politics are therefore mixed at all levels of cultural life. However, in Girard's terms, attempts to loosen this bond have tended to be more religious rather than less outside church boundaries. The evidence is not that the unchurched are less violent. If anything the reverse is true. Nationalism, whether Irish or British, seems itself religious. Conor Cruise O'Brien has talked of Irish nationalism's deification of Ireland, Godland. Ian Paisley constantly identifies the struggle of Ulster Protestantism as the struggle of the chosen people against evil. Hunger strikers in 1981 were explicitly compared to the crucified Christ. It is already clear, not just in Northern Ireland, that once aroused, the national cause, demanding loyalty, orthodoxy and blood sacrifice is quickly considered sufficient justification for enormous cruelty.

However even if conflict will not end, the inability of the churches in Northern Ireland to find ways beyond violence remains a serious problem for the churches and their faith. As we have seen, the churches are so integrally linked into the structures and perceptions of the society that they cannot be separated from some responsibility for the present outcome. The failure of the churches to offer serious models of change may have serious consequences for their and Northern Ireland's future.

REFERENCES

Andersonstown News (1980/81), various issues.
Bardon, J. (1992) *A History of Ulster.* Belfast, Blackstaff Press.
Boyd, R. (1987) *Christianity in Ireland.* Geneva, World Council of Churches.
Brooke, P. (1987) *Ulster Presbyterianism.* Dublin, Gill and Macmillan.
Bruce, S. (1986) *God Save Ulster.* Oxford, Oxford University Press.
Cairns, E. (1991) 'Is Northern Ireland a Conservative Society?' in Social Attitudes in Northern Ireland, ed. by P. Stringer and G. Robinson. Belfast, Blackstaff Press.
Chilver Report (1980) *Chilver Report.* Belfast, HMSO.
Daly, C. (1992) *The Price of Peace.* Belfast, Blackstaff Press.
Foster, R. (1988) *Modern Ireland 1600–1972.* London, Penguin.
Girard, R. (1973) *Violence and the Sacred.* Baltimore and London, Johns Hopkins University Press.
Girard, R. (1987) *Things Hidden since the Foundation of the World.* London, Athlone Press.
Hickey, J. (1984) *Religion and the Northern Ireland Problem.* Dublin, Gill and Macmillan.
Irish Inter-Church Meeting. (1991) *Challenge of the City: the Report of the Working Party on the Challenge of the Urban Situation in Ireland Today.*
Lee, S., ed. (1991) *Freedom from Fear.* Belfast, Institute of Irish Studies.
McElroy, G. (1991) *The Catholic Church and the Northern Ireland Crisis.* Dublin, Gill and Macmillan.
Millar, D. (1980) *Queen's Rebels.* Dublin, Gill and Macmillan.
Morrow, D. (1991) *The Churches and Inter-community Relationships.* Coleraine, Centre for the Study of Conflict, University of Ulster.
Moxon-Brown, E. (1983) *Nation, Class and Northern Ireland.* Aldershot, Gower.
Registrar General Northern Ireland, Department of Health and Social Services (1993) The Northern Ireland Census 1991 Religion Report. Belfast, HMSO.
Smyth, C. (1987) *Ian Paisley: Voice of Protestant Ulster.* Edinburgh, Scottish Academic Press.
Stewart, A. T. Q. (1984) *The Narrow Ground.* Belfast, Pretani Press.
Wilson, D. (1986) *An End to Silence.* Cork, Mercier Press.
Wright, F. (1973) 'Protestant Ideology and Politics in Ulster', European Journal of Sociology, 213–80.
Wright, F. (1987) *Northern Ireland: a Comparative Analysis.* Dublin, Gill and Macmillan.

11 Education and the Conflict in Northern Ireland

Alan Smith

A distinctive characteristic of the education system in Northern Ireland is segregation. The system is segregated by religion in that most children attend predominantly Protestant ('controlled') schools or Catholic ('maintained') schools; by ability (and some would argue social background) in that a selection system operates at age 11 to decide which children attend grammar schools (more than one-third of children in second-level education); and often by gender (particularly in second-level education where a quarter of the secondary schools and almost half of all grammar schools are single-sex).

Religious and cultural segregation is bound up with a long history which placed education at the centre of a struggle between the English state and the Catholic Church in Ireland. Until the late eighteenth century the Catholic population was excluded from any formal education by the Penal Laws established as a means of maintaining English control in Ireland. Murray writes that during this period,

> Catholic children got their education by means of illegal classes which took place in the open country, with lookouts posted to warn of any approaching authorities. These became known, for obvious reasons, as 'hedge schools' and by the end of the eighteenth century, the bulk of Catholic education was being achieved in this way. (Murray, 1985: 14–15)

The Act of Union in 1801 brought Ireland under direct rule from Westminster, the Penal Laws were relaxed and Catholic religious orders began to establish schools. First attempts at multi-denominational education emerged in 1812 following a commission of inquiry which recommended that grants be given to schools which 'educate Christians without any attempt to interfere with their respective religious beliefs'. For a short period it appeared that schools set up by the Kildare Place Society were fulfilling these conditions, but by 1830 it became clear that the Society was in fact a proselytising body.

168

Nevertheless, these years prepared the way for the principle of mixed schooling and in 1831 Ireland became the first country in Europe to introduce a National School system. The aspiration was to create a system of schools which provided mixed education for children of different creeds and avoided proselytisation. In practice this comprised a secular day plus time set aside for Bible readings 'without comment'. Each school was administered by a single manager, usually the local Catholic or Protestant clergyman and gradually, what had promised to be a non-denominational system, was eroded through mistrust and campaigns for concessions from clergy on both sides. By the end of the nineteenth century National Schools had become segregated and *de facto* denominational institutions.

Events in education following the establishment of Northern Ireland in 1921 are well documented (Akenson, 1973; Dunn, 1990) and indicate how the interests of different churches continued to shape the type of school provision. These interests led to a system comprised of controlled (*de facto* Protestant) schools and Catholic (voluntary) maintained schools which continues to be the predominant pattern of provision to the present day.

The current education system in Northern Ireland is relatively small. Statutory education encompasses approximately 300000 children within 970 primary, 166 secondary and 70 grammar schools. The system is administered by a Department of Education and five local authorities (known as Education and Library Boards). There also exists a statutory Council for Catholic Maintained Schools, and government funds the Northern Ireland Council for Integrated Education (NICIE) to coordinate the development of a small but growing number of integrated schools (17 primary and 4 secondary in 1993) which are attended by roughly equal numbers of Catholic and Protestant children. The education system also includes eight Irish language schools, of which three receive grant-aid from government, and ten independent Christian schools associated with the Free Presbyterian Church which do not receive government funds.

The past two decades have seen schools drawn more and more into the spotlight in terms of how their activities take account of the conflict which is taking place within the wider society. This has culminated in the introduction of new and significant initiatives, including legislation and government policies, which ascribe a more prominent role for schools in the improvement of relations between the two main religious and cultural communities in Northern Ireland. In broad terms, these policies support interventions in both the process of education (through curriculum reforms and associated inter-group contact) and the structure of education (through consideration of equity issues between existing schools and support for the creation of new, integrated schools).

EARLY DEVELOPMENTS

The pioneer in developments in Northern Ireland was a Belfast school principal (Malone, 1973) who persuaded the then Northern Ireland Ministry of Education to fund a project on education and community relations which was eventually based in the Queen's University, Belfast. This was essentially a curriculum development project, with some elements of joint school activities and meetings. It had quite ambitious plans for the production of curriculum support materials, but the funds for these were not, in the end, made available. Shortly after Malone's project, two parallel projects were established at the then New University of Ulster, one of which became a social sciences curriculum project (Skilbeck, 1973, 1976; Robinson, 1981), and the other concerned religious education (Greer and McElhinney, 1984, 1985a, b). These were experimental, relatively small-scale, and the success or otherwise of these projects is difficult to estimate. On the positive side they began a process and established a context which made future developments possible. On the negative side they did not become widely used or succeed in filling a permanent niche in the Northern Ireland school curriculum.

At the same time a large number of voluntary groups began to develop a role for themselves in this process. Many of these were able to supply resources of time, materials and personnel, to establish a variety of inter-school relationships between Catholic and Protestant schools. Others set up and ran residential courses where the issues could be debated and strategies developed. This trend has continued and a recent directory of such voluntary bodies indicates that more than twenty organisations are currently active in Northern Ireland in the field of community relations and schools (FOCUS, 1993).

These developments, taken as a whole, represented a patchwork of small, relatively isolated projects, geographically dispersed, each making a contribution towards the evolution of a more coherent and developed programme of work which included contributions to the mainstream curriculum, extra-curricular activities, conflict-resolution techniques, approaches to peace education, and inter-group contact

(Trew, 1986). There is little doubt that this range of activities provided an enormous stimulus in that it created a team of voluntary workers, teachers and academics who had expertise, interest in and commitment to community relations work through the schools. They provided a rationale and legitimacy for future developments in this area. It is difficult to see how later, more ambitious, projects could have come into existence without the basis which these earlier attempts provided.

SCHOOL LINKS AND CROSS COMMUNITY CONTACT

During the 1970s it became clear that little was known about the two school systems – the state system of 'controlled' schools and the 'maintained' system of Catholic schools. In 1976 a team of academics from the University of Ulster was funded from a Ford Foundation research initiative to carry out both a general survey within the Northern Ireland education system and a local case-study. This was published in 1977 as *Education and Community in Northern Ireland, Schools Apart?* (Darby et al.). It attempted to understand the ways in which the two systems were different, and, consequently, to give a meaning to the much-quoted notion of individual school ethos, a notion always used as a justification by protagonists of separation. Results suggested, among other things, that there was a genuinely segregated system, that is that there was little evidence of any significant level of crossover or interaction between the two sectors, but that in almost all the publicly measurable ways, few obvious differences could be found.

The findings suggested that the development of widespread integrated education was unlikely in the foreseeable future, but almost without exception, all interviewed expressed some anxiety about the effects, or even just the possible effects, of complete segregation. One possible way in which it seemed that these two views could be reconciled was for there to be as much contact as possible between pupils and teachers within the segregated system. A second research study, *Schools Together?*, set out to measure the amount of contact, of a sustained and important character, that actually existed between Catholic and Protestant schools. The results (Dunn, Darby and Mullan, 1984) suggested that very little contact existed even though quite extravagant claims are often made now about past levels of contact and cooperation between the two sectors.

A third research and development project known as *Inter School Links* followed. It was experimental and interventionist in that it set out to create linked programmes between a set of schools in one town on a routine and sustained basis. This project operated for four years between 1986 and 1990 and produced two reports. The first report (Dunn and Smith, 1989) outlined a development process by which all schools in the same town evolved regular, structured links. In the primary schools, Catholic and Protestant pupils were given opportunities to meet and work together on curriculum themes as part of the normal school day. Teachers in the post-primary schools worked together to create a programme of study in Irish history and this provided opportunities for joint field work and contact between pupils from the different schools.

The second report (Smith and Dunn, 1990) extended the project to schools in two other communities and evaluated some aspects of the work. The evaluation produced some evidence to suggest that the history programme had brought about a more questioning attitude amongst pupils toward interpretations of Irish history prevalent within their own cultural community. It also recommended that contact between Catholic and Protestant pupils appeared to be most successful when there was a strong curriculum focus. The project demonstrated that it was possible for such cross-community contact to become an accepted feature of the school curriculum and the evaluation also highlighted an extremely high level of support for such ventures amongst parents.

In 1987, midway through the project, the Department of Education introduced a scheme which provided approximately £0.4 million annually to encourage all schools in Northern Ireland to become involved in inter-school contact. Levels of participation have increased annually and recent figures indicate that almost a third of primary schools and over a half of post-primary schools are now involved in some form of inter-school contact which brings Catholic and Protestant pupils together.

THE DEVELOPMENT OF EDUCATION FOR MUTUAL UNDERSTANDING (EMU)

Although teachers and academics had been active from the early seventies, government was more hesitant and cautious about suggestions that schools should be involved with community relations issues. Its first public commitment of any sort was in the production in 1982 of a circular called *The Improvement of Community Relations: The Contribution of Schools* which stated that: 'Every teacher, every school manager, Board member and trustee, and every educational administrator within the system has a responsibility for helping children learn to understand and respect each other.' This signalled the beginning of formal government support. From its inception in 1983, the Northern Ireland Council for Educational Development (NICED), a quasi-government curriculum development body, became involved in the issues of education and community relations, and established a committee with a brief to develop ideas about what it decided to call Education for Mutual Understanding (EMU). The NICED committee appointed two field-officers, one for second level and one for first level, and eventually produced a guide to EMU for teachers (NICED, 1988) which tried to introduce schools to the procedures and techniques necessary for the promotion of EMU activities both within and between schools. This has been superseded by the Education Reform (NI) Order, 1989, which specifies that two 'cross-curricular themes' related to the issue of community relations are included in the Northern Ireland Curriculum. These are called *Education for Mutual Understanding (EMU)* and *Cultural Heritage.*

The statutory requirement to include these themes in the curriculum of all schools took effect from 1992 and the Northern Ireland Curriculum Council has produced guidance material which supports the definition that 'Education for Mutual Understanding is about self-respect, and respect for others, and the improvement of relationships between people of differing cultural traditions' (NICC, 1990). The aims and objectives state that as an integral part of their education the themes should enable pupils 'to learn to respect and value themselves and others; to appreciate the interdependence of people within society; to know about and understand what is shared as well as what is different about their cultural traditions; and to appreciate how conflict may be handled in non-violent ways' (NICC, 1990).

The Education Reform Order, 1989, also places a statutory responsibility on school governors to report annually to parents on steps taken to promote Education for Mutual Understanding. This is the only aspect of the Northern Ireland Curriculum which has this reporting requirement. There will be no direct assessment of individual pupils as part of EMU. It is envisaged that its aims and objectives will form an integral part of programmes of study in all subjects. However, it has become clear that many schools also see the aims being communicated less formally by the nature of relationships within the schools, and between the school and the wider community. In this sense many schools claim that the aims of EMU are already implicit in their whole-school ethos. While the themes are a mandatory feature of the curriculum, cross-community contact with pupils of other schools remains an optional strategy which teachers are encouraged to use.

The period between the introduction of legislation to include EMU in the curriculum and its impact on schools has provided a limited opportunity to consider the implications of EMU's transition from a voluntary activity to a statutory requirement. Initial research and evaluation confirms that the inclusion of EMU in the statutory curriculum was largely unanticipated with less than a third of schools having a policy in place (Smith and Robinson, 1992a). As EMU finds its place within the curriculum it has also become clear that teachers' perceptions of the theme and its purpose are diverse and varied and not restricted to community relations issues in Northern Ireland. More universal aspects, such as gender relations, human rights, and ethnic diversity in an international context, may be increasingly emphasised as EMU becomes interpreted by a larger number of teachers. In the short term, however, it appears that most schools will rely heavily on a strategy which focuses narrowly on generating more inter-school contact between Catholic and Protestant pupils.

The most pressing issue in the 1990s will be a comprehensive plan for education and training and many teachers have requested particular support regarding controversial issues and how these might be addressed in the context of the classroom and with mixed groups. In Northern Ireland approximately 17500 teachers are in daily contact with 330000 children in over 1200 schools so the target is large, the resource implications considerable and coordination between statutory, voluntary and academic agencies will be necessary.

It will take some time for the impact of these changes to become clear and it is unlikely that the themes will be afforded a high priority while schools still face other major changes in the main subject areas, assessment and financial delegation. Indeed the initial indications from Britain have already raised questions about the concept of cross-curricular themes as an educational strategy. Research by Whitty and Rowe (1993) suggests that pupils do not experience cross-curricular themes in a coherent fashion because their messages are dissipated across many subjects involving a number of teachers.

THE EMERGENCE OF INTEGRATED EDUCATION

In some ways the most dramatic development in education in Northern Ireland over the past twenty years has been the creation of integrated schools, that is schools which are attended in roughly equal numbers by Protestants and Catholics. In 1974 a group called All Children Together (ACT) was established, composed of parents in favour of children being educated together. This organisation opened up the arguments, promoted discussion and debate and allowed various strategies for the generation of change to be tested. The group lobbied successfully for legislation which would allow state schools to become integrated (Education (NI) Act, 1977), but this was only invoked on one occasion as an attempt to prevent a school closure. Eventually, some parents within ACT decided to establish a new school which would exemplify their commitment to integrated education and the first planned, integrated school, Lagan College, was established in Belfast in 1981. This was followed by the opening of three further integrated schools in Belfast in 1985 and a pattern was established whereby at least one new integrated school has been established in Northern Ireland every year since. By 1993 there were 21 integrated schools (17 primary and 4 post-primary) attended by approximately 3500 pupils (approximately 1 per cent of the school population).

The integrated schools have all been initiated by groups of parents working together to establish new institutions which are jointly managed and staffed on a cross-community basis. The aim of the integrated schools is that they should be attended by children from both Protestant and Catholic backgrounds, and should be open to children from other religious backgrounds and to children from backgrounds where there are no religious beliefs at all (Wilson and Dunn, 1989). In practice the schools are Christian in character and the founders, parents, teachers and managers have developed workable procedures for the teaching of religion.

The Education Reform (NI) Order, 1989, included a number of provisions for the encouragement of the development of integrated schools, created a mechanism for funding them and placed a statutory responsibility on government to support and promote integrated education. The increasing number of integrated schools, the fact that they had generated a central organising council, the Northern Ireland Council for Integrated Education (NICIE), and the new atmosphere of general government support, also led the government to include mechanisms in legislation to transform existing schools into integrated institutions, although this route seems more problematic (Moffat, 1993).

The schools have attracted considerable research interest. Studies have been completed on their impact on parental choice of school (Cairns, 1989); the views of parents (Agnew et al., 1992); the role of parents and teachers (Morgan et al., 1992); friendship patterns (Irwin, 1991); and a number of postgraduate case-studies.

Despite the strides which have been made within the past two decades, integrated education is still in its infancy and the number of schools is limited. Currently the movement for integrated education faces difficult strategic issues concerning further development at secondary level within the competitive climate of a selective education system, and at a time of government financial constraint on capital development. The introduction of a policy of 'open enrolment' may also pose difficulties for the schools in terms of maintaining pupil enrolments which draw from both cultural traditions in equal proportions. It will only be possible to judge what the eventual level of uptake will be once a system of integrated schools becomes established on a more widespread basis.

EQUITY ISSUES

The conflict has also focused attention on relative advantage and disadvantage between the Catholic and Protestant communities in Northern Ireland. One aspect of this was a review of fair employment legislation by the Standing Advisory Commission on Human Rights (SACHR, 1987) which indicated that Catholics were twice as likely to be unemployed as Protestants. In part this highlighted the ineffectiveness of the earlier 1976 Fair Employment Act and became the impetus for more rigorous fair employment legislation. Current legislation now requires employers to monitor the religious composition of their workforce and, where significant gaps exist, to adopt recruitment procedures which are likely to encourage applications for employment from members of the under-represented community.

The debate about the underlying explanations for unemployment differentials between the two communities also focused attention on the relationship between the labour market and the education system. In this respect the segregated system of schools once again came under closer scrutiny and Gallagher et al. (1993) suggest that this needs to be understood within the historical framework whereby,

> the importance of separate Catholic schools was not only ideological or cultural, but, in a very real sense, material. Apart from the Church itself, the Catholic school system represented the only significant social institution of civil society over which the catholic community, through the Church, exercised a degree of control ... In this context separate Catholic schools provided one of the few routes to social mobility in Northern Ireland, albeit largely into certain professional occupations involved in servicing the Catholic community.

In an effort to understand whether aspects of the segregated system of schooling had contributed to higher levels of unemployment amongst Catholics, the Standing Advisory Commission on Human Rights (SACHR, 1989, 1990, 1991, 1992) commissioned a number of research studies which investigated various explanations. In particular it was noted that a higher proportion of Catholics left school with low or no qualifications (Osborne, 1986; Cormack, Gallagher, Osborne and Fisher, 1992) and that more Protestants chose scientific subjects at school and university (Cormack and Osborne, 1983). This led to research which identified underlying differentials in funding between Catholic and Protestant schools (SACHR, 1991).

An unanticipated finding concerning recurrent funding revealed consistently higher levels of per capita funding in favour of Protestant pupils within primary, secondary and grammar schools (Cormack, Gallagher and Osborne, 1991). Various explanations were advanced to explain this including differences in school size and different provision of specialist teaching space (Cormack, Gallagher and Osborne, 1992), and it was suggested that for historical and perceptual reasons Catholic schools were less disposed to approach government for funding (Murray, 1992). The research concluded that the overall impact of a number of factors such as these had contributed to consistently lower levels of recurrent funding for Catholic schools (Gallagher, Osborne and Cormack, 1993). The Education Reform (NI) Order, 1989 included provision for the local management of schools (LMS) whereby each school is allocated a recurrent budget which is determined by a formula largely dependent on pupil numbers. It is anticipated that one consequence of this will be a more equitable distribution of funds between all schools. Eventually, through monitoring, it should become possible to judge whether this new system of financial input has any significant impact on the educational outcomes from the different schools which serve the Catholic and Protestant communities.

A further equity issue concerns the capital funding of Catholic schools. Historically the voluntary nature of Catholic schools had meant that the school trustees were largely responsible for the buildings and capital development of schools. This changed over a period of time following the establishment of Northern Ireland until, by the late sixties, Catholic voluntary maintained schools were receiving 85 per cent grant towards approved capital costs. Change towards fuller funding was incremental and involved a series of negotiations between the Catholic authorities and government. In general, the *quid pro quo* for higher levels of capital funding from government was a reduction in Church representation on school management boards. By the late 1980s a number of arguments contributed to a further change in the level of capital funding for Catholic schools. The introduction of a statutory curriculum meant that all schools are now required by law to provide the same educational opportunities to their pupils. For many schools this meant upgrading or providing specialist teaching facilities and it was questionable whether government could place part of the financial burden for this on the Catholic community. It was accepted that the differential in unemployment levels between Catholics and Protestants was linked in part to school provision and the political drive to tackle this problem made it less acceptable to have differential capital funding between schools. The example of 100 per cent capital funding for Catholic schools in Scotland was cited and arrangements for 100 per cent funding of integrated schools illustrated that it is possible for schools to retain a distinctive ethos without any single interest group forming a majority within each governing body. The outcome of these arguments was that government, in consultation with the Catholic bishops, introduced a mechanism by which Catholic schools could opt for 100 per cent capital funding (Osborne, 1993) and legislation to make this possible was enacted in 1993.

Finally, the existence of grammar schools and a selective education system in Northern Ireland has also been the focus for research on equity in education. Early research (Gallagher, 1988) had indicated higher overall attainment levels among pupils leaving grammar schools and this had obvious implications for employment and career opportunities. A recent analysis (Cormack, Gallagher and Osborne,

1992) indicated that fewer grammar school places are available within the Catholic school sector even if all grammar schools were enrolled to capacity. Government has responded by announcing plans to increase the number of places available in Catholic grammar schools.

The research outlined above highlights how important it is to investigate and monitor equity issues within a divided society. These initial studies have concentrated on the relative advantage and disadvantage between Catholics and Protestants, the two major communal blocks in Northern Ireland. Over time it will also be important that the concept of equity which evolves is comprehensive so that it also includes minority interests in education and takes account of other sources of division within the society.

DIVERSITY OF SCHOOLS

The history of developments in education in Northern Ireland since the most recent outbreak of violence in 1969 constitutes a complex case study in the development of a theory about the role of education in societies experiencing violent conflict. A range of approaches have emerged from within the community itself, and from government agencies, and the interaction of these raises interesting questions about the relative merits of interventions in the structure and process of education.

At a structural level the segregation within the education system in Northern Ireland appears to be resistant to change. Most children continue to be educated in predominantly Catholic or Protestant schools and equity issues tend to be addressed in terms of these two blocks. However, the past twenty years have also brought new types of school which, despite their small numbers, introduce a potential for change and raise questions about the overall administration and control of education within the society.

The 1980s saw the emergence of new integrated schools, founded by parents from both communities, now funded by government and incorporated in legislation. There is also the appearance of Irish language schools where all instruction is through the medium of Irish. There are now seven of these at primary level, and a secondary school has recently been established in West Belfast. In addition there are ten independent Christian schools, mostly attached to the Free Presbyterian Church which was founded by the Reverend Ian

Paisley. The model for these schools appears to be the Bible Christian schools in the southern states of the USA. They are financially independent of the state and are normally quite small, although they enrol children of all ages from 5 to 18. The schools follow a curriculum which eschews such things as the teaching of evolution and adheres to fundamentalist interpretations of the Bible on moral and sexual issues.

So there are, currently, three new types of school, all relatively small, but all healthy and growing, albeit slowly. Apart from the integrated schools, very little research has been carried out on other types of new school, and it is not at all clear what social forces are at work to make them appear now. Taken together they represent a relatively small, but significant potential for fragmentation or diversification within the overall school system. It may also be of significance that none of them is secular and it is unclear whether such diversity in school type is constrained by or a consequence of the current conflict.

REORGANISATION OF EDUCATIONAL ADMINISTRATION

Alongside the emergence of new types of school, questions have been raised about the role of different interest groups in the overall management of the education system. This has taken place in the context of a government review of arrangements for the administration of education in Northern Ireland. State schools (known as 'controlled' schools) are organised through five local authorities, called Education and Library Area Boards. In practice this has meant that these schools have had a degree of cohesion and uniformity of funding and treatment. This contrasted with the 'maintained' (Catholic) schools each of which was, in a sense, an individual unit. In 1987 the Catholic Church came to the view that this lack of a central management system was not in the best interests of the individual Catholic schools and persuaded the government to establish a Council for Catholic Maintained Schools (CCMS). The purpose of this body is to promote high standards of education in the schools for which it is responsible, and to negotiate, establish and implement educational policy both in general educational matters and in areas of management of the Catholic maintained schools sector in accordance with the statement of aims of Catholic schools.

The Education Reform (NI) Order, 1989, made provision for the Council and defines aspects of the Council's activities and functions.

Similarly the increase in the number of integrated schools led to the creation of a central organisation called the Northern Ireland Council for Integrated Education (NICIE). This is now funded mainly by government, although it was created out of substantial funding and support from charitable trusts. It has no statutory powers in relation to the integrated schools and no mandatory claim on public money. Primarily it has a developmental role in relation to the establishment of integrated schools, but it also undertakes the same sort of coordinating function as CCMS and the Area Boards. The existence of these bodies, along with public debate about the future of Area Boards in the administration of education has also been responsible for the recent demand by the Protestant churches for the creation of another body to look after the interests of the controlled (Protestant related) schools (McKelvey, 1993).

These developments suggest an interesting dynamic whereby the converse of movement toward greater diversity of school type at the level of provision, seems to be a movement toward greater coherence and coordination at the level of administration. However, it is not clear if the extent to which this potential convergence of educational providers at the level of administration represents the emergence of new relationships of trust. The impetus could equally be attributed to a realignment of competing interests at a new level of control within the system.

THE EDUCATIONAL PROCESS AND WIDER PERSPECTIVES

Irrespective of changes in the administration and control of education, there is little doubt that the 1970s and 1980s saw significant changes with regard to certain aspects of the school curriculum and how the educational process is perceived in Northern Ireland. The introduction of a common curriculum for all schools has provided an opportunity to develop programmes of study which take account of the two main cultural traditions in Northern Ireland, particularly within sensitive subjects such as history and religious education (Richardson, 1990), and many schools now routinely provide their pupils with opportunities to meet and work with pupils from another cultural tradition.

There has been considerable movement away from the situation in the early days of the conflict when schools regarded themselves as 'oases of peace', providing children with an environment relatively protected from the violence, but also insulated from the social issues around them. There is still debate about the extent to which schools can play a reconstructionist role in leading change, but changes have been accepted at a number of levels and there is an expectation that teachers will increasingly find themselves dealing with issues which are socially relevant, related to the conflict and at times, controversial.

In this respect schools in Northern Ireland have been part of a more global movement which looks to education to take account of cultural diversity and conflict within societies. In Britain this has been reflected in the debates surrounding multicultural education, anti-racist education and demands from ethnic minorities for separate schools (Lynch, 1986; Troyna, 1987; Banks, 1988; Massey, 1991). In the Republic of Ireland it is anticipated that controversial issues will be addressed by the introduction of *Civic, Social and Political Education* as a compulsory component of the school curriculum (National Council for Curriculum and Assessment, 1993). Further afield, deeply divided societies such as Israel have thrown up broadly similar educational strategies as Northern Ireland including inter-group contact, curriculum programmes and new forms of institutions. Lemish (1993) suggests that some of these may merely represent morphological change at a relatively superficial level which does little to challenge the existing power relationships within the society. Other initiatives may have the potential to bring about deeper, structural, change, but the extent to which this is possible may be related to the form of democracy which operates within the society. In this context, the concept of democracy, and the extent to which it can sustain religious and cultural diversity, has taken on new significance with the re-emergence of ethnic nationalisms in the former Yugoslavia and Eastern Europe (Eros, 1993).

In the United States, where the concept of a multicultural approach to education emerged, McCarthy (1991) has examined the ideological assumptions and desired outcomes of programmes designed to replace earlier, assimilationist approaches to education. He concludes that cultural understanding programmes fall short of their aspiration to generate more harmonious relationships within society when they 'abandon the crucial issues of structural inequality and differential power relations in society' and 'end up placing an enormous responsibility on the shoulders of the classroom teacher'.

The educational strategies which have emerged in Northern Ireland over the past twenty years are interrelated. Each places a different emphasis on how religious and cultural diversity might be addressed by the education system, but they all interact within the same social and political environment. The classroom teacher will have difficulty nurturing tolerance and respect of difference while basic inequalities within society remain unaddressed. Similarly, when members of a particular group feel that the state does not adequately take account of their interests, they are likely to demand separate institutions to protect their traditions and beliefs. Tension between social cohesion and pluralism is therefore inevitable. Ultimately it may not be the individual strategies which matter so much as the extent to which they enable all members of society to experience new and just relationships.

REFERENCES

Agnew, U., A. McEwan, J. Salters and M. Salters (1992) *Integrated Education: the Views of Parents*. Belfast, Queen's University School of Education.

Akenson, D.H. (1973) *Education and Enmity: the Control of Schooling in Northern Ireland 1920–50*. Newton Abbot, David & Charles.

Banks, J.A. (1988) *Multi-ethnic Education: Theory and Practice*. Boston, Allyn & Bacon.

Cairns, E. (1987) *Caught in Crossfire*. Belfast, Appletree Press.

Cairns, E. (1989) 'Integrated Education in Northern Ireland: the Impact of Real Choice', *Education North*, 2.

Cormack, R. J., A. M. Gallagher and R. D. Osborne (1991) 'Religious Affiliation and Educational Attainment in Northern Ireland: the Financing of Schools in Northern Ireland,' in *Sixteenth Report of the Standing Advisory Commission on Human Rights, Report for 1990–1991 Annex E*. London, HMSO.

Cormack, R. J., A. M. Gallagher and R. D. Osborne (1992) 'Access to Grammar Schools' in *Seventeenth Report of the Standing Advisory Commission on Human Rights Annex E*. London. HMSO.

Cormack, R. J., A. M. Gallagher and R. D. Osborne (1992) 'Report on School Size' in *Seventeenth Report of the Standing Advisory Commission on Human Rights Annex B*. London, HMSO.

Cormack, R. J., A. M. Gallagher, R. D. Osborne and M. Fisher (1992) 'Secondary Analysis of the School Leavers Survey (1989)' in *Seventeenth Report of the Standing Advisory Commission and Human Rights, Report for 1991–1992 Annex D*. London, HMSO.

Cormack, R. J. and R. D. Osborne, eds. (1983) *Religion, Education and Employment: Aspects of Equal Opportunity in Northern Ireland*. Belfast. Appletree Press.

Darby, J., D. Batts, S. Dunn, J. Harris and S. Farren (1977) *Education and Community in Northern Ireland, Schools Apart?* Coleraine, University of Ulster.

Dunn, S. (1986) 'The Role of Education in the Northern Ireland Conflict', *Oxford Review of Education*, 12: 3, 233–42.

Dunn, S. (1990) 'A History of Education in Northern Ireland Since 1920' in *Fifteenth Report of the Standing Advisory Commission on Human Rights*. London, HMSO.

Dunn, S., J. Darby and K. Mullan (1984) *Schools Together?* Coleraine, Centre for the Study of Conflict, University of Ulster.

Dunn, S. and A. Smith (1989) *Inter School Links*. Coleraine, Centre for the Study of Conflict, University of Ulster.

Education (Northern Ireland) Act (1977) An Amendment to the Northern Education and Libraries Order, 1972 (Dunleath Act).

Eros, F. (1993) 'The new democracies in Eastern Europe and the challenge of ethnocentrism'. Paper presented at the International Conference on Education for Democracy in a Multicultural Society, Jerusalem, June 1993.

FOCUS (1993) *Who's Who in EMU*. Belfast, The FOCUS Group, Peace Education Resource Centre, 48 Elmwood Avenue, Belfast.

Gallagher, A. M. (1988) *Transfer Pupils at 16*. Belfast, Northern Ireland Council for Educational Research.

Gallagher, A. M., R. D. Osborne and R. J. Cormack (1993) 'Community Relations, Equality and Education' in *After the Reforms: Education and Policy in Northern Ireland*, ed. by R. D. Osborne, R. J. Cormack and A. M. Gallagher. Aldershot, Avebury.

Greer, J. and E. P. McElhinney (1984) 'The Project Religion in Ireland: an Experiment in Reconstruction', *Lumen Vitae*, 39: 3.

Greer, J. and E. P. McElhinney (1985a) *Irish Christianity: Five Units for Secondary Pupils*. Dublin, Gill and Macmillan.

Greer, J. and E. P. McElhinney (1985b) *Irish Christianity: a Guide for Teachers*. Dublin, Gill and Macmillan.

Harbison, J., ed. (1990) *Growing Up in Northern Ireland*. Belfast, NI Learning Resources Unit, Stranmillis College.

Irwin, C. (1991) *Education and the Development of Social Integration in Divided Societies*. Belfast, Queen's University.

Lemish, P. (1993) 'Politics of Difference; Educators as Enlightened Oppressors'. Paper presented at the Annual Meeting of the American Educational Research Association, Atlanta, Georgia, April 1993.

Lynch, J. (1986) *Multicultural Education – Principles and Practice*. London, Routledge & Kegan Paul.

McCarthy, C. (1991), 'Multicultural Approaches to Racial Inequality in the United States', *Oxford Review of Education*, 17: 3.

McKelvey, H. (1993) *Church of Ireland Annual Synod*, Report of the Northern Education Committee.

Malone, J. (1973) 'Schools and Community Relations', *The Northern Teacher*, 11: 1, Winter.

Massey, I. (1991) *More Than Skin Deep: Developing anti-racist multicultural education in schools*. London, Hodder & Stoughton.

Moffat, C. (1993) *Education Together for a Change. Integrated Education and Community Relations in Northern Ireland.* Belfast, Fortnight Educational Trust.

Morgan, V., S. Dunn, E. Cairns and G. Fraser (1992) *Breaking the Mould. The Role of Parents and Teachers in the Integrated Schools in Northern Ireland.* Coleraine, Centre for the Study of Conflict, University of Ulster.

Murray, D. (1985) *Worlds Apart: Segregated Schools in Northern Ireland.* Belfast, Appletree Press.

Murray, D. (1992) 'Science and Funding in Northern Ireland Grammar Schools: a Case Study Approach' in *Seventeenth Report of the Standing Advisory Commission on Human Rights, Annex G.* London, HMSO.

National Council for Curriculum and Assessment (1993) *Civic, Social and Political Education – Draft Syllabus.* Dublin, NCCA.

Northern Ireland Council for Educational Development (1988) *Education for Mutual Understanding – a Guide.* Belfast, NICED.

Northern Ireland Council for Integrated Education (1992) *The Growth of Integrated Education: an Outline* (pamphlet). Belfast, NICIE.

Northern Ireland Council for Integrated Education (1992, 1993) *Annual Reports.* Belfast, Mount Charles.

Northern Ireland Curriculum Council (1990) *Cross-curricular Themes – Guidance Materials.* Belfast, NICC.

Northern Ireland, Department of Education (1982) *The Improvement of Community Relations: the Contribution of Schools.* DENI, Circular 1982/21.

Northern Ireland, Department of Education (1987) *The Cross Community Contact Scheme.* DENI Circular 1987/47.

Northern Ireland, Department of Education (1991) *Report of the Inspectorate on the Cross Community Contact Scheme.* Bangor, Co. Down, DENI.

Osborne, R. D. (1986) 'Segregated Schools and Examination Results in Northern Ireland', *Educational Research,* 28, 1.

Osborne, R. D. (1993) 'Research and Policy: a Northern Ireland perspective', *Environment and Planning: Government and Policy,* vol. 11.

Richardson, N. (1990) *Religious Education as if EMU Really Mattered.* Belfast, Christian Education Movement.

Robinson, A. (1981) *The Schools Cultural Studies Project: a Contribution to Peace in Northern Ireland.* Coleraine, New University of Ulster.

Skilbeck, M. (1973) 'The School and Cultural Development', *The Northern Teacher,* 11: 1, Winter.

Skilbeck, M. (1976) 'Education and Cultural Change', *Compass: Journal of the Irish Association for Curriculum Development,* 5: 2.

Smith, A. and S. Dunn (1990) *Extending Inter School Links: an Evaluation of Contact Between Protestant and Catholic Pupils in Northern Ireland.* Coleraine, Centre for the Study of Conflict, University of Ulster.

Smith, A. and A. Robinson (1992a) *Education for Mutual Understanding: Perceptions and Policy.* Coleraine, Centre for the Study of Conflict, University of Ulster.

Smith, A. and A. Robinson (1992b) *EMU in Transition: Report of a Conference on Education for Mutual Understanding.* Coleraine, Centre for the Study of Conflict, University of Ulster.

Spencer, A. E. C. W. (1987) 'Arguments for an Integrated School System' in *Education and Policy in Northern Ireland*, ed. by R. D. Osborne, R. J. Cormack and R. L. Miller. Belfast, Policy Research Institute.

Standing Advisory Commission on Human Rights (1987) Report on Fair Employment. London, HMSO, Cmnd 237.

Standing Advisory Commission on Human Rights (1989, 1990, 1991, 1992) *Fourteenth Report* to *Seventeenth Report*. London, HMSO.

Trew, K. (1986) 'Catholic and Protestant Encounter in Northern Ireland' in *Contact and Conflict in Intergroup Encounters*, ed. by M. Hewstone and R. Brown. Oxford, Blackwell.

Troyna, B., ed (1987) *Racial Inequality in Education*. London, Tavistock.

Whitty, G. and G. Rowe (1993) 'Five Themes Remain in the Shadows', *Times Educational Supplement*, 9 April.

Wilson, D. and S. Dunn (1989) *Integrated Education: Information for Parents*. Coleraine, Centre for the Study of Conflict, University of Ulster.

12 Policing a Divided Society
Andrew Hamilton and Linda Moore

Issues concerning policing policies, structures and practices – and the administration of justice in general – have been central to the polarisation of Northern Irish society since the establishment of the state, and they continue to divide the two communities. On the one hand, most unionists see the various institutional arrangements and legislative framework for the maintenance of law and order as essential to the preservation of the constitutional status quo, faced with the threat from militant republicanism. On the other hand, most nationalists view the same institutions and legislation as yet another example – and one of the most blatant and important examples – of the sectarian nature of the state. Indeed, as Hillyard (1983: 35) points out, from the outset the law and order strategy adopted by successive unionist governments continually alienated the minority community from both the law and the state. This has proved to be a difficult legacy for successive British governments striving to deal with the security problems facing the province, at the same time as trying to establish some degree of confidence in the law and order institutions among the Catholic population. And it has also proved a particularly difficult legacy for the Royal Ulster Constabulary (RUC). In order to win the 'hearts and minds' of the Catholic community the RUC must prove itself to be a non-political, non-partisan force. However, this is problematic in a society where the legitimacy of the state itself is contested. If it is seen to be protecting the status quo the RUC will be viewed by many in the nationalist community as an obstacle to change. However, if the RUC is involved in the policing of political initiatives such as the Anglo-Irish Agreement, it risks alienating the support which it has traditionally had from the unionist community.

HISTORICAL BACKGROUND

Towards the end of 1921, in accordance with the provisions of the Government of Ireland Act, responsibility for the maintenance of law and order in the province was transferred to the Northern Ireland government, with which it was to remain until March 1972 when the Westminster government suspended the Northern Ireland government and parliament and, among other functions, took over direct responsibility for law and order. In June 1922 the RUC officially came into being with an initial establishment of 3000 members. Only 1100 of these were recruited from the old Royal Irish Constabulary and although it was intended that a third of the force should be Catholic (roughly proportionate to the religious composition of the Northern population as a whole), that figure has never come close to being met though it must be stressed that the RUC has never been an exclusively Protestant force.

From the outset the RUC was trained to perform not only the normal functions of a civilian police force, but also a paramilitary role to counter the threat posed by the Irish Republican Army (IRA). In that role it was to be supported by the Ulster Special Constabulary (USC), consisting mainly of a part-time auxiliary force known locally as the B Specials, which could be called upon in an emergency. While membership of the USC was not in theory confined to Protestants, the selection and screening practices – allied to the risks of Catholic members becoming especial targets of the IRA – meant that in practice it had been a wholly Protestant force since its formation in 1920 (Darby, 1976: 61).

The USC played a central role in helping establish the authority of the new government in Northern Ireland and from the outset it was surrounded in controversy and viewed with suspicion, resentment and even hatred by most Catholics. The Scarman Tribunal which investigated the riots and shootings in the summer of 1969 concluded that the USC was 'totally distrusted by the Catholics' who saw it as 'the strong arm of the Protestant ascendancy' (Flackes and Elliott, 1989: 384).

It has been argued that the sectarian conduct of members of the USC contributed to the anti-police sentiment amongst the Catholic population, since not only were the USC and the RUC linked together in the public mind, but also half the initial recruits for the RUC came from the Specials (Hillyard, 1983: 33). Whatever the precise reasons, by 1969 the lack of confidence in the RUC among the Catholic population was clear to the Scarman Tribunal which, while rejecting the charge that the RUC was a partisan force which had cooperated with Protestant mobs to attack Catholics, concluded that the events of August 1969 had resulted in a complete loss of confidence by the Catholic community in the police force as it was then constituted

(Flackes and Elliott, 1989: 250 and 385–6). In particular, the poor quality of the leadership in the force was a common criticism in all investigations into police conduct during the Civil Rights period (Darby, 1976: 61–2).

The distrust felt by most Catholics was exacerbated by what was seen as politically repressive legislation dating back to the establishment of the Northern Ireland government. In 1922 the Stormont parliament passed the Civil Authorities (Special Powers) Act which gave the Northern Ireland Minister of Home Affairs sweeping emergency powers, including the power of internment, justified by the high level of political violence that accompanied partition. The Act (generally referred to as the 'Special Powers Act') conferred wide powers of arrest, questioning, search and detention on the police. Although originally intended as a temporary measure which was required to be renewed annually, in 1933 the Act was made permanent, and since it was used almost exclusively against Catholics it added to the widespread sense of resentment and lack of confidence among the Catholic community and 'ensured that the RUC was seen as an instrument of the Unionist government' (Guelke, 1992: 96).

This lack of confidence among Northern Irish Catholics in the impartial enforcement of law and order was further exacerbated by a lack of confidence in the courts, primarily due to the strong imbalance between Protestants and Catholics in the composition of both the judiciary and juries (Darby, 1976: 63–5; Hillyard, 1973: 35).

DEVELOPMENTS IN THE PERIOD 1969–75

In August 1969, the Northern Ireland government, faced with the inability of the RUC to contain the violent disturbances in Belfast and in Derry, was forced to request the deployment of British troops to attempt to stabilise the situation. Prior to this there had always been a British army presence in Northern Ireland, but at a fairly low level and solely to deal with any external threat to the Northern Ireland state. The new situation provided the British government with the opportunity to pressurise the Northern Ireland parliament into a series of reforms intended to reduce discrimination and increase Catholic confidence in the institutions of the state. It was inevitable, given the new involvement of the army and the widespread criticism of previous policing practices, that the arrangements for the maintenance of law and order should be a primary area for attention.

Following the recommendations of the Hunt Committee (1969), the USC was disbanded and replaced in April 1970 by the Ulster Defence Regiment (UDR), a locally raised force within the British army structure. The RUC was to be remodelled along the same lines as police forces in Great Britain, with the objective of establishing a wholly civilian force, with no military role; it was intended that the British army would take over the primary responsibility for security. Furthermore, to free the RUC from direct political control, the Police Act 1970 established a new Police Authority for Northern Ireland (PANI), which was to be representative of the main sections of the community and was given the responsibility to maintain an adequate and efficient police force. The size of the force, which had previously been limited to 3500, was increased to 4940 in 1970 and a series of subsequent increases led to a full-time force of 8478 by 1992, when there was also a full-time Reserve of 3160 and a part-time Reserve of 1432 (Flackes and Elliott, 1989: 386; Royal Ulster Constabulary, 1992).

However, in the light of increasing political violence, the plans to disarm and civilianise the police were quickly dropped, and the RUC returned to its old dual roles of 'normal' and security policing, although it was still to be subordinate to the army in the security field. In the process, any initial increase in acceptability of the RUC in Catholic areas quickly disappeared and the force became the target of renewed suspicions and distrust.

The reforms – resulting firstly from British pressure on the Northern Ireland government and subsequently from the introduction of direct rule by the Westminster government following the suspension of Stormont in March 1972 – were not restricted to the structure and control of the security forces. In 1972 a new office of 'Director of Public Prosecutions' was set up with full responsibility for the selection and prosecution of all serious criminal charges. There was a change in the internment process, which was now referred to as detention (without trial) and involved a system of judicial hearings rather than a decision by a government minister. In August 1973 the Special Powers Act was replaced by the Northern Ireland (Emergency Provisions) Act (EPA) which implemented most of the recommendations of the Diplock Commission (1972). The EPA provided the police and the army with extensive powers to question, search, arrest and detain. It also introduced non-jury trials for a wide range of 'scheduled' offences – the so-called Diplock Courts in which the guilt or innocence of the accused, as well as any sentence, is determined by a single judge, sitting alone – and introduced far-reaching changes in the rules of evidence. In 1974 the EPA was supplemented by the Prevention of Terrorism (Temporary Provisions) Act (PTA), which unlike the EPA relates to the whole of the UK but was originally designed only to deal with violence associated with Northern Ireland (in 1984 it was extended to apply to international terrorism). Both the EPA and the PTA have since been amended and updated on several occasions and, operating in tandem, continue to provide the legislative framework for combating political violence in Northern Ireland and Great Britain.

DEVELOPMENTS IN THE PERIOD 1975–90

By the mid-1970s it had become clear to the British government that there was no likelihood of any early agreed devolution of powers to some form of local assembly and that direct rule by the Westminster government was likely to continue for the foreseeable future. In those circumstances the government produced a radical overhaul of its security strategy, designed to criminalise political violence and to de-emphasise its political dimensions. This involved stopping the use of detention without trial – though it stopped short of actually abolishing the power – and relying on the courts instead.

Another central element of this new strategy was the policy of returning the primary responsibility for law and order, including security, to the police, with the army now operating in a support role. This policy of re-establishing the primacy of the police, and restoring the main responsibility for law and order to the local security forces in general, including the UDR, became known as 'Ulsterisation'. Not only did it result in a further remilitarisation of the RUC, but the continuing IRA campaign inevitably led to significant increases in the size of both the RUC and the UDR. Although the UDR was originally intended to be primarily a part-time force, by 1988 46 per cent of its overall strength of 6300 was full-time (Flackes and Elliott, 1989: 398). As Hillyard (1986: 44) points out, since the vast majority of the personnel in both the UDR and RUC were Protestant, 'the effect of the Ulsterisation policy, whatever its intention, was to replace British security personnel by Ulster Protestants'.

The RUC quickly became involved in renewed controversy. Initially this focused on allegations of physical maltreatment of suspects being interrogated in the Castlereagh holding centre. By the early 1980s the use, sometimes with fatal consequences, of plastic bullets by the security forces had become a major issue, and 1982 saw the first allegations of an RUC 'shoot-to-kill' policy. This latter issue led to the so-called Stalker affair, in which John Stalker, the Deputy Chief Constable of Manchester, was suspended from an inquiry into a number of incidents involving the use of lethal force by the RUC. Although this suspension was ostensibly related to allegations, subsequently found to be unjustified, surrounding aspects of his conduct within the Manchester police force, there was widespread suspicion that it was designed to abort the inquiry at a time when he seemed to be about to implicate senior RUC officers in either authorising or covering up such operations. The investigation was taken over by Colin Sampson, the Chief Constable of West Yorkshire, and ultimately resulted in disciplinary proceedings against more than 20 police officers, including two superintendents. The Police Authority decided, by a majority of only one, not to pursue disciplinary action against the then Chief Constable, Sir John Hermon, and two other senior RUC officers.

Just as the retirement of Hermon in 1989 seemed likely to put that controversy to rest, the new Chief Constable, Hugh Annesley, was faced by almost equally damaging allegations of the leaking of security force documents to loyalist paramilitaries. An inquiry carried out by John Stevens, the Deputy Chief Constable of Cambridgeshire, found that while there had been collusion between security forces and loyalist paramilitaries, it was 'restricted to a small number of members of the security forces and is neither widespread nor institutionalised' (quoted in Bew and Gillespie 1993: 234) and Stevens focused his main criticisms on the UDR rather than the RUC. Nevertheless, allegations of collusion continue to damage the prospects of improved relations between the RUC and the Catholic community.

The 1980s also saw the first real weakening of what had previously seemed the virtually unconditional support accorded to the RUC by the Protestant community. The enforcement of restrictions on some loyalist parades, and Protestant anger and frustration at the Anglo-Irish Agreement, resulted in over 500 incidents of attacks against the homes of RUC members and intimidation of their families within loyalist areas in 1986 (Royal Ulster Constabulary, 1986: x). While such overt manifestations of this hostility have largely died away, there is clear evidence of a continuing, and possibly increasing, antipathy towards the police in many Protestant working-class areas.

DEVELOPMENTS SINCE 1990

The 1990s have already seen a number of further attempts to improve the acceptability of the forces of law and order, particularly as regards relations with the Catholic community. Possibly the most significant move so far related to the UDR.

From the time of its establishment the UDR was seen by most Catholics as an undisciplined and sectarian force. Although it did attract up to 18 per cent Catholic membership in its early days, by the end of the 1980s this had fallen to some 3 per cent (Flackes and Elliott, 1989: 396). While this may have to some extent resulted from an IRA campaign against Catholic members, it also clearly indicated that the regiment had a major credibility problem in the eyes of the Catholic community, a problem which has been exacerbated by the conviction of some of its members, or ex-members, on sectarian murder charges and on charges of links with loyalist paramilitaries.

In July 1992 the UDR was merged with the Royal Irish Rangers – a 'regular' regiment in the British army – to form a new unit, the Royal Irish Regiment (RIR). The RIR, which like the UDR would have both full- and part-time soldiers, was to consist of one general service battalion of 900 soldiers with worldwide responsibilities and up to seven home service battalions (with a total strength of 6000) for duty in Northern Ireland. Other regiments of the British army will continue to operate in Northern Ireland as required.

Although this amalgamation was first announced in the context of overall cutbacks in defence expenditure, it was widely perceived by Protestants to be the result of pressure from the Catholic community, supported by the government of the Republic of Ireland operating within the context of the 1985 Anglo-Irish Agreement. Unfortunately the hostile reaction which this provoked from large sections of the Protestant community does not appear to have been matched by a more positive attitude towards this new body on the part of the Catholic community. There have also been a number of developments with the twin objectives of safeguarding those in police custody and helping to develop public confidence in the police.

In 1991, PANI, with the agreement of the Chief Constable, established five panels of lay visitors to monitor the treatment of persons held in those police stations which are designated for holding people in police custody who are suspected of involvement in non-terrorist criminal offences. Pressure to extend the lay visiting scheme to the holding centres for those suspected of involvement in terrorist crime has so far been strongly, and successfully, resisted by the RUC. However, in January 1993 the Secretary of State announced the appointment of Sir Louis Blom-Cooper QC as the first Independent Commissioner for the Holding Centres. The main role of the Commissioner is to observe, comment and report on the conditions under which persons are detained in the holding centres in Derry, Castlereagh and Armagh, and to ensure that both statutory and administrative safeguards are being properly applied.

In January 1993 the first Independent Assessor for Military Complaints Procedures was appointed. His remit is, however, significantly more limited than that of Blom-Cooper. The Assessor is responsible for looking at the systems and procedures for dealing with formal non-criminal complaints and he can recommend changes in procedures. He is not responsible for individual complaints, for compensation cases, nor for complaints which could involve criminal charges.

CURRENT ISSUES

Policing in Northern Ireland faces all the problems associated with policing in any modern industrial society, but with several extra dimensions. Firstly, the police are dealing with a very divided society, comprised of two communities which have so far been unable to reach any political or constitutional consensus, and in which the police have historically been closely associated with one of those communities. Secondly, as a result of the failure to reach any consensus, the police continue to be required to fulfil a role which goes far beyond the role of normal policing. Finally, the normal dangers associated with policing are greatly increased in a situation where, between 1969 and 1992, paramilitary activity has cost the lives of 189 police officers and of 98 members of the police reserve (RUCR) (Royal Ulster Constabulary, 1992: 82).

It can, of course, be argued that in a 'normal' society the provision of security, in the sense in which that term is used in this chapter, would not be a central issue for the civilian police. Indeed, if Northern Ireland is to become such a society, it ought to be at least an aspiration that security becomes a low priority for the RUC. The fact that this is not the case, and is not likely to be so in the foreseeable future, is a function of the apparent intractability of the political and constitutional issues. Within the present context, therefore, the overriding question is whether it is possible to construct in Northern Ireland structures and practices for the maintenance of law and order, which can provide adequate security while at the same time gaining the confidence of both the Catholic and the Protestant communities and respecting basic human rights and civil liberties.

The Opsahl Report accepted that, as with political structures, the key questions about policing in Northern Ireland have to do with accountability and responsibility (Pollak, 1993: 61–2). Policing in Northern Ireland is, theoretically, a tripartite responsibility shared by (1) PANI, which is responsible for the maintenance of an adequate and efficient police service; (2) the Chief Constable, who is responsible for the direction and control of the RUC; and (3) the Secretary of State for Northern Ireland, who is responsible for security policy. However, in practice the role of PANI is primarily that of a provider body, with no real authority over policing policies or operations. While it is by no means certain that even extending the powers of PANI would entice the SDLP to take up a place on the Authority, what does seems clear is that it is essential that representatives of both the nationalist and unionist communities are given a proper input into both policymaking and the administration of policing in the province.

The RUC argues that over the last twenty years it has made strenuous efforts to improve its professionalism and to gain acceptance by both communities in Northern Ireland as a non-political, non-partisan force. There would be a large level of agreement that through stricter recruitment policies and better training and management it has made significant progress in the first objective. However, it is clear that it has been less successful in achieving a sense of confidence and legitimacy in the eyes of the Catholic community. Surveys have consistently shown a majority of Catholics as believing that, to some extent at least, the police continue to discriminate against Catholics.

Furthermore, the commitment to trying to promote greater Catholic participation in the RUC is faced not only with this continuing suspicion of the force among large sections of the Catholic community, but also with the dangers posed by the IRA to any Catholics who do join. The percentage of Catholics in the force has never approached the 33 per cent advocated in 1921 and, indeed, in 1961 only 12 per cent of the force was comprised of Catholics (Darby, 1976: 59). Between the late 1960s and the mid-1980s, even this figure fell back sharply, partly as a result of an increasing sense of alienation within the Catholic community and partly because of the physical risks involved in joining. Despite recent efforts to boost Catholic recruitment, by 1992 the level of Catholics serving in the main force was only 7.7 per cent and in the same year only some 10 per cent of new applicants were Catholics. Just under 6 per cent of the full-time Reserve was comprised of Catholics (*Belfast Telegraph*, 28 January 1993).

In its most recent position statement PANI (1991), while accepting that the security situation imposes unique demands on the police, states that if the RUC is to be effective in tackling crime, including terrorist crime, it must have the wholehearted support of all sections of the community. The Police Authority has pledged itself to monitor public opinion and to seek to promote the wider acceptability of the RUC. However, this has proved and will continue to prove a difficult task since, as we have seen, there is a long legacy of complaints by the Catholic community against the RUC, with allegations ranging from general harassment, particularly of young Catholic males, to the operation of a 'shoot-to-kill' policy and collusion with loyalist paramilitaries.

One particular area of concern has been the procedures for investigating and pursuing complaints against the police. In 1988 a new Independent Commission for Police Complaints (ICPC) was established and given the primary responsibility for supervising the investigation of complaints against the RUC, although the Police Authority acts as the 'complaints and discipline' authority for chief officers and also has reserve powers to refer any matter relating to the conduct of a police officer to the Commission. It must be stressed, however, that the actual investigation of all complaints against the police is carried out by the police themselves and there remains widespread scepticism among the Catholic community as to the effectiveness of such procedures. Indeed, in his evidence to the Opsahl Commission Dr Brice Dickson, Professor of Law at the University of Ulster, points out that from the creation of the ICPC in 1988 until the end of 1991, there had been no fewer than 1019 allegations of assault laid against police officers by people arrested under the anti-terrorism laws. He continues:

> The stark truth is that not one of those allegations has been sub-stantiated after a police investigation. Now even allowing for the inevitable proportion of completely bogus cases, this nil rate of substantiation frankly beggars belief. (Pollak, 1993: 262)

It is probably fair to say that the establishment of credible and speedy processes for dealing with complaints, preferably carried out by independent investigators, would be the single measure most likely to increase the legitimacy accorded to the police among the Catholic community.

Another major area of complaint, particularly from the Catholic community has been that the RUC seems only to be interested in dealing with political crime and not with 'ordinary' crime. This links in with a widespread regret, within both communities, about the general absence of community policing.

The senior management of the RUC remain highly committed to the principle of community, or 'neighbourhood', policing, even in the most troubled areas of Northern Ireland. However, since the security of their officers has to be the first priority of the RUC management, the actual form of neighbourhood policing is clearly influenced by the security situation in particular areas. In extreme circumstances it could involve two RUC officers accompanied by possibly fourteen soldiers; it is highly questionable if this can really be considered to constitute a genuine form of community policing. Additionally, the policing of 'ordinary' crime cannot ever be effectively separated from the policing of political crime; nor have the RUC chosen to emphasise any such separation. The 'community policeman or woman' is not seen in most Catholic areas of Northern Ireland as being separate from the RUC as a whole. The use of informers by the RUC is a case in point, where the overlapping of 'normal' and 'security' policing becomes apparent. Fielding (1991: 166) notes that: 'To police, the most convincing argument for community policing is the gain in terms of information.' This has an important and unfortunate consequence in working-class Catholic areas, since to be seen talking to a police officer is to be suspected of giving information. Thus, while in some societies the process of acquiring local knowledge by the community police can be seen as simply bringing police officer and community closer together, in some communities in Northern Ireland even the activities of the community police officer are viewed as sinister.

These problems are exacerbated by a process of social distancing, in which police officers are increasingly unlikely to live in the working-class communities which they patrol. Reference has already been made to the low Catholic representation within the RUC, and for safety reasons few, if indeed any, of the Catholic officers would live within working-class Catholic areas. Furthermore, higher salaries and increased opportunities for 'overtime' payments because of the continuing violence have meant that Protestant officers now also tend to live in the more middle-class suburbs. This process of embourgeoisement was accelerated by the attacks in the mid-1980s on RUC personnel and their families living within Protestant working-class areas. The RUC in general, and the Police Federation (the police officers' union) in particular, are well aware of the dangers arising from such physical and social distancing.

It is clear, therefore, that despite its often restated commitment to professional and non-partisan policing, the RUC continues to be faced with major difficulties in seeking acceptance across the divided communities in Northern Ireland. Indeed, it has sometimes been suggested that it is a no-win situation, since it is still seen by many Catholics as essentially there to support British rule, which is therefore unionist and Protestant rule. On the other hand, any attempts to exhibit its professed neutralism is almost bound to risk alienating its Protestant support. To a large extent the RUC in particular, and the security forces in general, continue to pay the price of a failure on the part of successive governments to accept that institutional reform could not, in itself, be a substitute for fundamental political and constitutional change.

REFERENCES

Bew, P. and G. Gillespie (1993) *Northern Ireland: a Chronology of the Troubles 1968–1993.* Dublin, Gill and Macmillan.
Brewer, J. D. (1991) *Inside the RUC.* Oxford, Oxford University Press.
Darby, J. (1976) *Conflict in Northern Ireland: the Development of a Polarised Community.* Dublin, Gill and Macmillan.
Fielding, N. G. (1991) *The Police and Social Conflict.* London, Athlone Press.
Flackes, W. D. and S. Elliott (1989) *Northern Ireland: a Political Directory 1968–88.* Belfast, Blackstaff Press.
Guelke, A. (1992) 'Policing in Northern Ireland' in *Northern Ireland: Politics and the Constitution* (9th edn), ed. by B. Hadfield. Buckingham, Open University Press.
Hillyard, P. (1983) 'Law and Order' in *Northern Ireland: the Background to the Conflict,* ed. by J. Darby. Belfast, Appletree Press.
Police Authority for Northern Ireland (1991) *A Strategy for 1991/1992 and Beyond.* Belfast.
Pollak, A., ed. (1993) *A Citizen's Inquiry: the Opsahl Report on Northern Ireland.* Dublin, Lilliput Press; Belfast, Initiative 92.
Royal Ulster Constabulary (1986 and 1992) *Chief Constable's Report.* Belfast.

13 Sport, Community Relations and Community Conflict in Northern Ireland

John Sugden

For 25 years Northern Ireland has endured civil disobedience, terrorism, counter-terrorism and sectarian violence. Throughout this period, while politicians have sought in vain to discover ways through which a political settlement might be achieved, others, working at street level, have attempted to develop channels of communication between the province's divided communities. In recognition of the role which they will play in the future of Northern Ireland, much of the focus of community relations work has been directed towards the young. Based largely on its supposed popularity among the young, a belief in its fraternal and democratic qualities and its reputation in the international arena as a neutral medium for the promotion of peace and understanding, sport is one of the most popular choices for community relations work with young people in Northern Ireland. However, these assumptions are open to question and before sport can be effectively harnessed in the service of community relations it is important to distinguish between the 'ideal' and the 'real' world of sport.

It has been amply demonstrated that sport does not opt out of its host society, but is deeply and intrinsically bound up with events in the social and political mainstream (Allison, 1993). Sport in the modern world provides one of the most significant forums within which people can publicly display their community identity and, in some cases, their political aspirations. Northern Ireland provides plenty of evidence to support the proposition that sports not only reflect prevailing community structures, but, in several important ways, actively contribute to the content of community life and the definition of rival community boundaries (Sugden and Bairner,

1993). Of all the impediments to using sport as a community relations resource in Northern Ireland this is the most serious.

The relationship between sport and community identity in Northern Ireland is emotive and deep-seated. Play, games and sport are overlapping spheres of social interaction which reach back into our earliest memories and help to frame our perceptions of who we are and what we stand for. To a certain extent, in Northern Ireland we are what we play and, because play is essentially a social activity, it has an important role to perform in helping to determine the nature of the relationship between self and community. Play is the medium through which young people make sense of and come to terms with the social universe which surrounds them. It is the main vehicle for early childhood socialisation and, as such, of critical importance to the process of character formation. As toddlers, Protestant and Catholic children participate in similar unstructured forms of play, but, because most play exclusively in the company of others from the same religious tradition, from a very early age play develops as an important medium for learning the difference between 'us' Catholics and 'them' Protestants and vice versa. In other societies children's play becomes less insular and more integrative once the social territory of childhood moves away from the home and its immediate surroundings. In Northern Ireland, however, differential social learning is reinforced when children's play gives way to a network of organised games and sports which themselves tend to be rooted in separate institutions belonging to different religious organisations and cultural traditions.

The fact that Protestants are taught alongside Protestants and Catholics alongside Catholics, in separate institutions, is bound to have a limiting effect on the interpersonal horizons of impressionable young people and a negative impact on community relations. The school is one of, if not the, most important agency for promoting sports and games. The games curriculum of many, if not most, of Northern Ireland's schools is different according to whether those schools are predominantly Catholic or Protestant. Gaelic sports prevail in most Catholic schools whereas games with British pedigree such as rugby union, hockey and cricket dominate in many Protestant establishments. As part of a study of segregated schools in Northern Ireland, Dominic Murray surveyed games playing and his findings confirm that the sports curriculum tends to be divided according to different cultural associations which 'have traditionally been along lines which might be broadly defined as "British" and "Irish/Gaelic"'. However, he also points out that there is a group of sports, including soccer, basketball and net-ball which 'cut across the denominational split' (Murray, 1985: 44–5). Nevertheless, simply playing a game which is played by people in the other community counts little towards assimilation if it is only done 'against them' and in the company of those from 'your own side'. When schools participate in a common game, such as soccer, they often do so in ways which ensure that most Protestant and Catholic children never play together in the same team, but only against one another: and this can lead to conflict both on and off the field. Only a small minority, the best of the best, get selected onto those representative teams which have a blend of both religions and offer the greatest opportunity for longer term, cross-community exchanges.

It is true that in recent years sport and related forms of recreation have become popular vehicles for schools attempting to meet some of the community relations objectives contained within the 1989 Educational Reform Order. Organising combined sports days, sharing sports tours and joining together to visit leisure facilities and/or areas of geographical and historical interest are some of the means through which groups of Protestant and Catholic school-children have been brought together. However, the effectiveness of ephemeral initiatives such as these is yet to be established. Latest research suggests that, at present, while sport and related forms of recreation may be used for 'one-off' cross-community contact between schools, there is considerable resistance to any long-term alteration of the school physical education curriculum to service the objectives of community relations (McLaughlan, 1993).

A subtle form of sporting apartheid is carried on outside the school gates by a vast network of voluntary sports organisations and governing bodies through which separate community affiliation is confirmed in terms of what games are played and watched, which teams are supported, and which clubs and societies are joined and patronised in later life. In this respect sport has developed as one of Northern Ireland's most important symbols of national and community identity. It has been estimated that, outside of schools, up to a quarter of a million people are actively involved in sport in Northern Ireland (Sugden and Harvie, 1993). Because sport occu-pies such a significant place in this society, it is helpful to take a brief look at some of the province's more popular and high profile sports to see what role they play in community life and to identify what les-sons, if any, can be learned by those hoping to utilise sport for community relations purposes. Three sports, Gaelic football, hurling and camogie will be looked at by reviewing the activities of the GAA (Gaelic Athletic Association) while three other sports, rugby union, association football and boxing will be treated separately.

By a long way the Gaelic Athletic Association is the leading provider of sporting activities for Catholics in Northern Ireland (Sugden and Harvie, 1993). Its history provides perhaps the clearest evidence of the inseparability of sport and politics in Northern Ireland. The GAA's political roots are deep. It is not a coincidence that the organisation was founded in the last quarter of the nineteenth century at the same time as other important vehicles for Irish political and cultural nationalism were beginning to take shape. While a general concern over the physical/sporting health of the nation may have been in the minds of some of the organisation's founder members and patrons, for people such as Archbishop Croke, the land leaguer Michael Davitt and C. S. Parnell the development of an indigenous, all-Ireland sporting movement was also viewed as an opportunity for nurturing a sense of Irish national identity. At the same time the GAA was seen as a bulwark against the spread of English influence in the shape of 'foreign' (English) sports and pastimes.

The political character of the GAA has never been straightforward, largely because the factionalism which has been characteristic of Irish nationalist political life in general has been reproduced within its ranks. The organisation was united in its desire to see a united and independent Ireland, but it barely survived the opening decade of the twentieth century because of serious internal conflict between those who sought to throw off British rule by military means and those who favoured using the constitutionally approved political process. Likewise, in the early twenties, after partition sparked a civil war in the Free State, Gaelic men found themselves taking up arms against one another. It was through dealing with such internecine turmoil that the fathers of the GAA learned that, for the organisation to survive and continue to serve as a broad base for Irish nationalism, it had to distance itself from any formal association with one or other political faction. However, this does not mean that the GAA became apolitical. To this day its constitution relates to a 32-county Ireland and, more importantly, contains a series of articles designed to exclude the Northern Ireland and GB police and the UK armed forces from membership.

While in the Republic of Ireland the GAA has grown into one of the state's more important socio-cultural buttresses, the fact that the ban continues to operate in the six counties of Northern Ireland is evidence of the oppositional stance which the GAA adopts in terms of its relationship with the British state. In the North the GAA, as a body, has been careful to avoid direct association with any of the various strands of republicanism. However, individual Gaelic clubs and members have been implicated in the province's political turmoil through a variety of actions including vociferous support for the hunger strikers. In addition to actions such as these and the ban, it is possible to point to a list of other signs that do little to encourage Northern Ireland's Protestant community that the GAA are anything other than a symbolic rallying point for the enemy within. These include the flying of the Irish national flag at Gaelic games; the use of Gaelic as the official language for meetings of the Association's Ulster Council; the brandishing of the hurley in demonstrations and its use by punishment squads; the naming of the stadium in Belfast, Casement Park, in honour of the republican hero, Sir Roger Casement, executed by the British for treason; and the discovery of IRA arms caches on GAA property.

For their part, the various branches of government in Northern Ireland treat the GAA in a range of sometimes contradictory ways including benevolence, suspicion and harassment. Operating from an agenda which views any form of organised sport as good for social discipline and moral enhancement, the Sports Council for Northern Ireland provides a certain amount of grant aid for Gaelic clubs within its jurisdiction. There is some logic in this strategy. The GAA does symbolise Irish rather than British nationality, and so active members of Gaelic clubs tend to direct their nationalism into events on the field of play so allowing many thousands of young Catholics to display an affinity with the general cause of Irish nationalism while finding sanctuary from the violence of the republican political struggle. However, because of the ban, the level of government funding is strictly limited.

The fact that the GAA is funded at all by any government body in Northern Ireland causes great consternation among many of the province's unionist politicians. In one case the unionist-dominated Craigavon Borough Council refused planning permission to a local Gaelic club which wished to build new playing fields in the town. St Peter's Gaelic Athletic Club took the Council to court and won its case. The Council was given a heavy financial penalty because, according to the presiding High Court judge, it had been guilty of discriminating against St Peter's out of 'sectarian bias'. This is an extreme example of the hostility of elected unionist politicians towards the GAA which is present in all of the province's 26 district council areas.

Likewise, because of the ban and a traditional mistrust of anything celebratory of Gaelic-Irishness in the North, the security forces are not endeared towards the GAA and monitor its activities very closely. It is possible to point to incidents such as the construction of a military barracks on Gaelic playing fields in Crossmaglen, the temporary occupation of Casement Park and the regular stopping and searching of players and supporters on their way to and from Gaelic games. The result is that many GAA members feel that this monitoring is part of a systematic tradition of harassment which can be traced back continuously to the first 'Bloody Sunday', 21 November 1920, when a detachment of Black and Tans entered Croke Park in Dublin and shot dead 12 spectators and players enjoying a Gaelic football match.

Certainly, outside of the Catholic church itself, there is no greater rallying point for Irish national culture in Northern Ireland than the GAA. This was clearly demonstrated during the three consecutive years, between 1991 and 1993, when counties from Ulster (Down, Donegal and Derry) were crowned all-Ireland Gaelic football champions. While this led to considerable jubilation within the nationalist community, the response from Protestants and loyalists, to say the least, was ambivalent.

The heightening of the GAA's profile in Northern Ireland increased resentment in loyalist circles because of their perception of it as an organisation associated with nationalist political aspirations. The most extreme expressions of this have came from loyalist terrorist organisations who burned down GAA premises and threatened the lives of Gaelic players and administrators.

What of rugby union and association football, two of the major 'foreign' games which the GAA, at least in part, was incarnated to resist? At first glance the main difference between rugby union and association football is that the former has been more successful than the latter in establishing and maintaining links between the two parts of Ireland. It is well known for example that the Irish international rugby team is drawn from the whole of Ireland, whereas Northern Ireland and the Republic of Ireland are represented separately in international soccer. In addition, all-Ireland rugby leagues were established in the 1990–91 season to no small degree facilitated by the good cross-border relationships which had existed at the level of club rugby for many years previously.

Although it can be generally accepted that rugby union and association football are different features of the Irish political landscape, it would be an over-simplification to conclude that the former is integrative and the latter divisive. One of the most common explanations as to why rugby is able to function in an all-Ireland context, is that it is an essentially middle-class game. Just as in England, in Ireland, north and south, the game is central to the physical education curriculum of elite public schools and grammar schools and is an important focus for university sport. There is also a widespread all-Ireland network of private rugby clubs through which contacts and values acquired in school are developed and extended. In general the Irish middle classes have been happy to maintain cross-border contacts regardless of their political affiliations. Links made through sports such as golf, cricket, hockey and show-jumping emphasise the point, as does the existence at a different level, of a whole range of all-Irish professional and business associations. The result is a veneer of civilised behaviour which may conceal deeper feelings, but which transcends these for specific purposes. This includes the playing and enjoying of a good game of rugby which, after all, is only sport and thus, according to cherished middle-class values, has nothing to do with politics. However, while at the level of culture and to a limited extent only, the rugby fraternity may help to bind an all-Ireland middle class, it tends at the same time to exacerbate other social divisions by alienating working-class communities on both sides of the border. Thus, any horizontal integrative function rugby may perform must be balanced against those vertical class divisions which it helps to sustain.

In addition to class, another explanation for the harmonious nature of Irish rugby revolves around its low profile and its amateur status. Until very recently, with the exception of international fixtures, rugby has had a relatively small public following and a commensurately low level of media attention. In short, it has not been accompanied by the passionate partisan following which so often accompanies Gaelic football and soccer. In this way the potential of the game to act as a catalyst for cross-border and cross-community conflict has been diminished. This is not to say that rugby union in Ireland has been totally free of politics. In the past, questions concerning what flag should be flown, whose anthem should be aired and where internationals should be played have all led to political controversy within the Irish Rugby Football Union. At present, the hiring and firing of managers and coaches and the selection of players for the international team continues to stir emotions on each side of the border.

Under closer scrutiny the claims for the integrative power of rugby union are weakened. This is especially the case within the boundaries

of Northern Ireland where the game is almost exclusively middle-
class and Protestant. Rugby clubs in Northern Ireland do not make
constitutional statements concerning the union with Britain and
neither do they bar any Catholics from membership. Thus, they
claim to be non-sectarian. However, the vast majority of rugby clubs
in the province are grounded in an education system which is divided
along sectarian lines and which offers an equally divided games
curriculum. This informal sporting segregation is reproduced after
school through a network of rugby clubs which become the focuses
of a subculture which has an important role to play in maintaining
the social cohesion of Northern Ireland's Protestant middle classes.
Recently in Northern Ireland, driven largely by the need to produce
more and better rugby players, there have been a number of
attempts to broaden the sport's hinterland of recruitment by including primary schools, state secondary schools and Catholic grammar
schools in a variety of exercises such as leprechaun rugby and rugby
'blitz' tournaments (Snowling, 1993). In the short term this has led
to more cross-community youth rugby taking place, but in the longer
term it is doubtful whether such small-scale experiments can
seriously alter the sport's Protestant, middle-class complexion in
Northern Ireland.

This again is in marked contrast to the situation in association
football which is much more of a working-class sport than rugby and
where, since Partition, separate administrative bodies based in Dublin
and Belfast have presided over strictly delineated league and cup competitions. Attempts to create closer cross-border contacts have met
with considerable resistance in Northern Ireland where there are real
fears that closer ties would ultimately diminish the province's independent international status within FIFA. Furthermore, competitions
and individual matches involving teams from Northern Ireland and
the Irish Republic have frequently been marred by crowd trouble
which, in the eyes of many administrators, could only get worse if an
all-Ireland league or cup competition were to be introduced in the
present political context. Underlying these pragmatic considerations,
however, is the weight of opinion of the vast majority of Protestant
supporters in the North who are opposed to any form of unity as a
matter of political principle. So clearly have the battle lines been
drawn that for Derry City, a club based in Northern Ireland but
with a predominantly Catholic following and a ground situated in
the nationalist Bogside, it has proved easier to gain admission to the
southern based League of Ireland than be allowed re-entry into the

northern Irish League which it had been obliged to leave in 1972 because of the security situation.

Nevertheless, association football is often regarded as having a unique power to bring together people of all nationalities, classes, religious and ethnic groupings and political affiliations. In Ireland therefore, it might be assumed that unlike Gaelic games and rugby union with their particular forms of exclusivity, soccer has the integrative potential which peacemakers so avidly seek in sport. This is particularly so as the game appears to be growing in popularity in the Republic of Ireland with the possible long-term threat to support for Gaelic games. Although it may be that the performances of the national side have created what is merely a temporary upsurge in interest in the 'foreign' game, there is no doubt that the Irish have enjoyed their taste of something which the Gaelic sports movement had effectively denied to them: namely, the opportunity to compete at the highest international level and, indeed, to beat the English at their own game.

In contrast, north of the border soccer at an international level is currently going through a transitional period. Attendances at international matches are lower than at any time since the early 1970s and in part this is a reflection of a series of poor performances. However, although Northern Ireland recruits its players from both communities in the province, the context in which home games are played at Windsor Park in Belfast, the headquarters of Linfield FC, is so heavily laden with loyalist imagery that many Catholics find it increasingly difficult to identify with their national side and many have changed their allegiance to the relatively more successful Irish Republic side. Alternatively, because the Northern Ireland football team remains as one of the strongest reminders of the province's separate political identity, Protestant supporters have remained loyal and regard Catholic shifts in allegiance as the latest example of treachery which they believe to be endemic within that section of the community. While the rising popularity of soccer in the Republic may have a progressive impact in terms of loosening the cultural stranglehold of the GAA, in Northern Ireland its effect has been to polarise further the two communities.

Ironically, it is doubtful that the Republic could have achieved so much had it not been for the appointment of the Englishman Jack Charlton as manager, and his creative use of FIFA's rules governing qualification for international duty. By pursuing players who qualify to play for Ireland through their eligibility to hold an Irish passport, which includes people who had at least one Irish grandparent, Charlton has effected a massive increase in the demographic base of Ireland's recruitment, enabling him to construct a team which owes as much to Ireland's diaspora as it does to the country's indigenous population. The Irish from the west of Scotland, from Wales, from London and other parts of England have all been represented during Charlton's period as manager. Indeed, Charlton's somewhat promiscuous selection policy has provided northern Protestants with a particular source of grievance.

Until earlier this year the rules governing the selection of players for Northern Ireland were dictated by an agreement made with the home associations which restricted choice on the basis of place of birth of players or their parents. This rule was introduced to avoid confusion among the English, Welsh, Scottish and Northern Irish football associations when selecting players for the home internationals which were discontinued in the early 1980s. Along with the other home associations the IFA have now adopted FIFA's passport rule, but too late to select Alan Kernaghan, who was raised in Northern Ireland, who played schoolboy international football there and who is married to an Ulster woman. Although he could not qualify to play for Northern Ireland before the rule change, the fact that his grandparents were born in Belfast before Partition in 1921 has permitted him to play for the Republic! Indeed, the fact that both the FAI and the IFA are now in pursuit of players on the basis of what passport they are entitled to hold is certain to lead to conflict as players from Northern Ireland can claim both British and Irish citizenship. There are already signs at youth level that as the Republic's achievements eclipse those of Northern Ireland, increasing numbers of talented players, particularly those from the nationalist community, are looking towards the FAI rather than the IFA for the development of their international careers.

Indeed, if there is one single sport which does most to emphasise the polarity of Northern Irish society it is association football. This is because soccer is popular within both communities and, unlike Gaelic games and rugby union, there are many opportunities within the game for cross-community contact which can result in sectarian confrontation and even violence. The history of football in Northern Ireland is littered with manifestations of sectarian rivalry both on and off the pitch. Patterns of support for local teams and for the 'old firm' (Glasgow Celtic and Glasgow Rangers) tend to follow existing lines of community division. Also, at a lower level, leagues and teams within leagues tend to be organised in such a way that some degree of separation between Catholic and Protestant players is maintained.

All of this seems to suggest that soccer in the Northern Ireland context is inherently divisive. However, in other important ways the sport achieves far more than either Gaelic games or rugby union in terms of providing common ground for Catholics and Protestants. At a senior level it is usual for Catholics and Protestants to play together in the same teams. In the 1992–3 season even Linfield FC broke its Protestants-only taboo by signing several Catholic players, albeit from the Republic of Ireland. Neither is it unknown for Catholics and Protestants to support the same senior teams. Although support for the 'old firm' mirrors community division, this is not the case with regard to support for English league teams. It is common for Catholics and Protestants to support the same team and to travel together to England to do so. Indeed, this also provides opportunity for the development of cross-border soccer friendships through encounters with the large volume of travelling support from the Republic of Ireland. Finally, despite the segregated school system, soccer is the main sport of many Protestant and Catholic schools and a network of inter-school leagues and representative schoolboy teams makes it possible to provide points of cross-community contact for many young players. Thus, while in terms of direct sectarian conflict, soccer may be the most politically volatile sport in Northern Ireland, it may also be the team game that has the greatest potential to have a positive impact on the province's deeply divided popular culture. For this reason soccer has been one of the most frequently chosen sports for community relations initiatives (Sugden, 1991).

Take a violent sport such as boxing and locate it in the heart of a violent society and one would not be surprised to discover evidence of the sport exacerbating existing community divisions and worsening conflict. However, evidence suggests that while boxing is an intrinsic part of Northern Ireland's inner-city culture, to some extent the boxing fraternity manages to remain apart from those forces which promote cross-community conflict (Sugden, 1993). Throughout the darkest days of the troubles, in the early 1970s, when sectarian murders and random bombings were common and parts of Belfast were effectively no-go areas, many sports ceased to operate because of the difficulties associated with getting from one place to another. The City's boxing clubs, most of which are located in the heart of sectarian ghettos, remained open. Catholics and Protestants trained alongside one another and fought in tournaments in each other's clubs, free of the fear of sectarian attack. Little has changed and boxing continues to be the only working-class sport which, at least within its own boundaries, has managed to remain aloof from the divisive effects of sectarianism. How can this be so?

The capacity of boxing to attract people from both communities is helped by the fact that the sport is not automatically associated with one or other cultural tradition. Even though the English may have been responsible for the initial development of boxing in its modern form, in no way could the sport be specifically associated with England. Boxing has been able to develop as a genuinely universal sport which is not intrinsically bound up with a particular nationalist or post-colonial tradition. Boxing is perceived as a neutral sport. Being a boxer is not taken as an indication of a person's religious or political persuasion and so Catholics and Protestants can mix in the name of their sport without fear of sectarian stigma.

Also, while amateur boxers are members of and often compete for particular clubs, boxing is more of an individual than a team sport. Teams are not built in boxing clubs in the same sense that they are when the context is association, Gaelic or rugby football. The further a boxer advances in his career, the more individualistic he becomes and the further away he gets from identification with groups of other fighters and the cultural tradition of the neighbourhood within which his club may be located. Much of a serious fighter's training is conducted alone, outside of the gym. Even though he may train regularly at his club in the company of fellow members, the nature of that training is quite solitary and there is little time set aside for social bonding. Very little intimate social interaction takes place among senior fighters within clubs and even less occurs outside of the boundaries of the sport. It is only on the few occasions when a club travels away from home to box as a team that any significant socialisation takes place and even then the themes for communication are invariably selected from the world of boxing. The lack of an intimate social dimension to boxing means that there is no serious exchange of the views and values which bear upon wider social and political divisions.

More than anything else, however, it is the ethos that surrounds boxing in Northern Ireland which enables the sport to thrive against considerable odds. In Belfast boxing is sustained by old-fashioned working-class traditions and values. It is a sport for 'hard men', but in a pre-1950s rather than post-1960s vintage. The boundless violence which seems to be endemic within the modern inner-city, whether it be random, gangland or politically motivated has no place within the subculture of the boxer and this is as true in Belfast as it is in Chicago, Detroit and Mexico City. Along with a decision to become a serious boxer, therefore, comes an implicit rejection of many of the degrading aspects of life in working-class Northern Ireland, including terrorism and the subculture which sustains violence. Moreover, outside of the ring boxers are themselves respected on both sides of the sectarian divide. They are allowed to keep themselves to themselves and are not pressurised to get involved with political causes. The gatekeepers of boxing are well aware of this and they carefully police their boundaries to ensure that the malevolence, wildness and disrespect often associated with street youth culture are not allowed to contaminate the atmosphere of their sport. In addition, because politics and sectarianism are such close relatives of violence in Belfast, great efforts are made to ensure that these influences are left at the gymnasium door. Without such conventions of truce and their careful policing, boxing in Northern Ireland would surely degenerate into barbarism and soon would be proscribed. Thus, the truth of the matter is that boxing thrives in Belfast not because of the City's violent heart, but despite that violence.

However, boxing's apparent capacity to insulate itself from the violence of local community also means that the ethos of the sport does not travel far beyond the threshold of the gymnasium. It is unlikely that the individual fighter's informed rejection of sectarianism has much impact on the underpinning structure of cross-community conflict. While boxing can integrate participants in the name of their sport, there is little evidence to suggest that this has an impact on generalised attitudes and beliefs in the wider society. Moreover, as Wayne McCullough and Barry McGuigan have discovered to their cost, in Northern Ireland the moment a sport reveals its potential to have a positive impact on community relations beyond its own boundaries, no matter how slight, is the same moment that sport becomes a target for political exploitation by the forces which thrive on community division.

Wayne McCullough won a silver medal for Ireland at the Barcelona Olympics and, as Ireland's youngest competitor, he carried the Irish national flag in the opening ceremony of the Seoul Olympics in 1988. McCullough is a Protestant from Belfast's Shankill Road. Northern Irish amateur fighters must box under the governance of the IABA (Irish Amateur Boxing Association) and in international tournaments, with the exception of the Commonwealth

Games, must represent Ireland. This is not necessarily appreciated outside of boxing circles in Northern Ireland, especially in hard-line loyalist areas such as the Shankill Road where representing the Irish Republic is considered by some to be nothing short of treason. The glare of publicity which accompanied McCullough carrying the Irish Tricolour in Seoul reflected badly on his family back home who were intimidated and beaten by hard-line loyalist elements. More recently the politics of national division were more formally revealed by the actions of the unionist dominated Belfast City Council. After taking (what was for them) the enlightened step of hosting a civic reception at City Hall for McCullough on his return from Barcelona, they refused to invite fellow team member and Olympic champion, Michael Carruth, from county Cork, even though McCullough had been guest of honour at the reception held in Dublin for Carruth a few days earlier. The council argued that they could not honour Carruth because he was a corporal in the army of a state which still claimed constitutional jurisdiction over Northern Ireland. With this kind of treatment fresh in his mind, McCullough has spurned opportunities to join professional boxing stables in both England and Ireland electing instead to box professionally in the United States.

Circumstances in the career of Barry McGuigan, arguably the best boxer to emanate from the island of Ireland in recent memory, may also have influenced McCullough's decision to fight professionally in the United States. McGuigan was born and brought up in Clones, County Monaghan, in that part of Ulster which is in the Irish Republic. As an amateur, like all Ulstermen, McGuigan fought within the embrace of the IABA. However, when he turned professional he was advised by his then mentor/manager B. J. Eastwood to box in pursuit of British rather than Irish titles – presumably because the former offered a more lucrative return than the latter and a better chance of world recognition. In an attempt to appease Irish nationalists while at the same time not offend unionists, McGuigan entered the ring under the flag of the United Nations and the Londonderry Air ('Danny Boy'), rather than the British or Irish anthems was played. However, many Irish nationalists outside of the boxing fraternity never forgave McGuigan for fighting for British titles, becoming, as they saw it, a 'turncoat'. When the boxer paraded through the streets of Belfast with his world title, slogans such as 'Barry the Brit – sold his soul for English gold' were daubed around many nationalist areas of the city. Since retiring from the ring

McGuigan has elected to set up home in southern England: it is possible that in deciding whether to live in England or Ulster, death threats which McGuigan received from nationalists helped to tip the balance in favour of Kent over Armagh.

It has been demonstrated that sport is part and parcel of the society within which it is located and this seriously questions the extent to which sport in Northern Ireland can opt out of social divisions and act as a neutral medium for community reconciliation. Nevertheless, sport has no intrinsic values. It is the people who play, support, teach and administer sport who introduce an ideological dimension. The reality is that sport is an extremely malleable social medium which can be engineered in the service of social justice, but which can just as easily be exploited in the service of social conflict. By their very nature many forms of sport and related forms of recreation are social activities which are especially appealing to young people and it is not surprising that they have been incorporated into what is rapidly emerging as a community relations industry in Northern Ireland. Clearly, given what has already been said about the relationship between sport and community division in Northern Ireland, there are strict limits on the scope of such initiatives. However, there is some evidence to suggest that, if the context of the experience is carefully managed at an interpersonal level, as tends to be the case within the world of boxing, sport can assist in broadening the outlook of young people. Many such projects are currently being supported by the government and a variety of voluntary organisations. It is worth mentioning two for illustration.

The first, which is called Belfast United, is a cross-community sports programme involving soccer and basketball. Essentially, youngsters are recruited from Catholic and Protestant areas of Belfast to be trained and coached as members of integrated teams. The fact that both sports involved are already played, albeit usually separately, by both sections of the community provides an important common denominator which is initially measured in terms of interest and skill in the games themselves but which also serves as an interactive medium for the underpinning community relations work. The highlight of the Belfast United project involves residential playing/coaching experiences in the United States. The youngsters are required to live with American families in mixed pairs (Catholic and Protestant). Project evaluations have shown that it is during these extended periods away from home, in the intimate company of peers from a different religious background, that the best community relations work can be done (Sugden, 1991).

The second example is an experiment which is attempting to introduce rugby union to Belfast's Catholic community. In this case a number of Catholic secondary schools and non-rugby playing Protestant secondary schools have been encouraged to send teams to Malone Rugby Club to participate in a series of tournaments using a simplified form of the game. From these tournaments three integrated rugby teams have been selected (under-18s, under-16s and under-14s) and are currently playing regular junior rugby on Saturday mornings in Belfast as well as going on tour together. This project is especially significant because it requires persuading Catholic youngsters to take up a sport which in Northern Ireland, as we have seen, is clearly associated with a British cultural tradition (Snowling, 1993).

The range and number of community relations programmes which use sport in the ways outlined above will continue to expand so long as government and other agencies are willing to provide the finance. It would be a mistake to make grand claims as to the impact such programmes are having on community relations in the province. Nevertheless, it is quite clear that these practical, grass-roots experiments in social engineering can have some impact on the relatively small numbers of individuals who experience them. The view taken by many of those who are involved in the development and supervision of such initiatives is that after a quarter of a century of serious sectarian violence and in the absence of any impending political panacea, this very gradual grass-roots work is the only way forward. At least it is better than doing nothing.

REFERENCES

Allison, L. (1993) *The Changing Politics of Sport*. Manchester, Manchester University Press.

McLaughlan, J. (1993) *Sport, Physical Education and the Common Curriculum in Northern Ireland*. PhD thesis, University of Ulster.

Murray, D. (1985) *Worlds Apart: Segregated Schools in Northern Ireland*. Belfast, Appletree Press.

Snowling, R. (1993) *The Malone Experiment. Rugby Union as a Cross-Community Sport*. MA dissertation, University of Ulster.

Sugden, J. (1991) 'Belfast United: Encouraging Cross-Community Relations through Sport in Northern Ireland', *Journal of Sport and Social Issues*, 15: 1, 59–80.

Sugden, J. (1993) *Fighting for the Holy Family*, Television Documentary in the 'Under the Sun' series, BBC2, Bristol.

Sugden, J. and A. Bairner (1993) *Sport, Sectarianism and Society in a Divided Ireland*. Leicester, Leicester University Press.

Sugden, J. and S. Harvie (1993) *Sport and Community in Northern Ireland: a Governing Body Perspective*. Unpublished Central Community Relations Unit Report.

14 Culture, Religion and Violence in Northern Ireland
Dominic Murray

During his whistle-stop tour of Northern Ireland in spring 1994 to protest against the joint Downing Street Declaration of the British and Irish governments, Dr Ian Paisley claimed that when 'his people' (the Protestants of the seventeenth-century Plantation of Ulster) came to Ireland, they encountered a 'bog country, inhabited by a bog people'. He would seem to be suggesting that ethnic differences have contributed to a conflict which has never been far from the surface since that time. However, few other observers would perceive the violence in Northern Ireland in terms of an ethnic war. On the other hand, there has been persistent debate with regard to the relative influence of culture and religion on the provenance and maintenance of the conflict there.

RELIGION

There is no doubt that religious difference plays a role in the perpetuation of the conflict but not to the extent that is often suggested by outside commentators. It is true that historically the indigenous Catholic Irish have continued to identify more with Ireland as a whole than with Britain, while the descendants of the Protestants of the Plantation have maintained strong emotional links with their ancestral British heritage. It is important to note, however, that the violence has little to do with religion *per se* but rather with the perceptions and aspirations which have come to be associated with the major religious groups in the region. It is quite usual, for example, for Catholics to perceive political symbols in Northern Ireland (Stormont buildings, the union flag) in terms of a Protestant establishment. Protestants on the other hand often associate manifestations of Catholicism (the papal flag) with a desire for a united Ireland.

Much has also been written recently about the increasing degree of alienation being experienced by Protestants in Northern Ireland. This has come about partly because the process of redressing the historical discrimination which has operated against Catholics is resulting in more occupational opportunities being presented to members of that religious group. In addition there is a common perception among Protestants that their rights are being eroded, and indeed threatened, by the British government through processes such as the Anglo-Irish Agreement and the Downing Street Declaration. There is a temptation to perceive all of this in terms of capitulation to the ever-increasing demands of Northern Irish Catholics and the government of the Republic of Ireland. It is possible therefore that Northern Irish Protestants who have never identified with the Republic of Ireland, and who are becoming increasingly suspicious of what they perceive as 'perfidious Albion', are tending to emphasise their Protestantism in attempting to forge a common identity. Finally there is genuine apprehension that the perceived religious hegemony of the Catholic church in the Republic of Ireland would inevitably result in the restriction of the religious freedom of Protestants within any form of united Ireland.

However, too often the conflict in Northern Ireland is presented in terms of a religious war which it certainly is not. It is important to restate that the violence there has little to do with confessional difference. The terms 'Catholic' and 'Protestant' simply provide convenient, and often misleading, labels under which the conflict can be compartmentalised.

CULTURE

Buckley (1986) has claimed that in Northern Ireland there exist both cultural diversity and cultural uniformity in the sense that

> There do not exist, in empirical fact, two (or three) 'traditions' in modern Ulster, and that the opposite claim, that there is a single Ulster or even Irish tradition is equally false.

Dunn et al. (1990) argue that 'Despite the mythologies, common elements (of culture) are now pervasive', while Murray (1985) states that 'there are as many elements of culture which unite people in Northern Ireland as there are those which separate.'

If these claims have any veracity, then one must ask why the view persists that culture is a significant element in the continuance of the conflict in Northern Ireland? Again it would appear that it is not difference itself that causes problems but rather people's inability to handle difference. Nor is it the existence of differing cultures that sustains violence but rather the associations and appendages which accompany their manifestations. An Orange parade provides a good example of this. To those involved it may be seen as a natural and enjoyable demonstration of Protestant culture. However in a divided society, the enactment of such ritual is of less importance than how it is perceived. Nationalists may (and do) see such events as examples of Protestant ascendancy, cultural dominance, and as 'coat trailing' exercises. Therefore symbols, as manifestations of cultural identity, are very important in Northern Ireland and one problem in the past was that people of the unionist tradition experienced total freedom to display and proclaim their culture while severe legal restrictions operated against nationalists doing likewise. However, changes such as the repeal in 1987 of the Flags and Emblems Act (1954) have eased the situation considerably.

In any analysis of the connection between culture and conflict in Northern Ireland it is advisable to define one's terms. I believe that culture is the whole set of norms, values, attitudes, mores and behaviours which make us what we are. In this context, culture and violence may well be related since the elements of the two major cultures (if two there are) tend not only to be different, which would be healthy and manageable, but also antipathetic and exclusive. It would be hard to imagine for example the aspiration for a united Ireland being able to accommodate to the existence of Northern Ireland as a distinct political entity. Mutualism may therefore be impossible at the moment since, to a very large degree, the elements and aspirations of one culture can only flourish and succeed at the expense of the other. On the other hand, the character and manifestations of culture may not be immutable. Recent loyalist banners and gable-wall graffiti for example now seem to have conscripted Cuchulainn to their cause. This Ulster hero of Irish mythology stoutly defended the province from the marauding Queen Maeve from the south.

There is a close relationship between religion and culture in Northern Ireland, the former being part of, and allowing access to, the latter. For this reason, it has been argued that attempts to separate them will prove unproductive. Therefore, in order to illuminate and understand the violence in Northern Ireland, we should consider the religio-cultural groups in the social contexts in which they exist.

DEMOGRAPHY

There has always been a fair degree of physical separation between Catholics and Protestants in Northern Ireland, especially in the larger cities. This has come about as a result of historical factors, and of a perceived need for safety. In some cases it was also a consequence of government and local government policy, for example the gerrymandering of electoral divisions to maintain a unionist majority. This was particularly so in the city of Londonderry, which, though in numerical terms a predominantly nationalist city, was carefully constructed electorally to ensure a unionist majority. Nonetheless, in the years between 1921 and 1968, a significant increase in the degree of mixing between the two groups did occur. However, the onset of the most recent spate of violence in 1969 heralded what was described at the time as the biggest enforced movement of population in Europe since the Second World War. This again was precipitated by a combination of intimidation, suspicion and fear.

An analysis of the 1991 Census reveals that about half of the region's one and a half million population lives in areas more than 90 per cent Catholic or 90 per cent Protestant. Fewer than 110 000 live in areas of roughly equal numbers of Catholics and Protestants. Of Belfast's 51 wards, 35 are at least 90 per cent one religion or the other. McKittrick (1993) has argued that this geographical separation means that people can, in a fashion that seems natural to them, lead lives of near-apartheid and rarely, if ever, mix or socialise across the religious, cultural or demographic divide. Some 24 years of sectarian violence have served to deepen these existing divisions.

Obviously there is a perceived sense of safety in 'being among your own'. However, in terms of the use of violence, such separation of the major groups allows for the easy and clear identification of targets; the recent bombing of the Shankill Road for example. It also means that any response can be similarly targeted at the other community; the shooting dead of seven people in the Greysteel bar is a case in point. Both were sectarian acts which were carried out in the near-certainty that only Catholics or Protestants would be affected on each occasion. In the past such blatant sectarian attacks have tended to be rare in Northern Ireland. It is more normal that some 'justification' is given for each killing. These explanations can take the form of the victim being 'accused' of being a member of the security forces or of one of the many paramilitary groups. It can simply be for doing manual work for the security forces, as was the case in 1992 with the killing of eight workers returning from such employment at Teebane in County Tyrone. As these 'tit for tat' murders continue, individuals and families are becoming increasingly fearful of working in, or travelling through, the wrong area. As a result, social segregation is likely to have become even more marked, with one community meeting less and less of the other community. Thus they then have less knowledge of each other as cultures, families or human beings. This increases suspicion, fear and ultimately the potential for sectarian violence.

Concomitant with this rise in sectarian segregation has been an increase in a kind of siege mentality within the two communities. In many regions the sense of fear and threat has become almost palpable, and this has permitted the paramilitaries to present themselves in the role of defending, and indeed policing, the 'ghettos'. This role seems to have had an attraction for the young people of the areas in terms of emulation and recruitment, this despite (or perhaps because of) the fact that some of the justice meted out has included killing, kneecapping, tarring, beatings and exile of members of the community for such crimes as theft, drug abuse or joyriding. It should not be surprising therefore that many of the young people of these areas become involved in the ambient violence since many see it as exciting and legitimised. Quite apart from a commitment to any cause, such involvement can provide status and esteem which would not easily be experienced otherwise.

With regard to culture, the physical separation between the two communities, and the accompanying suspicion and ignorance, makes it possible for them to maintain separate elements of culture. A Catholic parish will generate and support a Gaelic football team; its Protestant counterpart will produce a flute band. The practices and day-to-day experiences of the two will emphasise differing sets of priorities and will place differing levels of importance on particular forms of behaviour. Even when this involves the larger world – for example the support of English or Scottish football teams – local values will be transported out. Glasgow Rangers becomes a Protestant team and Celtic a Catholic one. And, even though the modern international culture of Ramsey Street and pop groups becomes a common feature, they are enjoyed separately.

EMPLOYMENT

People may be socialised into violence because of frustration with their standard of living or quality of life. Both of these concerns are likely to be critically affected by levels of unemployment. The Cameron Commission, reporting on the disturbances of 1968 and 1969, concluded that a sense of injustice felt by Catholics had been a major contributory factor to the violence. This sense of injustice was related to complaints about discrimination in employment and was one of the main reasons for the street protests of civil rights groups at that time.

Cormack and Osborne (1991) record that the official male unemployment rate in Northern Ireland in 1989 was 19.3 per cent. This global figure conceals several significant disparities. For example, the rates are much higher in the west of the country where Catholics form the majority. In addition, Catholic men are 2.6 times more likely to be unemployed than their Protestant counterparts. This difference has remained almost unchanged despite the creation of the most sophisticated Fair Employment Act in western Europe. Nowadays this disparity is probably explained by the existence of what Gallagher (1991) has termed 'indirect discrimination'. These are employment practices which may have the effect of discriminating against Catholics but which are not necessarily designed to so do. For example, research demonstrates that school leavers in Northern Ireland use informal networks (personal contacts, for example) to gain employment. Because unemployment tends to be higher among Catholic families, Protestant school leavers may have more access to those in work and so are more successful in obtaining employment. The consequence is that, while unemployment rates are high in both communities, they tend to be higher in Catholic working-class areas. The effect in Catholic communities is to engender a sense of grievance and a belief that such differentials are the result of discrimination and injustice. However, although unemployment is proportionally less among Protestants it is still high in absolute terms and this is increasingly perceived among Protestant communities as a result of special treatment for Catholics. I believe that the importance of the unemployment issue has consistently been underestimated in terms of its contribution to violence. In some Catholic areas, for example, the unemployment rate may be 30 per cent and whole families have never worked and may never be employed. In these areas, frustration and a sense of injustice are attributed to a political power base with which the majority there have never identified. The situation is seen clearly as a sectarian issue. It makes little difference if this analysis is correct in fact. That it is perceived to be true exacerbates feelings of separation and suspicion and provides the paramilitaries with persuasive propaganda material.

It also helps to support and sustain long-term myths about the basic cultural values of each separate group. For the Protestants the Catholics are lazy, have large families, exploit the welfare state system, and so benefit far more from the system than Protestants. For Catholics, the Protestants discriminate routinely and are internally focused with no regard for other groups, or their needs.

EDUCATION

The family unit and education system are probably the strongest forces of socialisation and enculturation in any society. One of the normal functions of a school system is to pass on to the next generation that which is culturally cherished by the present one. In Northern Ireland, schools are segregated along religious lines. Research (Darby et al., 1977: 15–18) suggests that in 71 per cent of schools all of the children come from one of the two major group-ings. The polarisation of teachers is just as pronounced. There now exists a small number of integrated schools (about 17) but these cater for only a tiny percentage of the school-going population. My own research interest (Murray, 1985) has been in the extent to which schools can influence the formation or reinforcement of national identity. To this end I have spent long periods observing and participating in both Catholic and Protestant schools. In all of this time I have never observed one instance of the use of violence being encouraged. What was commonplace however was that each type of school tended to idealise and extol different aspects of culture and, indeed, history. As one teacher put it: 'In Catholic schools they give a biased version of history. Here, we teach it as it was.'

These different accounts of history may well be reinforced by the myths and legends learned in the home. A British army officer tells the story of apprehending a seven-year-old child for throwing stones at his patrol. When asked why he was doing it, the child replied: 'You bastards have been exploiting us for 300 years and we are not putting up with it anymore'!

In this story it would seem that the child was simply parroting the logic of the adults in the community. The point is that children may carry out acts of violence which they have come to realise are acceptable to their parents, and indeed reinforced by their parents' attitudes. The daily rituals and symbols carried out within the separate schools also highlight difference rather than commonality. This can sometimes be seen within the broad categories of unionism or nationalism. More often, however, it can be observed through the celebration of more cultural events such as Commonwealth Day or the Queen's birthday or the flying of the 'Union Jack' in the Protestant schools. In Catholic schools, celebrations of occasions such as First Communion or Confirmation or Ash Wednesday are normal aspects of the school year. It is important to emphasise that such events, while common and natural, are also totally school-type specific. It would be inconceivable for example that the former list of events would ever be celebrated (or even recognised) in a Catholic school. In fact it can be argued that each demonstrates a cultural position which is anathema to the other.

I have argued elsewhere (Murray, 1985: 77–90) that in Northern Irish schools, culture is caught rather than taught. But, since the process takes place in separate and segregated establishments, emerging identities may be all the more strong and exclusive. Children, albeit unconsciously, are socialised into an awareness of difference and distinctiveness. In any democracy this should be both natural and desirable. In Northern Ireland, however, there tends to be a general inability to handle difference: the display of symbols is interpreted as provocation, and distinctiveness is seen as synonymous with divisiveness. This is exacerbated by the fact that when children from different schools meet each other, the interaction often takes place in a competitive context. On one occasion for example I was researching in a Catholic primary school and the ten-year-old soccer team was playing the local Protestant school. One of the Catholic teachers present was getting quite animated, and when I teased him about it he replied darkly: 'There is more to this than just football'.

Schools are rarely accused of contributing consciously to the violence but they can be fairly criticised for not doing more to promote mutual understanding and tolerance. At the moment, it would seem that children in both types of school are being denied the means to understand each other's culture. However, within the formal curriculum of Northern Irish schools, programmes such as 'The Schools Cultural Studies Programme', 'Education for Mutual

Understanding' (EMU), 'Cultural Heritage' and 'The Cross-Community Contact Scheme' are attempting to bring about increased awareness among children. EMU and Cultural Heritage are compulsory cross-curricular components for all school pupils. These operate at the attitudinal level in trying to bring about increased tolerance. However, the problem with attitudes is that the more strongly we feel about something, the less likely we are to be tolerant of opposing views. We can all examine our consciences in this regard in terms of such issues as smoking, conservation, contraception, divorce, homosexuality or abortion. If we have problems with any of these, or indeed with any issue, then think how much more demanding it will be to expect tolerance from children whose fathers or mothers have been killed by Catholic or Protestant paramilitaries or the armed forces. Consider too how attitudes must have been affected by events such as Bloody Sunday, internment or the Enniskillen or Teebane bombings.

The attitudinal approach to increasing tolerance in schools and lessening violence afterwards is therefore a difficult and sometimes hazardous pursuit. The strategy of increasing contact between schools has been employed to this end through such approaches as joint classes and cultural trails. These can yield results when planned and carried out with great care: but, if the contact is superficial, they can do more harm than good. I can remember for example on the occasion of one such joint trail the Protestant children being less than amused when being confronted, in a Catholic area, with the graffiti: 'Boom, Boom goes Mountbatten'. Similarly, the Catholic children were less than impressed with the scrawled scoreline: 'Paras 13, Derry nil' – a farewell message from that particular regiment to the people of the city after the events of Bloody Sunday, when 13 unarmed civilians had been killed by the army. I was convinced at that time that those children returned to their schools with less tolerance than when they left and that the potential for violence among and between them had increased rather than diminished. However, the much wider range and extent of experience of this kind of joint work means that schools and teachers are now more aware of the dangers.

Despite the difficulties, the Roman Catholic Church now supports the attitudinal approach. This is perhaps inevitable since it accommodates both the desire for schools to play a part in reducing violence and the conviction that separate Catholic schools have the right to exist.

THE USE OF VIOLENCE

In normal class politics, politicians and policies tend to be influenced by an expanding or contracting middle ground. The relative performance of the Liberal Democrats in England, for example, seems to have had a significant effect on the reactive measures adopted by the other two major parties. In Northern Ireland, however, conflict, rather than class, politics seems to obtain. In the context of strife, politicians tend to be more preoccupied with the possibility of being outdone, or outmanoeuvred, by the more extreme individuals in their own or other parties. In addition, within the 'politics of violence' it may well be tantamount to political suicide to be perceived as 'getting soft' with the other side. There is likely therefore to be an inextricable link between community violence and the development of political intransigence. Each act of violence causes hurt and fear. Fear engenders the demand for response and reassurance. Most often this demand is satisfied, at least in the short term, by the utterances of the more extreme politicians or the violent actions of the paramilitaries.

Conflict theorists have long been preoccupied with attempting to understand how it is that violence comes to be accepted as a means of settling conflict. The evidence suggests the simple truth that violence is inevitable in conflicts which involve minority and majority groupings. Generally the majority group tries to maintain power and social control. In Northern Ireland during the 50 years subsequent to the setting up of the state in 1921, this control tended to be maintained by a degree of gerrymandering, voting restrictions and discrimination against Catholics in housing and employment. Although the situation has now improved significantly, in 1969 such policies had become part of the social fabric to such a degree that when the civil rights movement took to the streets in non-violent protest, this in itself was seen by the institutional powers as an act of subversion against the state and was responded to accordingly. In other words, the establishment perception of violence actually precipitated and reified that violence. It seems likely that, in any conflict involving a majority and a minority, the demonstration of legitimate grievance by one side will inevitably be perceived as an act of unacceptable violence by the other. Actual violence may be the ultimate and inevitable development. Unfortunately, recent world events seem to reinforce this view.

At another level, it is extremely difficult for outside observers to understand, never mind condone, the use of violence. The temptation is therefore to attempt to impose objective, yet judgemental, analyses on the conflict. However, it is relatively easy to be tolerant and objective if one does not feel under threat, and at the moment, both communities in Northern Ireland feel themselves to be under threat to varying degrees. For the participants, therefore, violence may have become not only essential but also functional. It can, for example, be used at the outset as a form of defence, then attack, and perhaps, ultimately, to achieve some political objective. Most of the violence perpetrated in Northern Ireland is not mindless. This is an uncomfortable yet important observation, and one which those with a genuine concern for the region will have to come to terms with. The violence is often presented in terms of amoral 'godfathers' seducing young people into criminal acts. If this were the case, then solutions would be much easier to achieve. As an explanation or a way of apportioning blame, such a depiction has a comforting ring to it. However it is neither accurate nor helpful. There are many highly motivated people who are actively engaged in violence on both sides. If ever proof were needed of this it was provided by events such as the hunger strikes when activists were prepared to die for their principles and, in fact, ten did. In the past, politicians, especially in England, have failed to appreciate this degree of conviction and strength of commitment. Strategies for dealing with the conflict have been adversely affected as a result.

This may explain changing attitude both in Britain and the Republic of Ireland towards the policy of internment. In the past it was believed that internment without trial was an effective procedure for curtailing and containing 'godfather' criminals. Currently the view is that it can be counterproductive in the treatment of individuals who are highly committed to a cause, and that it can serve (and has served) to increase such commitment and motivation.

The two sides, Protestant and Catholic, in Northern Ireland are Christian: that is they belong to the Christian tradition of peace and love. This acknowledged affiliation raises the crucial question, how does it come about that they are prepared to use violence in a religious conflict? As I have already said, I do not see the conflict in Northern Ireland to be a predominately religious one. But even if it were, this would not distinguish it from the many other altercations which are extremely violent *precisely because* they arose as a result of religious difference and dissent. The point is that the extent to which people are prepared to resort to violence as a possible solution to conflict is largely determined by the strength of commitment and identity with respective, and presumably conflicting, aspirations. For some people in Northern Ireland, an identity with either Britain or a united Ireland is the single most important facet of their lives. Indeed, for some it is almost a *sine qua non.* It should not be surprising therefore that they will go to any lengths to protect and promote their respective identities both for themselves and for their children. I believe that in the context of resorting to violence, no one would be any different. The only thing that would distinguish between us would be the required strength of the threshold stimulus.

It is interesting that the violence emanating from each side over the years has tended to take different forms, or at least has been so perceived. Since the IRA is attempting to achieve a withdrawal of the British presence, then almost anything British or which represents the establishment is viewed by them as a legitimate target. Hence, they would argue that government offices, banks, police and army barracks and even buildings such as post offices can be attacked. In addition, they would claim, their human targets very often wear uniforms. It has to be stated, however, that these carefully made distinctions are regularly contradicted by their actions.

On the other hand, loyalist paramilitaries have a dilemma in this regard. To attack official property or personnel would be an assault on the very establishment that they purport to cherish and defend. They have therefore tended to concentrate their attentions on those elements and locations from which, in their perception, the attack on their world emanates: that is targets that can be identified with nationalism and Catholicism. They have therefore very often attacked targets like Catholic churches, Gaelic football grounds, the homes of Catholics and Catholic civilians. For this reason, loyalist violence often appears to be more sectarian than its IRA counterpart. However, it is becoming ever more debatable if even the perception of this difference remains widespread.

When one poses the question 'why is violence acceptable?', often the answer given is that it achieves its desired effect. In Northern Ireland, many Catholics argue that the unionist government would not have granted them any concessions were it not for the original civil rights upheaval and the subsequent IRA violence. In fact, since the introduction of direct rule in 1972, the Catholic population has experienced significant improvements especially in terms of housing and standard of living. Many Protestants on the other hand perceive this equalling-up process in terms of capitulation to the violence of republican paramilitaries. They are right in the sense that the violence has certainly speeded up the process. This was especially important in December 1993 when it would appear that, for whatever reasons, the unionist population were represented as being obstructive towards the highly publicised peace process. But they are simply articulating a genuine sense of outrage that, despite the protestations of the British government, Sinn Féin (the political counterpart of the Provisional Irish Republican Army) has almost succeeded in achieving a place at the conference table through its support for violent action. Similar processes have been observed in places like Cyprus, Palestine, Kenya and many others. It is remarkable how quickly the use of violence has expedited the metamorphosis from 'terrorist' through 'freedom fighter' to 'statesman'.

There is however a responsibility to subject the concept of violence to intellectual scrutiny and try to advance alternatives to it. Such a process will have little relevance for highly motivated and totally committed individuals on both sides who are actively engaged in a war. These people are likely to be convinced, not only of the justness of their own cause, but also of the immorality of the establishment which is opposing them. In addition many of these participants may never have considered an alternative to violence as a means to achieve their goal since they have no experience of any other means of negotiating. In this context, psychologists tell us that abused children are more likely than others to become abusers when they grow up. If this is so, then violence in Northern Ireland is likely to be self-perpetuating in the same way. For many people in the worst-affected areas, violence is part of their everyday lives and can take the form of bomb scares or actual bombs, sectarian attacks, road blocks and checks, and so on. In addition, since the principal attempts at arriving at a solution to the political problem to date have been by military means, then, *ipso facto*, violence becomes not only legitimised, but also an accepted part of the problem. In addition, when people study topics such as 'violence as a means of resolving conflict', they tend to consider only the violence emanating from the paramilitaries engaged in the conflict and not that being perpetrated by the state forces confronting it. It is in the nature of armies to use violence and in Northern Ireland this is manifest from time to time. Such violence can take the form of house searches, verbal abuse, baiting and harassment at identity checks or in its most extreme form, the events of 'Bloody Sunday'. Even if such behaviour arises from laudable intentions, it is inevitable that it will precipitate reactive violence and indeed it often has. Thus, very rapidly the state's 'solutions' become part of the problem and violence may become cyclical and almost endemic.

CONCLUSION

The more obvious manifestations of cultural life in Northern Ireland are inextricably built into the separated communities. The normal avenues of communication and contact between people which would provide a tendency towards the creation of a single shared culture are closed. The groups go to different schools and attend different churches; they live relatively separate social lives, even when they are not physically segregated; they play and support different games, and even when the game is the same, the teams are often defined as in some way culturally singular. They are suspicious of each other in the group sense, even when there are good interpersonal relations between individuals. Attempts to build bridges between these two differently perceived and experienced worlds continue at school level, among individual church-people, and in a great range of associations and centres. However, the problem of measuring or understanding their effectiveness is an enduring one, and the power of the bomb or the assassination to destroy or weaken bridges is difficult to overestimate.

REFERENCES

Buckley, A. (1986) Collecting Ulster's Culture: Are there really Two Traditions? Paper presented to the British Association for the Advancement of Science, Annual Meeting, Bristol.

Cameron Report (1969) *Disturbances in Northern Ireland.* Belfast, HMSO.

Cormack, R.J. and R.D. Osborne (1991) *Discrimination and Public Policy in Northern Ireland.* Oxford, Clarendon Press.

Darby, J., ed. (1983). *Northern Ireland: The Background to the Conflict.* Belfast, Appletree Press.

Darby, J., D. Murray, D. Batts, S. Dunn, S. Farren and J. Harris (1977) *Education and Community in Northern Ireland: Schools Apart?* Coleraine, University of Ulster.

Dunn, S., V. Morgan and C. Bowring-Carr (1990) *All the Things We Are.* Unpublished paper, Centre for the Study of Conflict, University of Ulster.

Gallagher, A.M. (1991) *Majority Minority Review 2: Employment, Unemployment and Religion in Northern Ireland.* Coleraine, Centre for the Study of Conflict, University of Ulster.

McKittrick, D. (1993) *Independent,* London, 21 March.

Murray, D. (1985). *Worlds Apart: Segregated Schools in Northern Ireland.* Belfast, Appletree Press.

15 Institutions for Conciliation and Mediation
Derick Wilson and Jerry Tyrrell

THE ORIGINS OF COMMUNITY RECONCILIATION GROUPS IN NORTHERN IRELAND

Reconciliation groups, as we now understand them, emerged in Northern Ireland for the first time in 1964. Although many of the leaders of these groups came from Northern Ireland, a surprisingly high proportion of them had the common characteristic that, prior to initiating projects within Northern Ireland, they all had some broadening experience outside Northern Ireland (Wilson, 1986: 7). The range of experience included work with the trade union movement, in international companies, in overseas development agencies, in non-governmental organisations and in ecumenical initiatives within different religious traditions. These people returned to Northern Ireland wishing to be part of the changes taking place here. There were of course others involved, including people from abroad living in Northern Ireland.

Reconciliation groups mushroomed in the post-1969 period after the outbreak of communal violence (Gallagher and Worrall, 1982; Bowman and Shivers, 1984). The focus of their activities varied and included addressing political issues, developing ecumenical understanding and bringing children and families from the different traditions together. The work often involved people from different and often opposed traditions meeting together for discussion, working together on community programmes and organising proposals for changes in government policy. Their common agenda was the improvement of community relations in Northern Ireland.

Initially resources were very limited and what financial support there was came from a number of (mainly new) agencies such as the Ministry of Community Relations, the Northern Ireland Community Relations Commission and the Ministry of Education.

When people from different traditions came together in mixed groups they often met harsh reactions from members of their own tradition. Many were not prepared for these reactions and learning how to deal with them was often the first lesson. In addition people were often surprised at the range of the cultural and historical differences that surfaced within mixed groups. This range extended from different understandings of history to different procedures for discussion and decision-making. These differences emerged in the most unexpected ways and often reflected and illuminated similar – if more crucial – differences in the wider society. For example, decision-making processes for Catholics did not necessarily mean the use of simple majority voting. Such procedures, however, dominated the experience of the political majority and Protestants often did not realise how this approach mirrored their own experiences in the wider society. In this way the majority–minority history, politics and fears existing in the wider society would often invade group meetings.

Much to the surprise of the wider public, and perhaps even to the participants, those mixed groups developed and thrived even though their members were unprepared for the experience of meeting each other, and had little experience of working together. Successful approaches included ensuring that the different traditions were formally represented within their structures, and the establishment of constitutions where equality of regard for all traditions was demanded (for example Protestant and Catholic Encounter – PACE). This accommodation of all was not always easily accomplished.

These reconciliation groups were signs that new relationships were possible even though they had to learn to survive the stress caused by communal violence and sectarian hatred. They learned about differing understandings of the role of the police, of the nature of government and about the law. They learned that responses to questions and problems are coloured by traditions and by perceptions of being under threat. Times of stress are especially difficult in the life of the cross-tradition group in that political and other events have the potential to drive people apart, especially when the groups have little understanding of the dynamic dominating them. The crucial factor is trust, and where this exists it acts as a contrast to the separating force that often accompanies communal violence and sectarian hatred.

Where relationships of this kind were able to survive and remain strong, people were able to meet together and enter into each other's experience. The Corrymeela Community is perhaps the most famous example. In this case the group predated the outbreak of the troubles and this was an important factor in its influence. In the beginning it helped people simply to address issues together and to learn to live with differences. More recently it has played an important part in the generation of materials which have identified and highlighted debilitating features in social interactions. These have included in particular the culture of 'politeness, avoidance and separation' which enables people to avoid contentious issues especially in company which is religiously mixed. In Northern Ireland, people do not often have the experience of dealing with each other openly and directly in mixed company. So initiatives in this area depend on finding ways to meet together openly but beyond this protective politeness in the initial stages.

Groups such as the Northern Ireland Community Relations Council (NICRC) and PACE have always felt it necessary to reflect critically on their work and on the nature of the Northern Ireland society. As part of this process they publish material, promote conferences and support educational developments. This has resulted in the emergence of critical thinking about the role of government policy and of religious, political and community institutions. A wider level of public discussion has followed and the emergence of a greater space within which it is possible to experience new ways of living together. As community-based programmes evolved, mainly within the voluntary sector, and as the people concerned gained experience, their influence began to be felt in such areas as education (Richardson, 1992a, 1992b; Wright, 1993); youth work (McCartney, 1985; Youth Council for Northern Ireland, 1991); and community development (Griffiths, 1974). Eventually long-term programmes developed as experiences of joint work accumulated. The importance of some of this work was later accepted by central government, albeit after 15–20 years, in the policy changes made with respect to Education for Mutual Understanding (Smith and Robinson, 1992); the Youth Service and community relations (Department of Education, Northern Ireland (DENI), 1987) and the establishing of the Northern Ireland Community Relations Council (Fraser and Fitzduff, 1986).

More recent examples of this critical reconciliation tradition are the positive responses of government to some proposals from the Committee on the Administration of Justice (CAJ) on Police accountability (CAJ, 1988); the lay visitor programme and documents on the need for race relations legislation in Northern Ireland (CAJ, 1985).

'Initiative 92' has recently published its first report (Pollak, 1993) based on 554 submissions from individuals from all sections of the people of Northern Ireland. Its findings build on a history of smaller initiatives within the reconciliation group field such as the New Ireland Movement political debates; the New Ulster Movement; the Glencree and Corrymeela political alternative conferences (Rea, 1982); the British and Irish Council of Churches initiatives on themes such as human rights in Britain and Ireland (Bailey, 1988); Quaker Peace initiatives; and the Inter Church Group on Faith and Politics pamphlets (1989).

At significant times in the history of the past 25 years the response to violent incidents has been to design schemes and projects which are intended to provide young people with opportunities to learn about other contexts and to understand how peaceful societies can be managed. Examples include the development of the Peace People's link with Norway, the Spirit of Enniskillen bursary scheme and, more recently, the scheme for children emerging from the aftermath of the Warrington bomb. Each of these events, and the subsequent responses, has helped build a movement within Northern Ireland which is about contrasts and alternatives to violent knee-jerk responses.

A CLASSIFICATION OF GROUPS

The range of reconciliation groups can be classified in a number of ways, and we have chosen the following four categories: (a) The work of intentional communities of reconciliation; (b) Local groups formed in the midst of hostility; (c) Groups formed out of the experience of violent bereavement and (d) Children's community relations holidays. We will now look at each of these in turn.

The work of intentional communities of reconciliation

The first category contains groups formed with the specific intention of acting as centres for reconciliation. They include Corrymeela (founded 1965), the Rostrevor Centre for Christian Renewal (founded in the early 1970s), the Columbanus community, the Cornerstone community and the Curragh community (1992). Each of these communities has evolved a distinctive programme of activities. For example: Corrymeela is associated with direct work with local community groups and supports this with all-age residential programmes; Rostrevor provides ecumenical retreats; Cornerstone and Curragh have developed a local presence within North and West Belfast linked with community development; and Columbanus promotes extra-mural certificate courses in Ecumenics.

Their existence is, intentionally and deliberately, a contrast to the experience of separation which is so dominant within the religious traditions (Greer and Wilson, 1993). They provide contexts within which people from the Catholic and Protestant communities can work together and develop legal, liturgical and symbolic ways to assist the evolution of new forms of ecumenical community. Within them people experience relationships which cross the different Christian traditions. They have, for example, created legal structures, outside the formal church structures, where people from both traditions become responsible, together, for a common programme. They have brought new experiences of cross-community life into the church traditions and so have been able on occasions to take important initiatives to lessen movements towards revenge and retaliation. They have also assisted in the development of other local initiatives, such as the Ulster Peoples College (UPC), and the Northern Ireland Mixed Marriage Association (NIMMA).

In the sectarian climate of Northern Ireland, reconciliation groups have had to concentrate these energies on the Catholic/Protestant, unionist/nationalist conflict. The result has been that there is little energy left for work with those who belong to traditions other than Christian in Northern Ireland. In numerical terms these ethnic communities are small but they have experienced racial harassment and are easily targeted as people to be abused (Gibson et al., 1993; CCRU, 1992; CAJ, 1985). There is growing concern among those involved in community relations work in the province that their work should also address equity issues not restricted to the Protestant/Catholic debate (Northern Ireland Community Relations Council, 1993).

Local groups formed in the midst of hostility

This second category relates to reconciliation groups which have emerged in places where there is great communal hostility. These groups seek primarily to bridge the communal divisions within their own membership in the context of an often pervasive social disunity. The result is that they are often the focus of a great deal of distrust and even hatred. The statements below are a sample from those gathered in the course of research (Wilson, 1986).

I have been spat on while holding a collection box in the city centre for peace and reconciliation work. (A mother supporting reconciliation work)

The day after our reconciliation group went public I was hissed at as I took up the offering in Church. (Co-founder of a cross-community group)

My daughter was getting abused and humiliated at school because her dad was for peace and reconciliation. (Father who established a reconciliation group)

Examples of such groups include the Peace and Reconciliation Group, Derry, the Northern Ireland Political Study Group and the Ballynafeigh Community House Group.

Groups formed out of the experience of violent bereavement

The third category consists of groups made up of individuals who have lost family or others close to them as a result of violence. A forgiving spirit has been the hallmark of such groups and this attitude is general and independent of side.

Perhaps the best known of these groups is the Peace People which began in 1976 as a response to the death of three children. This became a major and widespread movement which brought thousands of people into a new movement for peace and had a wide range of often invisible side-effects. In a smaller and more concentrated way this group continues to do important work with families of bereaved people, families of prisoners and cross-community youth programmes.

There have been many other such groups including the Cross Group, which was formed by a group of bereaved mothers and wives. Maura Kiely and Joan Orr were the originators when their sons were killed in sectarian shootings (McCreary, 1981). Other examples include Women Together and the work of Pat Campbell; the development of Widows Against Violence (WAVE); Families Against Intimidation and Terror (FAIT); and a help-line organised by Mrs Statham whose daughter Julie committed suicide in the aftermath of her boyfriend being assassinated. Dr Hylda Armstrong was inspired to help initiate Glebe House in memory of her son, Sean Armstrong, who was assassinated in 1973 as a cross-community worker. International Voluntary Service (IVS) (the organisation Sean worked for) joined with Harmony Community Group to establish Glebe House as a children's centre. IVS and Harmony Community Trust have committed themselves to promoting local and international experiences for young people in community understanding and peace work.

The Reverend Joseph Parker formed the Witness for Peace Organisation in 1972 when his son was killed while delivering newspapers, on a bike to which a bomb was attached. One of their initiatives was an annual ceremony where relatives planted plain white crosses at the City Hall, Belfast, to remember people who had lost their lives through violent action. In the latter years of this activity the backs of some of the crosses were written on with sentiments which demonstrated the deep hurt people felt and their difficulty with the spirit of forgiveness. The organisers felt that the original spirit of forgiveness which had prompted the event was not one they could force on others; and so, rather than allow the event to deteriorate into an expression of communal bitterness with each death being regained for a particular tradition or group and used against the other group, they ended the ceremony and found other public ways to continue their work through the 'Witness for Peace' Award associated with the Corrymeela Community.

The bomb which ripped through a public commemoration of Remembrance Sunday in November 1987 at Enniskillen took eleven lives and injured over 100 people, among them Marie Wilson, a young nurse. In the immediate aftermath, instead of the violent reaction that was expected by many, the community of Enniskillen reacted with a deep and significant dignity. Gordon Wilson, Marie's father, identified himself with the launch of young people's bursaries (called the 'The Spirit of Enniskillen') to allow young Catholics and Protestants to travel together abroad to examine attempts to heal division in other countries. There have been a number of other projects and developments in Enniskillen as a result of the bomb, including a new integrated school.

These are only some examples of the ways in which communities have found ways to respond to the effects of violence and deaths on themselves and their friends. The long-term effects of experiences of this kind have been the subject of some recent academic study which looked closely at the concept of bereavement, and at the personal and social supports needed to retain balance and sanity (Dillenberger, 1992).

Children's community relations holidays
Right from the beginning of the current violence, the social consequences for Northern Ireland children have been a matter of wide

concern. One common response to this has been to organise and provide holidays for religiously mixed groups of children normally from those areas of the province that experience the violence at its worst. These schemes have resulted in great part from the wide international interest generated by the media, and in particular the dramatic pictures of children in the midst of violence. The countries in which these holiday schemes are located include those with strong historical and other links with Northern Ireland, such as the USA, Britain, Holland and the Irish Republic.

> The initial impetus for children's holiday schemes came primarily from abroad and from Great Britain. In response to world-wide publicity about the troubles in N Ireland, offers of holidays came flooding in. (*Scope*, 1976: November–December)

Because the system grew as a result of individual responses, there was no central planning organisation involved, and so host bodies from the same country were often unaware of each other. In 1992 when all the US host bodies were invited to a conference in Newcastle, Co. Down, it became apparent that no single US agency was aware of the extent and diversity of the different host groups, and that this was the first time they had had the opportunity of discussing their common difficulties and learning experiences. If there was lack of coordination among the host bodies it was also true that few common channels existed within Northern Ireland for mixed groups of Protestant and Catholic children to be selected for the holidays. In Derry/ Londonderry in 1972 the then Community Development Team established a coordinating committee of representatives of Health and Social Services, teacher's unions, local charities and community workers in order to coordinate holidays for 800 children. This group was the 'Holiday Projects Derry 1972' committee. The fact that they included the year in the title illustrates the temporary, task-orientated nature of the group and their views at that time.

Other organisations like the Northern Ireland Children's Holiday Scheme (NICHS) were established in England initially by a group of Catholic seminarians, who later invited Protestant ordinands to join them. In other instances an individual council of churches in Britain worked through an individual known to them in Northern Ireland. Alternatively charitable organisations like Rotary in GB have worked with the equivalent body in Northern Ireland.

It soon became apparent that holidays offered a unique community relations opportunity in a society where segregated play, education and housing were common experiences. The government saw the benefits of promoting such holidays and provided funds to help pay for the travel of groups going to Britain. However the flood of children leaving the province to have holidays tended to add to the negative image of Northern Ireland, and led to growing doubts about their value. The Director of the Community Relations Commission in 1976 (David Rowlands) said that 'the responsibility of people here to provide holidays for their own children in their own country was taken away from them.'

The 'give the kids a break' approach was short term and immediate, very dependent on outside intervention. It was often initiated by groups who, while well motivated, did not have the time to develop analyses of the Northern Ireland society or to generate analyses of the effectiveness of the holiday scheme concept. Within the Northern Ireland community it became necessary to develop a critical analysis of the whole idea, and this began with the view that 'holidays are not the central issue', and that what happened after the holidays – particularly when the children went back to their own community – was a key issue. The result was that local people began to play a key role in the long-term development of holiday schemes in three particular areas:

1. the establishment of centres where children could meet on holiday and subsequently on follow-up weekends;
2. the use of regular follow-up activities accessible to the children's own areas where they could meet to continue the friendships formed on the holiday;
3. the development of holidays using facilities in Northern Ireland.

The government was conscious of the amount of money being spent on travel in holiday schemes, and, in an attempt to redirect resources locally, it withdrew the grant for travel to Great Britain. The result was that the following year (1977), there was only a small increase of 200 (15 per cent) local holidays which in no way compensated for the 800 (100 per cent) cut in holidays to Great Britain. It became clear that goodwill and sponsorship of host bodies outside Northern Ireland was based to some extent on the need to have children physically present in Leeds, or London or wherever the host body was based, rather than Rostrevor or Portrush. The result in practice was that the local holiday organisations that had sprung up in the early 1970s could no longer depend on outside host bodies to provide holidays, or fund-raise. The negative image of Northern Ireland also meant that representatives of individual host bodies were often reluctant to come and visit. When the venue of one holiday for a group of Derry children was changed from Donegal to Newcastle, Co. Down, the English helpers, concerned for the children's safety, were incredulous they should be allowed to go there.

As this variety of holiday projects and schemes evolved, the extent to which organisations and groups were interested in a fundamental change in the relationships and structures between people in Northern Ireland, and between Britain and Ireland, emerged as issues. Variations in the understanding of reconciliation emerged and so there were very different conceptual views among the different holiday programme groups, although this remained hidden for a long time. However, as experience accumulated, this variation of views began to come to the surface and, in acknowledging its existence, a constructive debate developed among the adults involved.

Other practical questions to emerge included: the quality of training for volunteers; the processes whereby children were selected; and the structure of the programme of activities used during holidays. One holiday organisation (Children's Community Holidays) based its practice on a model taken from Colony Holidays in Great Britain, but generally the others developed on the basis of trial and error.

Established reconciliation centres such as Corrymeela ran their own holiday programmes as part of ongoing, year-round work in different localities. In these cases, aims about reconciliation were explicitly stated. Other organisations involved in holidays were more ambivalent about stressing reconciliation while others, like Harmony Community Trust, were constrained by the term not being within their charitable deed and used instead a phrase like 'a children's centre'.

Groups like Holiday Projects West occasionally discovered that their volunteers, happy enough with bringing Protestant and Catholic children together, were ambivalent when it came to identifying community relations work as work for peace. One Catholic escort from a republican area said, 'If my mum thought this had anything to do with peace she wouldn't let me come here.' Whereas for members of the Protestant community to become involved in the same organisation, the issue was that they were mixing with Catholics. Their personal commitment to reconciliation led them to have to distance themselves from their own community.

In 1984, when Holiday Projects West had the opportunity of undertaking a major reconciliation project with Palestinians and Jews from *Neveh Shalom* in Israel, there was a debate within the executive committee of Holiday Projects West about whether it should be so closely linked to reconciliation. Its subsequent decision to do so was symptomatic of a trend within holiday organisations at that time to start taking a proactive stance in developing conflict resolution and anti-sectarian programmes.

With the development of EMU, and in particular Circular 1982/21 from the Department of Education, there was encouragement from official quarters to look more carefully at the potential of holiday schemes as a vehicle for community relations. A holiday often allowed an atmosphere of trust and safety to be built up between Protestant and Catholic children and, often, the children themselves expressed a wish to explore differences. This placed further pressure on those organisations which were unwilling or unable to address the local issues more openly. If holiday organisations were not prepared to take account of these issues in organisational terms it became clear that the young people would still raise the issues in unstructured ways.

By the late 1970s, DENI had acknowledged the benefit of training and was providing grant-aid and encouraging specialised training in conflict resolution. Holiday organisations began to develop materials, in particular building on experiences of using cooperative games to train volunteers in dealing with conflict. The International Voluntary Service and Glebe House (a community reconciliation centre) worked together on developing a programme of training; the Northern Ireland Children Holiday Scheme produced a pamphlet on 'introducing conflict management into holiday settings'; Holiday Projects West brought in an outside facilitator from the 'Children's Creative Response to Conflict' programme (New York), to work with children and volunteers in 1982 and 1983. The general result was that, by the late 1980s, conflict resolution and prejudice reduction components were featuring in most if not all of the training programmes.

Holiday organisations began to find that a percentage of the young people who went on holiday with them as children would subsequently train with them and become volunteers. One consequence was that the volunteers were drawn from the same areas as the children, and this added to the validity of the programmes in the eyes of communities. Another was that volunteers who might become involved with holiday organisations influenced their friends to join them.

The use of holidays, and the sending of young people together into new, different contexts (and later the bringing of children and young people together for more in-depth exploration of their similarities and differences), all these processes are human responses to internal conflict. Their success can be measured to some extent by their contribution to the development of current official structures and strategies on community relations within Northern Ireland. They have much in common with responses to be found in other conflicts such as the youth exchange programmes between conflicting countries after the 1939–45 war.

GOVERNMENT POLICY

There has recently been a raft of policy commitments by central government, with associated legislative changes, which have promoted discussion about community relations within government and public bodies. These have included legislative changes relating to Fair Employment, the new Education Order, school curriculum changes, the emergence of the Northern Ireland Community Relations Council, and the establishment of internal audits by the Central Community Relations Unit (CCRU) within many government bodies.

Initiatives which have evolved in the wake of these policy impulses include:

— the location of Community Relations Officers in 26 District Council areas (Knox et al., 1994);
— the promotion of cross community contact schemes for schools;
— the creation of youth service agencies and a youth cross community contact scheme;
— the anti-sectarian, anti-discrimination programmes of the trade union movement including Counteract.

With respect to this last, a range of initiatives have been taken by the Northern Ireland Congress of Trade Unions about such matters as threats to workers, intimidation and discrimination, and the Congress has established the project Counteract to develop local responses. In association with this, longer-term training programmes for a group of trade union trainees is now being established with 'The Understanding Conflict and Finding Ways Out of It' project. This is a step on from pilot work undertaken in 1992–3 (Morrow and Wilson, 1993). Other trade union related organisations, such as the Workers Educational Association, are developing related discussion work, and many employers are becoming more proactive in this area as the current climate, with the support of the law, slowly opens up the discussion.

A GROWING NETWORK OF COMMUNITY RECONCILIATION

Some recent projects (such as the Conflict and Mediation Network, INNATE – Irish Network for Nonviolent Action, Training and Education – the Quaker Peace Education Project and The Holywell Trust) are also involved in reconciliation work, and the Community Relations Council has taken on the role of providing training in relation to such matters as the facilitation of political discussion, antisectarian work and prejudice reduction. One result is the emergence of published material containing suggestions and advice about the sort of work that might be encouraged (Fitzduff, 1991; DENI, 1987).

A further consequence of the current supportive climate for community relations work is that it is possible for groups with years of experience in joint work between schools, youth and community projects to refine their approaches and programmes and develop their practice and thinking further. There are a great many such groups including Community Relations in Schools, FRAN (Finaghy, Rosario and Nubia youth clubs), the Crumlin Road Youth Opportunities Project, Protestant and Catholic Encounter, and the Drumcree Faith and Justice Group. In addition, the Charities Evaluation Service (CES) (Northern Ireland) is now available to help groups and reconciliation bodies of this kind to begin to measure the impact of their work.

In the wake of new policy initiatives about community relations some long-established organisations, which have traditionally worked within one only of the major traditions in Northern Ireland, now wish to develop on a wider basis. They have begun to look at their policies and to examine the extent to which their isolation enhances or diminishes local community development and its funding. Difficulties with matters such as poverty, housing and employment are not identified with one section of the community only, even though the two traditions often have differential experiences of such difficulties. If such work remains polarised, it acts against its own central principles. The value of single tradition work is therefore exercising community workers, and it is agreed that there needs to be a more open examination of such issues as the difficulty of involving people in Protestant areas in community work activities (Wright, 1991), or the ways in which play and related activities can be helpful within the community (Wilson, 1992). Another example of a long-established institution which has traditionally related to one side only is the YMCA, and the staff concerned have developed new staff roles and new programmes about community relations. The recent inter-church Youth Link body is another example of such work as is the recent appointment of staff by the Conference of Major Religious Superiors to assist community relations work.

The main Christian churches in Northern Ireland have also been the subject of criticism both from within, in the form of Irish Council of Churches documents, evangelical responses and Catholic critique; and from without, in particular by a research project from the Centre for the Study of Conflict which examines their contribution to community understanding (Morrow et al., 1991). In addition, the Conference of Major Religious Superiors is also undertaking a review of the work of Catholic orders in Northern Ireland (Greer and Wilson, 1993).

The Northern Ireland Youth Forum was established to give young people opportunities to develop political awareness and skills of debate. It was modelled along the district council boundaries and it was hoped that it might assist debate among young people and secure their greater involvement in youth affairs. Under the recent policy changes this organisation was enabled to develop a more active programme of community relations work and this was proposed by their mixed tradition membership.

A more recent feature has been the reconsideration of the training associated with cross-community work, sectarianism, prejudice and discrimination given to teachers (Smith and Robinson, 1992), youth workers (Youth Committee for Northern Ireland, 1989) and social workers. A number of models for courses on these have been developed in pilot form and the training of youth and community workers and social work training at the University of Ulster has been reorientated to address this challenge.

The Community Relations Council encourages trainers to identify training needs, and an ad hoc group is currently exploring the need for certification of the courses run by community relations trainers. These are very wide-ranging and include: teacher days and residential courses for secondary and primary teachers (under the auspices of local education boards and the Department of Education); the Northern Ireland Curriculum Council's work with history teachers; the Quaker Peace Education Group; and joint work between the two Belfast teacher training colleges. In a society where the segregation of education reflects the segregation of society, this inevitably leads to mixed feelings when the divisions of society are alluded to in a training programme. The challenge is to facilitate in-service training in a way that is relevant, engaging and reduces stress rather than adds to it.

REVIEW AND CONCLUSION

Community relations work has many levels and dimensions. In associated meetings people experience new relationships with others from different and often opposed traditions; they seek new ways of working with one another that become established in regular joint use of resources such as buildings and transport; they share insights across traditions on such disparate matters as housing designs, fund-raising, the needs of children, the creation of jobs and much more; they work together for changes in legislation and social policy such as the need for clearer systems for the administration of the police complaints procedures. All such activities are characterised by people from different traditions meeting together and breaking old, established patterns of cultural separation and distance. These are one layer of active mediation and conciliation in day to day living.

A central difficulty is to find ways to acknowledge the hurt people feel when they are with people from the other tradition. At the base of this difficulty is the experience of living in fear of 'the other, sharing the same place'. Often people from both sides speak about wishing to change and about being prepared to change 'as long as the other side move first'. Another important cause is the unwillingness to discuss the issues openly, or, at best, an expression of openness that is conditional.

One of the clichés about life in Northern Ireland is that 'people have carried on as normal'. The newspaper image of the mother shepherding her pram through a riot is a well-known example. This cliché is often a denial of the effect of the conflict on individual lives, and the denial has a legacy: on the one hand people are yearning to share their story; and on the other hand, even when it is no longer too painful to tell, it is often too painful to hear. People talk about the danger of expressing emotions when the more real danger is that the emotions will be acted out, with violence and killing taking the place of meeting together, dialogue and healing.

Historically many voluntary agencies in Northern Ireland were formed to represent the needs of one tradition only, often for understandable reasons at that time; or they grew out of old relationships which predated partition. These have been replaced by new attempts to structure the experiences of people in joint projects in ways which move them out of the old majority–minority politics which so dominates life here. In such a cross-community group the organisation is usually managed by a committee with representatives from both traditions and it is likely that this experience of joint work is new to most participants. Examples of this are within the management of the integrated schools and the cross-community arrangements between schools.

Working as equals with people from other traditions contrasts with most other experiences in a divided society. Where it works well, people move out from their previous experience of being a majority or a minority into a new structure with new possibilities, and show that it is possible for people from different traditions to manage community organisations together and so become an educational resource on which other transcending structures may be developed.

Northern Ireland has a population of 1.5 million, and over 3000 people have died as a result of the conflict during the past 25 years. Throughout this time there have been events which have shocked and stunned the population of the province; there have been hopes that these traumatic events might become turning-points. The idea has been expressed that a particlar event is so gross in its obscenity, that even those who created it would stop in their tracks and think again.

In a divided society where people are being killed for their beliefs or for being in the wrong place at the wrong time, there is an added edge to the work of reconciliation and mediation agencies. In 1968 there was a small number of organisations within a fairly traditional peace movement, with one or two innovative and prescient institutions such as Corrymeela. In contrast, in 1993 there are over 70 peace and reconciliation groups listed in *A Guide to Peace and Reconciliation Groups* published by the Northern Ireland Community Relations Council. Conferences and exhibitions continue but there is now an emphasis on training, on conflict resolution models, on mediation as a process and on the delivery of community relations and conflict resolution within the education system and the youth service. Statutory organisations have taken a proactive role in the delivery of community relations. For example, one of the objectives outlined in the *Policy for Youth Service in Northern Ireland* (Department of Education, Northern Ireland, 1987) is, 'to promote greater understanding of a society with diverse traditions by engaging where at all possible in programmes where there is a strong cross-community involvement'.

Since the early 1970s the government had taken an active interest in community relations, and this has had spin-offs in terms of alternative ways of resolving disputes, such as mediation. In 1985 the

Fellowship of Reconciliation organised a one-day mediation conference 'to consider the relevance of mediation techniques and their application in Northern Ireland'. An experimental project entitled 'Conflict and Change' is being piloted at one of the prisons at the moment, using among other programmes those of Alternatives to Violence Project (AVP) and the National Coalition Building Institute (NCBI). The establishment of the Northern Ireland Conflict and Mediation Association (NICMA), which subsequently became the Conflict Mediation Network illustrates the increasing need for work of this kind.

In 1993 more and more voluntary and statutory agencies are taking seriously the need to have definite policies regarding anti-sectarianism, fair employment and equal opportunities. Reconciliation and mediation agencies have received government funding for some time, and are encouraged to carry out evaluations of their work. The continuing climate of dialogue is essential in order that traumatic effects of individual atrocities do not either raise expectations of 'turning points', or dash hopes with predictions of outright civil war. The role of mediation projects and reconciliation agencies is to build a culture of dialogue in a divided society where the pull is to split into exclusive 'tribes' at times of crisis.

In the recent experiences of escalating 'tit for tat' murders in October 1993 in Belfast on the Shankill Road, Kennedy Way and in Greysteel a number of commentators have remarked that, while such violence would have served to split communities in the 1970s, it would not be so powerful now. There is little space for mediation and reconciliation in a divided society, it has to evolve and grow out of people meeting and finding new ways to structure their relationships in ways which act as alternatives and contrasts to many of the cultural models of separation and apartness. Out of such meetings and relationships new realities can grow.

REFERENCES

Bailey, S. D. (1988) *Human Rights and Responsibilities in Britain and Ireland, A Christian Perspective*. London, Macmillan.

Bowman, D. and L. Shivers (1984) *More than the Troubles*. Philadelphia, New Society Publishers.

Central Community Relations Unit (CCRU) (1992) *Race Relations in Northern Ireland*. Belfast.

Committee on the Administration of Justice (CAJ) (1985) *Ways of Protecting Minority Rights in Northern Ireland*, Pamphlet 7. Belfast.

Committee on the Administration of Justice (CAJ) (1988) *Police Accountability in Northern Ireland*, Pamphlet 11. Belfast.

Department of Education for Northern Ireland (DENI) (1987) *The Cross Community Contact Scheme*. Bangor, NI.

Dillenberger, K. (1992) *Violent Bereavement: Widows in Northern Ireland*. Aldershot, Avebury Press.

Fitzduff, M. (1991) *A Typology of Community Relations Work and Contextual Necessities*. Belfast, Northern Ireland Community Relations Council.

Frazer, H. and M. Fitzduff (1986) *Improving Community Relations, Paper for the Standing Advisory Commission on Human Rights (SACHR)*. Belfast.

Gallagher, E. and E. Worrall (1982) *Christians In Ulster, 1968-80*. Oxford, Oxford University Press.

Gibson, F., G. Michael and D. A. Wilson (1993) *Discrimination in Social Work in Northern Ireland*. Coleraine, University of Ulster.

Greer, J. and D. A. Wilson (1993) *Ways Forward for Religious in Northern Ireland, A Report to the Conference of Major Religious Superiors*. Dublin.

Griffiths, H. (1974) *Community Development in Northern Ireland*. Coleraine, University of Ulster.

Inter Church Group on Faith and Politics (1989) *Living the Kingdom*. Belfast.

Kaptein, R., D. Morrow, D. A. Wilson and F. Wright (1990) *Finding Ways Together*. Belfast, Corrymeela Press.

Knox, C., J. Hughes, D. Birrell and S. McCready (1994) *Community Relations and Local Government*. Coleraine, Centre for the Study of Conflict.

McCartney, C. (1985) 'Human Rights Education' in *Annual Report, Standing Advisory Commission for Human Rights*. London, HMSO.

McCreary, A., (1981) *Profiles of Hope*. Belfast, Christian Journals.

Morrow, D. et al. (1991) *The Churches and Inter-Community Relationships*. Coleraine, Centre for the Study of Conflict, University of Ulster.

Morrow, D. and D. A. Wilson (1993) *Three into Two Won't Go, From Mediation to New Relationships in Northern Ireland*. Washington, DC: National Institute for Dispute Resolution.

Northern Ireland Community Relations Council (1993) 'Lessons from Anti-Racism'. *Trainers Journal*, 3 Belfast.

Pollak, A., ed. (1993) *A Citizens Inquiry: The Opsahl Report on Northern Ireland*, Dublin, Lilliput Press; Belfast, Initiative 92.

Rea, D., ed. (1982) *Political Co-operation in Divided Societies*. Dublin, Gill and Macmillan.

Richardson, N. (1992a) *Where did EMU come from?* Coleraine, Centre for the Study of Conflict, University of Ulster.

Richardson, N. (1992b) *EMU in Transition*. Coleraine, Centre for the Study of Conflict, University of Ulster.

Smith, A. and A. Robinson (1992) *Education for Mutual Understanding: Perceptions and Policy*. Coleraine, Centre for the Study of Conflict, University of Ulster.

Wilson, D. A. (1986) *Innovation in Reconciliation*. London, Charitable Trust Administrators Group.

Wilson, D. A. (1992) *Play and Community Understanding*. Belfast, Playboard Northern Ireland.

Wright, F. (1991) 'Culture, Identity and The Protestant Community' in *Community Work in Protestant Areas*. Belfast.

Wright, F. (1993) *Integrated Education and New Beginnings in Northern Ireland*. Belfast, Corrymeela Press.

Youth Committee for Northern Ireland (1989) *Initial Proposals for the Promotion of Greater Community Understanding*. Belfast, Community Relations Working Group.

Youth Council for Northern Ireland (1991) *Community Relations in the Youth Service*. Belfast.

Part Five
Sources of
Information

16 Sources of Information: Books, Research and Data

Seamus Dunn, Ciarán Ó Maoláin and Sally McClean

This chapter is in three main parts. The first looks at the literature on the Northern Ireland conflict since about 1989 and concentrates on books and booklets. The second describes sources of information about research using three subheadings: registers and bibliographies; resource centres such as libraries and archives; and information services. The third part outlines the sources of quantitative or statistical data, and considers government sources, general and specialised surveys both national and local, and socio-demographic and economic data which may relate to the conflict.

BOOKS

The current conflict in Northern Ireland began in 1968, and since then has generated a very extensive literature. John Whyte (1990) estimated the total number of items as approaching 7000 and suggested that it was 'quite possible that, in proportion to size, Northern Ireland is the most researched area on earth'. There is no evidence that the deluge of material has decreased since that time, and the most recent register of research (Ó Maoláin, 1993) contained a total of 605 entries, indicating that much more material is in prospect. Of course the quantity of writing is no guide to quality and it would be fair to say that a proportion of what has been produced is ephemeral at best.

It would be impossible in one section of a book chapter to do very much about charting a path through this quantity of material, so some limits have been set. To begin with the material published up to about 1989 has been dealt with in a comprehensive and analytical manner in Whyte's excellent book, which could be described as a sustained commentary on and analysis of the whole range of serious academic literature. John Darby's book *Background to the Conflict*

(1983) also contains a valuable chapter on sources. For this reason, almost nothing referred to in Whyte or Darby is referred to again here, and the reader is recommended to go to these two books for information about earlier work. In addition it was felt to be impossible to do justice to the periodical and ephemeral literature, and so it was decided to deal only with books and booklets. It is of course recognised that, by leaving out periodical material, some significant and important contributions are not being dealt with. However, even with these limitations, a total of approximately one hundred books and booklets are referred to in the section that follows.

The basic intention, however, remains modest. It is to guide readers in their selection from the *most recent* literature related to the conflict, especially the literature in book form. It makes no claim to be comprehensive and has little space for any very extensive critical analysis. Because there is so much material it has been necessary to deal with it under relatively general headings to avoid producing an incoherent listing of unrelated items. On occasions this leads to slightly artificial assignments.

History

The writing of history is a controversial matter, especially in a contested society, and the history of Northern Ireland is no exception. Prior to the partition of Ireland in 1920 Northern Ireland was written about in the context of Ireland as a whole, and rarely received any great prominence. The recent much-praised book by Foster (1988) is no exception. However Jonathan Bardon's magisterial (and very long) survey of the history of Ulster (Bardon, 1992) tells the story in a comprehensive and readable way and is likely to be the standard text for some time. If this is thought to be too long, then shorter, if slightly out-of-date, histories have been written by Buckland (1981) and Harkness (1983). The events leading up to the outbreak of violence in 1968 are well described by Bob Purdie (1990) and, in relation to more recent events, Gaffikin and Morrissey (1990) make a clear analysis of the impact and conse-quences of Thatcherism on political, social and economic life in Northern Ireland.

The particular, and in some ways central, episode of the hunger strikes has been described and analysed with great, if depressing, insight and care by O'Malley (1990b) and Clarke (1987) has also made a contribution to our understanding of this painful episode. And, in some senses a contrast, there is a new edition of Eamonn McCann's stimulating description of the origins of the conflict from a Derry perspective (first published in 1974) which continues to provide witty and lively reading (McCann, 1993).

A carefully written and most useful reference book in the form of a detailed and clear chronological guide to the last 25 years – since the conflict began in 1968 – has been produced by Bew and Gillespie (1993). This adds to and brings up to date earlier chronologies by Deutsch and Magowan (1973, 1974, 1975), and Hall (1988). In addition Rolston (1993) has produced a useful index to the magazine *Fortnight*, the best and most regular – although not fortnightly! – journal on current affairs in Northern Ireland. The book has a comprehensive index showing over 55 categories, 2500 entries and a subject and author index, and will serve to guide readers to reporting and analysis of issues as they happened. Finally, the political directory produced by W. D. Flackes and Sydney Elliott in 1989 is still a most useful compendium, with a new edition due shortly.

Politics

Perhaps not surprisingly political scientists continue to provide a rich variety of analyses and modellings of the Irish condition. For a clear survey of the British government's legislative and institutional policies in Northern Ireland during the past twenty years, the carefully compiled work by Cunningham (1991) is indispensable – if not always lively – reading. Con O'Leary et al. (1988) describe in some detail the workings and achievements of the Northern Ireland Assembly, one example of a local elected chamber, and O'Malley (1990a) continues his careful analyses of internal Northern Ireland political perceptions, especially among politicians, and, although deeply pessimistic, has the virtue of being aware of the complexity and multi-dimensionality of the many issues. The extent to which Northern Ireland's experience of violence is unique is discussed in a book of comparative papers edited by Darby and his colleagues (1990), indicating perhaps where the debate about inter-group conflict must go in the future.

Marxist interpretations of Northern Ireland have shown little ability to agree. Patterson's analyses represent what John Whyte calls one of the revisionist schools, and his books have had a considerable influence on historical and political thinking about the North. His

1989 book *The Politics of Illusion* represents the most recent exposition of his views, which are clearly continuing to develop. In a similar area, the collection of papers by Hutton and Stewart (1991) deals with Marxist interpretations and provides an arena where some of the various ideologies can compete. In some contrast, the book edited by Roche and Barton (1991) might be thought of as unionist revisionism; it is about the need for a more rigorous analysis of unionism in Ireland and to this end it sets out to examine some of the myths and undeciphered assumptions about unionism and its history.

Brendan O'Leary and his colleagues, working mainly from a base in England, have produced a series of thoughtful and perceptive books and papers which take a constructivist approach based on what Whyte calls the 'internal conflict' interpretation. First in 1990 McGarry and O'Leary develop the refreshing – if much opposed – view that it is possible to find a solution to the Northern Ireland problem and that earlier apostles of pessimism such as Richard Rose (who argued that there was no solution) were wrong. In a later work O'Leary and McGarry (1992) look at the sequence of political initiatives and developments since 1969 and analyse why successive British governments have failed to produce a settlement acceptable to all. In a more recent work O'Leary and others (1993) provide a carefully delineated constitutional model which they feel would unblock the stalemate in the North. It proposes that there should be a sharing of Northern Ireland's sovereignty between Great Britain, Ireland and Northern Ireland in a way that both shares power and authority and provides protection for minority cultures and aspirations.

The constitutional issue was at the centre of the controversies surrounding the Anglo-Irish agreement. The result was an extended public debate that seemed incapable of any final definition. The book by Hadden and Boyle (1989) gives a clear and detailed analysis of the document itself for those wishing to follow the arguments. Still on the constitutional question, Hadfield (1993) provides a forum for political scientists and lawyers to exchange ideas, look closely at a range of constitutional ideas and reflect on forms of government. This leads to chapters on such matters as policing, the army, the judiciary and the electoral system, all written with a view to understanding how such institutions function and how they impact on the social and structural life of Northern Ireland. Hill and Marsh (1993) look at the history of Irish democratic institutions both North and South, and, although the majority of the material is related to the South, the contrast allows for some lively reflection on the North.

The interesting question of the inability of the relatively strong and lively trade union movement within Northern Ireland to make a political and constitutional impact on Northern Irish life is examined by Cradden (1993). Munck (1992) takes a clear-eyed and analytical look at the economics of Irish life, North and South, and tries to understand the consequences of a number of possible future scenarios. The degree and quality of contact between organisations and institutions, North and South, is also little researched and a valuable first step on this has been taken by Murray and O'Neill (1991).

A Citizens' Inquiry: The Opsahl Report on Northern Ireland (Pollak, 1993) provides a unique and endlessly stimulating series of reports and analyses of all aspects of Northern Irish life. To quote from the document itself, it is based on 'what around 3,000 people in 554 written and taped submissions said to Initiative '92's citizens' inquiry into ways forward for Northern Ireland, and the reflections on those submissions by seven eminent observers'.

The last book, edited by Keogh and Haltzel (1993), contains a set of papers delivered at a conference in the USA. These provide a disparate set of analyses and understandings of both the history and the politics of Northern Ireland without any very obvious central theme.

Law

A relatively diverse and small collection of material can be found under this heading. First Brice Dickson has produced a second edition (1993) of his invaluable survey and practical handbook on rights and civil liberties in Northern Ireland covering everything from education to prisoners to social security. The justification for such a book might be found in the set of illuminating if depressing papers edited by Jennings (1990) on abuses of civil liberties in Northern Ireland with regard to such issues as plastic bullets, powers of arrest and the alleged excessive use of lethal force by the police and army, usually referred to somewhat misleadingly as 'shoot-to-kill'. In addition, some of the chapters in Hadfield (1993) relate to security and legal issues. The question of policing in Northern Ireland is always at least a subtext in much discussion of the criminal justice system, although surprisingly little creative thinking is carried out in this area. Brewer's 1991 book on the RUC (with Kathleen Magee) remains the only ethnographic study of the police in Northern Ireland although other studies are in the offing. Hogan and Walker's 1990 book is a detailed and detached, if essentially conservative, compilation of factual material about the available legislation in respect of what they term 'political violence'.

The question of the use and the more general impact of special legislation aimed at such violence is examined by Hillyard (1993) with respect to the Prevention of Terrorism Acts. He looks in particular at the experience of Irish people living in Great Britain and provides considerable evidence about the abuse of such legislation.

General Social Issues

The establishment of the Northern Ireland Social Attitudes Survey in 1989 has meant that there now exists a three-year pool of attitude data with respect to a wide range of matters, which is available to scholars for analysis. For each of its three years in existence Stringer and Robinson (1991, 1992, 1993) have published a set of invaluable papers looking at a variety of these issues. Another social issue of some consequence is sport in Northern Ireland, and John Sugden and his colleagues have pioneered this work with respect to its community and general impact. A number of works have now been published (Sugden and Bairner, 1993; Sugden and Harvie, 1994). The effects of the deaths caused by the violence are also in need of more careful examination, and Karola Dillenburger (1993) has made an important contribution to this with a careful study of the lives of a number of women whose husbands or companions have been killed.

Employment/Unemployment

For many in Northern Ireland this is the most contentious issue of all and the one on which writers and commentators are most likely to disagree. Tony Gallagher (1991) produced a carefully organised set of tables and data illustrating Catholic/Protestant differences. Smith and Chambers (1991) and Cormack and Osborne (1991) have produced books of data and analysis which continue the debate described with some care in Whyte. McCormack and O'Hara (1990) write about the history of employment legislation and its relative lack of success, and about the attempts to deal with the differentials, especially about the debates leading up to the establishment of the 1989 legislation. Finally Rubenstein (1993) has described the results of the first years of the Fair Employment Tribunal which he perceives as efficient and unproblematic.

Aside from the statistics, the experience of being unemployed is difficult to represent and understand and the ethnographic study by

Howe (1990) is therefore of considerable value, especially for the light that it shines on the differing cultural experiences of unemployment as between Catholics and Protestants. Finally, McLaughlin (1993) has edited a set of conference papers examining the experience of being unemployed, both North and South.

Religion

For many commentators the issue of religion is central to any understanding of Northern Ireland. For a time much of the relevant literature tended to be descriptive and anecdotal, and there is an increasing range of biographies and personal statements, which are useful as background but are not included here.

The most interesting recent study is by Morrow and his colleagues (1991) and is based on research and close analyses of the two communities. It makes clear the impact of the conflict and the violence on the institutional churches, and their debilitating effect on the coherence and unity of many of them. It also points to the ambivalence created for many church-people by the inescapable closeness of the religious and political worlds of Northern Ireland. Fulton (1990) contributes to the debate with some discussion of the role of religion and of the difficulties that emerge when politics and religion become entangled. The churches and their leaders have publicly committed themselves to improving cross-community relations, and Lee (1990) has edited the proceedings of a conference and discussion attended by representatives of many of the churches on the subject of community relations, and the contribution which Christians might make.

With regard to Protestants, Bruce's study (1992) of the Protestant paramilitaries provides insights, if not into religion, then into the associated cultures on the Protestant side. A most interesting chapter by Boal and his colleagues in Roche and Barton (1991) makes clear the range of attitudes and positions among people lumped together under the single title of 'Protestant'. The dimensions of difference include religion, obviously, but also political and social attitudes.

On the Catholic side O'Connor's recent book (1993) on attitudes and perceptions among a relatively small sample of Catholics is full of insights and understandings, and occasional surprises, in relation to the current state of mind of the Catholic population.

Finally, McElroy (1991) looks at the history of the Catholic Church's response to the conflict, examines the attitudes of the clergy and attempts to understand the overall ethos of Catholic life in the North.

Education

A good deal of the recent work on education has been about the contribution that schools and the educational system might make to resolving community differences and about investigating inequities between the two communities. A summative report on Catholic–Protestant differentials in education (Gallagher, 1989) was published by the Centre for the Study of Conflict as part of a series of 'Majority–Minority' studies, and this allows for direct comparisons with respect to a number of variables. During the late 1980s the Standing Advisory Commission on Human Rights (SACHR) commissioned a series of researches on human rights aspects of educational provision in the province. The results were published originally in annual reports of SACHR (1989, 1990, 1991 and 1992) and they represent a rich, varied and unique set of accounts of many aspects of educational provision, funding, enrolment and management. A short, up-to-date survey of the history of education in Northern Ireland (Dunn, 1990) was also commissioned in order to provide a background to the rest of the work. In addition a book (*After the Reforms*) containing material arising out of this work was edited in 1993 by Osborne and his colleagues.

The new 'planned' integrated schools have begun to attract description (Wilson and Dunn, 1989) research and written analyses. The process of creating an integrated school normally starts at ground level (or within the community), with parents as the principal movers, and this produces a complex and relatively unprecedented form of parent–teacher interaction. A number of recent studies of this issue have been published (Morgan et al., 1992; Agnew et al., 1992), and a wide-ranging set of essays on the integrated schools has been edited by Moffat (1993).

The majority of pupils, however, continue to be educated in segregated schools, and for them the curricular initiatives, Education for Mutual Understanding (EMU) and Cultural Heritage and the school-contact programme are of some importance (Dunn and Smith, 1989; Smith and Dunn, 1990). Smith and Robinson (1992) have been trying to understand how these initiatives are perceived by the educational community in general, and to establish approaches to the evaluation of their impact that are subtle and valid. Finally, Burgess (1993) examines the moral context of education in Northern Ireland and analyses what he perceives to be the moral ambiguity of the churches.

One of the most interesting side-effects of the violence has been the development of a considerable industry associated with promoting children's holidays as a way of giving them respite from the violence. Recently a careful and insightful evaluation of one of these schemes has been produced by Smith and Murray (1993).

Paramilitaries

Perhaps not surprisingly the literature on the paramilitaries remains scanty and variable in quality, with a disproportionate interest in the republican side. One of the most recent of these is the book by O'Brien (1993), which is based on carefully accumulated field data and so bears careful reading. Bowyer Bell has also published on the subject again recently (1993), as have Alexander and O'Day (1991) who continue to gather papers which take a non-simplistic approach to the definition and understanding of the contested word 'terrorism'. The first substantial study of the INLA (Holland and McDonald, 1994) should help us to be clearer about how that group fits into the overall picture. Conor Foley (1992) has also produced a book on the IRA from an historical perspective, with a small final section devoted to the current conflict.

On the Protestant/unionist side, the book by Steve Bruce (1992) on Protestant paramilitaries breaks new ground and indicates where further work may need to be done. The book by McAuley (1994) is about the politics and ideology of a section of Belfast's Protestant working class, rather than simply the paramilitaries, but it nevertheless contains a good deal of useful information about the world in which the Protestant paramilitaries live.

Finally Raymond Murray has written a book on the SAS and related undercover security operations in Ireland (1990) which describes in some detail the work of the British secret forces.

Women

The literature on women and the conflict is relatively scant, in part because of the tension between the need to take up a position on the conflict itself, and the sometimes opposed issues of women's rights and needs. Morgan and Fraser have recently completed a report (1994) on women in rural communities, where there remain highly traditional social structures and important and influential religious roots. In their report they develop some complex analyses of the positions which women find themselves in and, in particular, the central importance for women of religion in defining their position in the home and family. Similar work in the urban communities indicates that these roots in traditional views of society prevail there also (Davies and McLaughlin, 1991; Rooney, 1993). The political violence also impacts on the high levels of domestic violence in the form of direct reaction to external events. These are sometimes justified within communities as a response to stress, and this also reflects the traditional roots of the discourse (McWilliams and McKernan, 1993). However, much more work needs to be done on the various interfaces between feminism and women's rights, political violence and concepts such as nationalism.

Cultural Issues

Although the central planks of the government's approach to the social and community issues relate to community relations and equity, there has also been a considerable emphasis placed on cultural issues. A series of conferences was held by the Cultural Traditions Group in the late eighties and early nineties and the proceedings of these have been edited by Crozier (1989, 1990, 1991). The same editor has combined with Sanders to produce a directory of cultural traditions organisations and institutions. In addition there have been a number of spin-off conferences including one on traditional music (McNamee, 1992), one on broadcasting and culture (McLoone, 1991) and one on the concept of 'discriminations' (Cullen, 1992). The idea of a cultural traditions group and of related conferences was exported to the Republic of Ireland, and one volume of proceedings has been edited by E. Longley (1991). Rolston (1991b, 1992) has also published the fruits of many years of study of the wall-paintings and murals from both sides in Northern Ireland and the resulting books make fascinating reading and viewing. Finally, a classic contribution to the understanding of cultural and community differences in Northern Ireland, originally published in 1973, has recently been republished (Evans, 1992). There is of course an extensive literature on literary culture and on what might be called 'high' culture. No attempt has been made to deal with this here.

Media

This is, surprisingly, one of the most neglected areas of study in Northern Ireland and there is little sign that this is going to change: for example, the words media and television do not appear in John Whyte's index. Curtis (1984) has carried out pioneering work on the attitudes and responses of the British media and Rolston (1991a) has made a start on the issues with a set of essays which, while containing some gaps, helps to establish the agenda. Martin McLoone (1991) has also edited the proceedings of a conference on Culture, Identity and Broadcasting in Ireland which reflects a wide range of opinions on some aspects of the issue.

INFORMATION ON RESEARCH

The sheer quantity of material published makes it difficult to identify exactly what is relevant to any particular research field or to know how to gain access to it. The problems include the variety of research exercises, and the number of individuals and institutions conducting research. Projects range from postgraduate theses, to broad socio-economic surveys by public bodies, to small local research efforts by non-governmental organisations. There is also the fact that a great deal of the research, even when completed, remains unpublished in the conventional sense; for example, theses and dissertations are usually accessible only through university libraries, and reports by voluntary groups are rarely circulated to libraries or reviewed in the media, and so do not enter the academic system. With these constraints, it is very likely that much work of value fails to reach its potential in terms of readership or impact on policy; it is also probable that some work is duplicated, that the potential synergies between separate projects in related fields are not recognised, and that some urgent research is not commissioned because funding agencies lack a clear picture of what the gaps in knowledge actually are.

Three ways of obtaining an overview of, and access to, the current research are publications such as registers and bibliographies;

resource centres such as libraries and archives; and information services.

Publications

Registers of research provide basic information on who is doing what, and where; some go into more detail, for example by providing abstracts of the research brief or of the findings, and some give details of funding. The compilation of these registers is expensive and time-consuming, and because of this only four registers have covered research on Northern Ireland society or the Northern Ireland conflict since the outbreak of the present troubles.

In 1972, Darby was asked by the Northern Ireland Community Relations Commission to produce the *Register of Research into the Irish Conflict* (Darby, 1972). This was a 33-page booklet listing a total of 175 projects, mainly, as the title suggests, concentrating on the violence and on community divisions. In 1981 Darby, by then Director of the Centre for the Study of Conflict at Coleraine, produced (with others) a similar booklet (Darby et al., 1981); this was followed in 1983 by a much more substantial volume funded by the Social Science Research Council, *A Register of Economic and Social Research on Northern Ireland 1980–83*, which as well as the violence-related work included socio-economic research relevant to an understanding of the background to the conflict. The 1983 work, with 517 entries, took in projects outside Northern Ireland and had an introductory essay outlining the state of research in each of the social science disciplines (Darby et al., 1983).

Also in 1983, Queen's University Belfast published *A Social Sciences Bibliography of Northern Ireland 1945–1983*, a compilation by Rolston and others, with 5482 entries for books, articles and other publications since 1945 on social science topics relating to Northern Ireland since 1921 (Rolston et al., 1983).

Over the following years it became increasingly hard for researchers, and users of research, to keep track of the publishing output and, in the case of government, to locate the pools of knowledge and expertise needed to evaluate and influence policy in what was a very difficult and sensitive political situation.

A new register was eventually commissioned from the Centre for the Study of Conflict by the Central Community Relations Unit, CCRU, and the Policy Planning and Research Unit, PPRU. These two units are especially concerned with monitoring and fine-tuning the way in which public expenditure and policy impact on the material well-being of, and the relations between, the two communities. The result was the publication of the 1993 edition of the *Register of Research on Northern Ireland* (Ó Maoláin, 1993). Although this lists a total of 605 projects, it makes no claim to be comprehensive. As in the 1983 book, there is an introductory essay (in this case by Pádraig O'Malley) and the projects are grouped under broad subject headings (conflict, economics, health and welfare, and so on).

While the 1993 register was in production, the World Bibliographical Series published by Clio Press (and in the USA by ABC-Clio) brought out a 640-page regional bibliography (Shannon, 1991); this overlaps to some extent with both Whyte and Rolston, but is less analytical than the former, and more descriptive than the latter.

There are a few specialist Northern Ireland registers and bibliographies on specific topics such as nursing and health care, or on specific regions. Northern Ireland is also covered in numerous bibliographies on Irish, British and international themes; for example, there are some 400 Northern Ireland items of varying relevance and importance in Amos Lakos's *International Terrorism: a Bibliography* (Lakos, 1986). In the field of education, 378 items are listed, with an extensive commentary, in Dunn's *Education and the Conflict in Northern Ireland* (Dunn, 1986).

Mention must also be made of several publications which cover wider areas, but are also useful in tracking down research on Northern Ireland. The Economic and Social Research Institute in Dublin (ESRI, 1988) produces, at irregular intervals, a *Register of Current Social Research in Ireland* (last produced in 1988, with a new one due in 1994); this provides brief entries for the title, location and staffing of research projects in Irish universities, colleges, institutes, research agencies and government departments, North and South.

Indexing and abstracting services which cover Northern Ireland research and publications with varying degrees of efficiency include, in the Longman/British Library *Current Research in Britain* series, *The Humanities* and *Social Sciences*; the *British Humanities Index*, covering some 400 journals, and the *US Humanities Index* which has limited UK coverage; the excellent *Aslib Index to Theses*, which is less useful for the Republic since many entries appear without abstracts; and three Institute for Scientific Information publications, all also available through the BIDS (Bath Information Data Service) on-line system: the *Social Sciences Citation Index*, the *Arts and Humanities Index* and *Current Contents*, together covering over 5000 journals.

Subject specialists will know of, and others can take libraries' guidance on, the many historical, sociological, psychological and other abstracting and indexing journals.

Libraries, Archives and Museums

Both the region's universities have good libraries which are dispersed between several sites. The University of Ulster has two libraries at Coleraine (with some specialist collections relating to Northern Ireland), one at Jordanstown, one in Derry at Magee College, and a small one in central Belfast for Art and Design. All are covered by a single computerised catalogue, although some holdings are located by the Library of Congress classification and the rest by the Dewey Decimal System. *Bona fide* scholars from outside the University may consult and photocopy material. Theses and dissertations are held in the libraries of the campuses where they were submitted, and are catalogued normally; however some are subject to temporary embargoes on access, of up to five years.

Most of Queen's University's holdings are in the Main Library, which also houses the University Archive, but theses and some other relevant materials are in the Science Library. The Institute of Clinical Science has the Health and Social Science Library, and specialist collections are held by some departments and faculties. Most of Queen's catalogue is card-index, rather than computerised; the opposite is the case in the University of Ulster. Both universities have very extensive holdings of official (HMSO) and European Union publications, and selective holdings of Northern Ireland Departmental and other public-sector publications.

Specialist libraries are in the teacher training colleges (Stranmillis and St Mary's), the agricultural colleges, the Union Theological College and other educational and vocational training institutions.

One of the oldest libraries in the region is also one of the best, and in terms of research on local political affairs is perhaps the most important. The Linen Hall Library opposite the City Hall in the centre of Belfast is a private institution dating from 1788. It is renowned for its collection of books of Irish interest, and above all for its Political Collection, which includes virtually every magazine, leaflet, position paper and manifesto published by local political parties, pressure groups and paramilitary organisations since the 1960s. The collection is available for purchase on microfiche. Non-members may consult the holdings but membership, which is inexpensive, covers a subscription to the *Linen Hall Review*.

The public library service in Northern Ireland is currently provided by the five Education and Library Boards. Researchers are most likely to make use of the Irish or Local Studies services, and these are particularly good in Coleraine (County Hall), Belfast (Belfast Central Library), Armagh (at SELB Headquarters) and Ballynahinch. Many libraries hold runs of the local press, but a virtually complete collection is held in the Newspaper Library, an annexe of Belfast Central.

Official papers may be consulted, normally after 30 years, at the Public Records Office for Northern Ireland. The General Register Office holds birth, marriage and death records.

Church archives of all denominations are only accessible to researchers with some difficulty, but that may change; the Catholic archdiocese of Armagh, for example, is planning to open a new archives building. The Church of Ireland has archives and libraries in St Columb's Cathedral, Derry, and in Belfast; the Presbyterian History Society has an archive at the Church headquarters, and Orange House has archives mainly of interest to historians of the Orange Order.

The Northern Ireland Assembly library at Stormont, which has been kept up to date with books and newspapers, is said to be one of the best in Northern Ireland, but while the Assembly remains suspended only civil servants normally have access to it.

A small Oral History Archive has been assembled by Ronnie Munck and others in the University of Ulster; it concentrates on the civil rights and labour movements, and the early period of the present troubles. Press cuttings archives include those of the Committee on the Administration of Justice (CAJ), concentrating on civil liberties themes, the Community Relations Council and the Business Library in Belfast Central Library, concentrating on business and economics. There are no general indexes to the region's daily press, but the University of Ulster at Jordanstown has a somewhat limited manual index of the *Belfast Telegraph*. (Neither the regional dailies, nor the local weeklies, are particularly receptive to requests for cooperation from researchers.)

The records of the defunct Irish Information Partnership, which compiled factual data including statistics on the troubles, are at present in store, but the Centre for the Study of Conflict hopes to acquire them at some future date; the Centre is also in contact with researchers who have private archives on fatalities and other aspects of the troubles. Reference is made above to a number of chronologies of the troubles (Bew and Gillespie, 1993; Deutsch, 1973, 1974, 1975; Hall, 1988) in book form; ongoing chronologies are published in the indispensable *Fortnight* magazine (see also the index to *Fortnight* produced by Rolston, 1993), in *Just News* (the journal of the CAJ) and in the bulletin of a US pressure group, American Protestants for Truth in Ireland.

Among the region's museums, both the Ulster Museum and the Ulster Folk and Transport Museum have some archival holdings and engage in research; other museums, interpretive centres, visitor centres and so on are of limited value to academics, but some interesting material is at the Tower Museum in Derry, Armagh County Museum in Armagh, and the Ulster-American Folk Park near Omagh.

Turning to journals, *Northern Ireland Research Briefing* is a free quarterly newsletter for the Northern Ireland research community – that is, researchers, academics, and those who commission or make use of research. It is published by the Centre for the Study of Conflict. Other journals giving information on current research and publications include the *Irish Review* (now published by the Institute of Irish Studies at Queen's University); *Causeway*, a new journal on cultural traditions in Ireland, focusing mainly on the North and published by the Community Relations Council; *History Ireland* and *Books Ireland*, both published in Dublin; *Scope*, published by the Northern Ireland Council on Voluntary Action, and the *Linen Hall Review* and *Fortnight* magazine, both mentioned above.

Information Services

We have referred above to the research data published by the various Northern Ireland government departments and agencies. The Northern Ireland Office Information Service, in London and Belfast, will assist researchers with inquiries, as will the Information Offices of each of the main Departments (Agriculture, Economic Development, Education, Environment, Finance and Personnel, and Health and Social Services). In all cases it is best to apply in writing to the appropriate section.

Among public agencies with research functions and information services are, in the economic field, LEDU and the IDB (responsible respectively for promoting small and large businesses), the Northern

Ireland Tourist Board, the Fair Employment Commission and the Equal Opportunities Commission.

It may not be surprising that the criminal justice system is not very open to researchers. Conflict-related publications are mentioned in the first part of this chapter. Access to other RUC statistics and to the data of the court, prison and probation services is limited, in part by valid considerations of security, confidentiality and staff resources, and in part by the culture of secrecy which is endemic in both the British and Irish public services.

The Community Relations Council can provide assistance to researchers, and holds and distributes a range of publications through its Information Centre. Many other voluntary-sector peace and reconciliation groups have libraries, archives or information services, and there is a Peace Education Resources Centre in Belfast, run by an inter-church programme, which holds a vast range of material in that field and is in contact with most Northern Ireland peace groups. It also publishes an annual catalogue of resources for peace education, education for mutual understanding and cultural heritage. The Centre for Research and Documentation, also in Belfast, holds material on Irish social and economic affairs which reflects the Third World experience and orientation of its staff. The Irish Congress of Trade Unions and the Irish Labour History Society provide easier access to material on labour relations than the individual unions, which are not geared to supporting research.

For those in the University of Ulster, or with access to a computer and modem, a resource of ever-increasing value is CWIS, the University's Campus-Wide Information System, which is on the same host system as the library catalogue and which provides several useful data sets including electronic versions of the 1993 *Register* and the 1983 Rolston bibliography.

As a general rule, political parties in the region are not well equipped to deal with outside enquiries; the most efficient in this respect is Sinn Féin, with a monthly newspaper, an international bulletin and a press and information office. Most of the others (the Ulster Unionist Party, the Social Democratic and Labour Party, the Democratic Unionist Party and Alliance being the largest) have internal members' bulletins and occasional policy publications, but they will generally respond to specific written enquiries. The same applies to the minor parties including the Workers' Party, Democratic Left, the Ulster Popular Unionist Party, the Ulster Democratic Party, the Green Party and the Communist Party of Ireland. It is neither easy, nor advisable, for inexperienced researchers to make contact with any of the illegal paramilitary groups such as the IRA, the UDA or the UVF.

There are many local history groups, mostly members of the Federation for Ulster Local Studies based in the Institute of Irish Studies at Queen's University; some local history and genealogy work is done by voluntary bodies such as Irish World, which has offices in many towns and also does some newspaper indexing, and by semi-commercial operations such as the Ulster Historical Foundation and the Ulster Genealogical and Historical Guild.

The European Commission has an information office in Belfast which is mainly geared to providing help to local business-people seeking to export to the other countries of the European Union, and also holds stocks of official publications of the European Union; however both Universities hold EU publications with a particularly extensive collection in Coleraine.

Finally, we will mention the Dissemination of Research project at the Centre for the Study of Conflict. The Centre's Information Officer is employed to make it easier for people to find out about research and to make use of it. There are four aspects to the work; firstly the compilation and maintenance of the *Register of Research*, both for publication and as an on-line database; secondly the production of the *Northern Ireland Research Briefing*; thirdly the organisation of public seminar series, and lastly, responding to written or faxed enquiries about research on any Northern Ireland topic. Researchers who have difficulty locating material or expertise on any topic, having checked the *Register*, are able to use the inquiry service free of charge.

STATISTICS DATA SOURCES

Much of the research carried out in the past into the Northern Ireland conflict has been of a qualitative rather than a quantitative nature. This has partly been due to problems of accessibility of data and partly due to a perception by researchers that such a complex problem necessitates an in-depth qualitative approach rather than a macro-level quantitative approach. However, access to government sources has become increasingly more possible, with the introduction of the Data Protection Act, and there have been various initiatives of the UK Economic and Social Research Council (ESRC) to extend their coverage to include more Northern Ireland sources. While a quantitative approach to the Northern Ireland conflict may not be adequate to illuminate all the intricate details of such a multi-faceted problem, it is nonetheless the case that such an approach may prove a useful means of studying the different aspects of the conflict and provide a framework for integrating micro-level results into a macro-level interpretation.

The collection of data for purposes of government is largely the responsibility of the Northern Ireland Civil Service, rather than the Imperial Civil Service which has responsibility for the rest of the United Kingdom. This has resulted in the past in Northern Ireland being omitted from some national surveys and, even where the coverage includes Northern Ireland, the data are collected separately which means that access must be negotiated separately with the Northern Ireland Civil Service. The government statisticians, while willing to cooperate with researchers and release information for particular projects, have a large number of data-gathering and dissemination exercises to carry out and do not always have time to extract and document specific data-sets for individual use. There are, however, a number of sources of macro-level secondary data published by the Northern Ireland Civil Service which may be of use to the researcher.

The ESRC has supported researchers into the Northern Ireland conflict by implementing a number of initiatives, principally the setting up of the Northern Ireland Regional Research Laboratory. A number of data sets on the conflict are held in the ESRC Data Archive in Essex along with Northern Ireland data collected as regional components of national surveys. The ESRC Data Archive has also facilitated researches by publishing a special issue of its bulletin in September 1992, devoted exclusively to research data on Northern Ireland (ESRC, 1992). This issue provides an excellent introduction to the various sources of Northern Ireland socio-economic data with discussions provided by some of the principal researchers in the various areas.

We will consider the data sources on the Northern Ireland conflict under three headings:

1. data collected by the Northern Ireland Civil Service – both for general purposes of Northern Ireland government and as the Northern Ireland component of national surveys;
2. data collected specifically on the Northern Ireland conflict as part of an ad hoc research exercise;

3.   data collected on socio-demographic and economic variables which relate to aspects of the conflict.

Government Data

Much of the information collected by the Northern Ireland Civil Service for purposes of government is disseminated as macro-level data in the form of tables in various government reports. Some of these, particularly those released by the Northern Ireland Office concerning the conflict, are specific to Northern Ireland, while others appear as a regional part of a more general UK or EU report. The most useful introduction to Northern Ireland data is the *Northern Ireland Annual Abstract of Statistics* which contains summary data on all aspects of society under the headings: Population and Vital Statistics; Households and Individuals; Social Services and Health; Law and Order; Education; Housing; Environment and Climate; Transport and Communications; Tourism; Labour; Earnings and Income; Production Output and Energy; Agriculture, Forestry and Fishing; Regional Accounts; Public Finance; Banking, Insurance and other Financial Institutions.

The section on Law and Order contains various tables on terrorist activities, deaths and injuries and legal proceedings and convictions. The Northern Ireland Office separately publishes the Annual Commentary on the Northern Ireland Crime Statistics which includes more details on the number of offences recorded by the police, court proceedings, sentencing, prison populations and international comparisons. Additional conflict data are published in the Royal Ulster Constabulary (RUC) *Chief Constable's Annual Report* which gives a breakdown of terrorist related crime, the reports of the Independent Commission for Police Complaints for Northern Ireland and the biennial Report of the Police Authority for Northern Ireland.

Northern Ireland data are also included in a number of UK and international statistical sources, principally *Social Trends* which provides a comprehensive overview of UK statistical series, *Regional Trends* and *Council of Europe Prison Statistics*. In addition, a number of the large-scale UK social surveys include coverage of Northern Ireland, principally the Continuous Household Survey (CHS), the Northern Ireland Family Expenditure Survey (FES), the Labour Force Survey (LFS) and the Northern Ireland Social Attitudes Survey (NISAS). Data from these surveys have been deposited in the ESRC

Data Archive and are therefore available at a micro level for secondary analysis. They provide a useful source of information to make comparisons between Northern Ireland and the rest of the United Kingdom on the basis of various social, demographic and economic indicators.

Ad hoc surveys are also carried out by the Northern Ireland Civil Service from time to time: either as part of a larger UK ad hoc study – for example the Survey of Disability which extended the main UK data collection exercise to cover needs for Northern Ireland more fully; or to examine issues of particular concern in Northern Ireland – for example, the incidence of seat-belt usage for the Road Casualty Reduction Unit of the Department of the Environment. The Northern Ireland Office Statistics Branch also produces a Statistics and Research Bulletin series which reports on findings from other various data sources available to them.

A number of research projects have collected data as a means of investigating specific aspects of the Northern Ireland conflict. Although much of this information is not available in the public domain, a number of studies have deposited their data in the ESRC Data Archive and these data are available for secondary analysis.

Related Data Sources

There are a number of areas of social sciences which have carried out research and collected data on matters which may either contribute to the conflict or be directly or indirectly affected by the conflict. In particular, demographic variables may both affect and be affected by the conflict; for example the number of young men in an appropriate age group may affect the intensity of the conflict while the number of migrations may be affected by it. The provision and uptake of health and social services may be an indicator of social deprivation and the general breakdown of the fabric of society, which may in turn both lead to future conflict and be exacerbated by conflict. Similarly housing may serve as an indicator of social deprivation and, as such, bad housing may be seen both to contribute to the conflict and to be a consequence of the conflict. Education has frequently been cited as both a source of division and hence conflict and, through a number of initiatives, as a possible means of reducing the conflict. Labour and economic variables also serve to highlight social deprivation and the effect of conflict on economic prosperity. Thus, economic factors such as unemployment may be seen as an underlying cause of conflict, whereas increasing conflict may have a negative effect on economic prosperity as reflected by various economic indicators. Religion is, of course, closely identified with the Northern Ireland conflict and, as such, data on the religious breakdown of the population is often of interest to the researcher. We discuss data sources under these headings, as follows.

Demographic Sources

The main source of demographic data is the Northern Ireland Census and the various Census Reports which emanate from this. Of particular note are the intercensal estimates, particularly when, as was the case for the 1981 Census, there is a severe problem with under-enumeration. However, under-reporting was not a problem with the 1991 Census, and it is hoped that, for the first time, anonymised individual level samples will be available in the near future. Information on births and marriages, and on deaths (by causes), are available in the Registrar General's annual reports.

Health and Social Services

The National Health Service reports its annual statistics in the Central Services Agency Annual Report; the Northern Ireland Department of Health and Social Services (DHSS) issues *Personal Social Statistics*, and health costs are covered in the *Northern Ireland Commentary on Public Expenditure Plans* and the DHSS *Health Costs Report*. Social security figures are reported in *Northern Ireland Social Security Statistics*. Hospital in-patients and out-patients are reported in DHSS *Hospital Statistics*.

Housing Statistics

The main sources of Northern Ireland macro-level housing data are the *Northern Ireland Census Housing Report*, *Northern Ireland Housing Statistics* and the Northern Ireland Housing Executive's *House Condition Surveys*.

Education Statistics

Most of the publicly available data on education in Northern Ireland is produced by the Department of Education for Northern Ireland (DENI). The major source of such information is the DENI *Basic Education Statistics Data Card*, which provides information on school, pupils and teachers along with basic information on enrolments in tertiary level education. Costings are provided in the *Northern Ireland Commentary on Public Expenditure Plans.* The *School Leavers Survey* provides information on qualifications and destinations of school leavers, while *First Destination of Primary Degree Graduates* does the same for university leavers.

Labour and Economic Data

The major sources of information on labour and economic variables have already been mentioned, namely the *Family Expenditure Survey, Regional Trends* and the *Northern Ireland Labour Force Study.* Of note also are *Economic Trends* (HMSO, monthly), and the *Northern Ireland Census Workforce and Travel to Work* report.

Data on Religion

The major source of information on religion for the Northern Ireland population is the *Northern Ireland Census Religion Report.* A religion trailer question is also included in the *Northern Ireland Labour Force Study.* Unfortunately, however, this information does not form part of the LFS deposition in the ESRC data archive.

REFERENCES

Agnew, U. et al. (1992) *Integrated Education: the Views of Parents.* Belfast, Queen's University, School of Education.

Alexander, Y. and A. O'Day, eds (1991) *The Irish Terrorism Experience.* Aldershot, Dartmouth.

Bardon, J. (1992) *A History of Ulster.* Belfast, Blackstaff Press.

Bew, P. and G. Gillespie (1993) *Northern Ireland: a Chronology of the Troubles 1968–1993.* Dublin, Gill and Macmillan.

Boal, F. et al. (1991) Chapter in *The Northern Ireland Question: Myth and Reality,* ed. by P. J. Roche and B. Barton. Aldershot, Avebury.

Bowyer Bell, J. (1993) *The Irish Troubles: a Generation of Violence.* Dublin, Gill and Macmillan.

Brewer, J. D. with Kathleen Magee (1991) *Inside the RUC.* Oxford, Clarendon Press.

Bruce, S. (1992) *The Red Hand: Protestant Paramilitaries in Northern Ireland.* Oxford, Oxford University Press.

Buckland, P. (1981) *A History of Northern Ireland.* Dublin, Gill and Macmillan.

Burgess, T. P. (1993) *A Crisis of Conscience: Moral Ambivalence and Education in Northern Ireland.* Aldershot, Avebury Press.

Clarke, L. (1987) *Broadening the Battlefield: The H-Blocks and the Rise of Sinn Féin*. Dublin, Gill and Macmillan.

Cormack, R. J. and R. D. Osborne, eds (1991) *Discrimination and Public Policy in Northern Ireland*. Oxford, Clarendon Press.

Cradden, T. (1993) *Trade Unionism, Socialism and Partition*. Belfast, December Publications.

Crozier, M., ed. (1989) *Cultural Traditions in Northern Ireland: Varieties of Irishness: Proceedings of the Cultural Traditions Group Conference*. Belfast, Institute of Irish Studies, Queen's University.

Crozier, M., ed. (1990) *Cultural Traditions in Northern Ireland: Varieties of Britishness: Proceedings of the Cultural Traditions Group Conference*. Belfast, Institute of Irish Studies, Queen's University.

Crozier, M., ed. (1991) *Cultural Traditions in Northern Ireland: All Europeans Now: Proceedings of the Cultural Traditions Group Conference*. Belfast, Institute of Irish Studies, Queen's University.

Crozier, M. and N. Sanders, eds (1991) *A Cultural Traditions Directory for Northern Ireland*. Belfast, Institute of Irish Studies, Queen's University.

Cullen, B., ed. (1992) *Discriminations Old and New: Aspects of Northern Ireland Today: Proceedings of the Irish Association Conference*. Belfast, Institute of Irish Studies, Queen's University.

Cunningham, M. J. (1991) *British Government Policy in Northern Ireland 1969-89: its Nature and Execution*. Manchester, Manchester University Press.

Curtis, L. (1984) *Ireland: the Propaganda War, the British Media and the 'Battle for Hearts and Minds'*. London, Pluto Press.

Darby, J. (1972) *Register of Research into the Irish Conflict*. Belfast Northern Ireland Community Relations Commission.

Darby, J., ed. (1983) *Northern Ireland: Background to the Conflict*. Belfast, Appletree Press.

Darby, J. et al. (1981) *Register of Research into the Irish Conflict, 1981*. Coleraine, Centre for the Study of Conflict, New University of Ulster.

Darby, J., et al. (1983) *A Register of Economic and Social Research on Northern Ireland, 1980–83, with an Introductory Essay*. Social Science Research Council Northern Ireland Panel.

Darby, J. et al., eds. (1990) *Political Violence: Ireland in a Comparative Perspective*. Belfast, Appletree Press.

Davies, C. and E. McLaughlin, eds (1991) *Women, Employment and Social Policy in Northern Ireland*. Belfast, Policy Research Institute.

Deutsch, R. and V. Magowan (1973, 1974, 1975) *Northern Ireland, a Chronology of Events*, vols. 1–3. Belfast, Blackstaff Press.

Dickson, B. (1993) *Civil Liberties in Northern Ireland*, second edition. Belfast, Committee on the Administration of Justice.

Dillenburger, K. (1993) *Violent Bereavement: Widows in Northern Ireland*. Aldershot, Avebury.

Dunn, S. (1986) *Education and the Conflict in Northern Ireland: a Guide to the Literature*. Coleraine, Centre for the Study of Conflict, University of Ulster.

Dunn, S. (1990) 'A History of Education in Northern Ireland since 1920' in *Fifteenth Report of the Standing Advisory Commission on Human Rights*. London, HMSO.

Dunn, S. and A. Smith (1989) *Inter School Links*. Coleraine, Centre for the Study of Conflict, University of Ulster.

Economic and Social Research Council (ESRC) (1992) 'Research Data on Northern Ireland'. *ESRC Data Archive Bulletin, Special Issue*, September 20.

Economic and Social Research Institute (ESRI) (1988) *Register of Current Social Research in Ireland*. Dublin, ESRI.

Evans, E. E. (1992, 1973) *The Personality of Ireland: Habitat, Heritage and History*. Dublin, Lilliput Press.

Flackes, W. D. and S. Elliott (1989) *Northern Ireland: a Political Directory 1968–1988*. Belfast, Blackstaff Press.

Foley, C. (1992) *Legion of the Rearguard: the IRA and the Modern Irish State*. London, Pluto Press.

Foster, R. (1988) *Modern Ireland 1600–1972*. Harmondsworth, Penguin Books.

Fulton, J. (1990) *The Tragedy of Belief: Division, Politics and Religion in Ireland*. Oxford, Clarendon Press.

Gaffikin, F. and M. Morrissey (1990) *Northern Ireland, the Thatcher Years*. London, Zed Books.

Gallagher, A. M. (1989) *Majority Minority Review 1: Education and Religion in Northern Ireland*. Coleraine, Centre for the Study of Conflict, University of Ulster.

Gallagher, A. M. (1991) *Majority Minority Review 2: Employment, Unemployment and Religion in Northern Ireland*. Coleraine, Centre for the Study of Conflict University of Ulster.

Hadden, T. and K. Boyle (1989) *The Anglo-Irish Agreement: Commentary, Text and Official Review*. London, Sweet & Maxwell; Dublin, Edwin Higel.

Hadfield, B., ed. (1993) *Northern Ireland: Politics and the Constitution*. Buckingham, Open University Press.

Hall, M. (1988) *Twenty Years: a Concise Chronology of Events in Northern Ireland from 1968–1988*. Newtownabbey, Island Publications.

Harkness, D. W. (1983) *Northern Ireland Since 1920*. Dublin, Gill and Macmillan.

Hill, R. J. and M. Marsh, eds (1993) *Modern Irish Democracy*. Dublin, Irish Academic Press.

Hillyard, P. (1993) *Suspect Community: People's Experience of the Prevention of Terrorism Acts in Great Britain*. London, Pluto Press.

Hogan, G. and C. Walker (1990) *Political Violence and the Law in Ireland*. Manchester, Manchester University Press.

Holland, J. and H. McDonald (1994) *The INLA: the Inside Story*. Dublin, Torc Press.

Howe, L. (1990) *Being Unemployed in Northern Ireland: an Ethnographic Study*. Cambridge, Cambridge University Press.

Hutton, S. and P. Stewart, eds (1991) *Ireland's Histories: Aspects of State, Society and Ideology*. London, Routledge.

Jennings, A., ed. (1990) *Justice Under Fire: the Abuse of Civil Liberties in Northern Ireland*. London, Pluto Press.

Keogh, D. and M. H. Haltzel, eds (1993) *Northern Ireland and the Politics of Reconciliation*. Cambridge University Press (UK and USA) for Woodrow Wilson Center Press.

Lakos, A. (1986) *International Terrorism: a Bibliography.* Boulder, Westview Press.

Lee, S., ed. (1991) *Freedom From Fear.* Belfast, Institute of Irish Studies, Queen's University.

Longley, E., ed. (1991) *Culture in Ireland: Division or Diversity: Proceedings of the Cultures of Ireland Group Conference.* Belfast, Institute of Irish Studies, Queen's University.

McAuley, J. W. (1994) *The Politics of Identity.* Aldershot, Avebury.

McCann, E. (1993, 1974) *War and an Irish Town.* London, Pluto Press.

McCormack, V. and J. O'Hara (1990) *Enduring Inequality: Religious Discrimination in Employment in Northern Ireland.* London, National Council for Civil Liberties.

McElroy, G. (1991) *The Catholic Church and the Northern Ireland Crisis.* Dublin, Gill and Macmillan.

McGarry, J. and B. O'Leary, eds (1990) *The Future of Northern Ireland.* Oxford, Clarendon Press.

McLaughlin, E., ed. (1993) *Beyond the Statistics: the Effects of Unemployment in Ireland.* Belfast and Dublin, Cooperation North.

McLoone, M., ed. (1991) *Culture, Identity and Broadcasting in Northern Ireland.* Belfast, Institute of Irish Studies, Queen's University.

McNamee, P., ed. (1992) *Traditional Music: Whose Music?* Belfast, Institute of Irish Studies, Queen's University.

McWilliams, M. and J. McKernan (1993) *Bringing it Out into the Open – Domestic Violence in Northern Ireland.* Belfast, HMSO.

Moffat, C., ed. (1993) *Education Together for a Change: Integrated Education and Community Relations in Northern Ireland.* Belfast, Fortnight Educational Trust.

Morgan, V. et al. (1992) *Breaking the Mould: the Role of Parents and Teachers in the Integrated Schools in Northern Ireland.* Coleraine, Centre for the Study of Conflict, University of Ulster.

Morgan, V. and G. Fraser (1994) *Women, Community and Organisations.* Coleraine, Centre for the Study of Conflict and Centre for Research on Women, University of Ulster.

Morrow, D. (1991) *The Churches and Inter-community Relationships.* Coleraine, Centre for the Study of Conflict, University of Ulster.

Munck, R. (1992) *The Irish Economy: Results and Prospects.* London, Pluto Press.

Murray, D. and J. O'Neill (1991) *Peace Building in a Political Impasse.* Coleraine, Centre for the Study of Conflict, University of Ulster.

Murray, R. (1990) *The SAS in Ireland.* Cork, Mercier Press.

O'Brien, B. (1993) *The Long War: the IRA and Sinn Féin, 1985 to Today.* O'Brien Press.

O'Connor, F. (1993) *In Search of a State: Catholics in Northern Ireland.* Belfast, Blackstaff Press.

O'Leary, B. et al. (1993) *Northern Ireland: Sharing Authority.* London, Institute for Public Policy Research.

O'Leary, B. and J. McGarry (1992) *The Politics of Antagonism: Understanding Northern Ireland.* London, Athlone Press.

O'Leary, C. et al. (1988) *The Northern Ireland Assembly 1982–1986: a Constitutional Experiment.* London, Hurst.

O'Malley, P. (1990a) *Northern Ireland: a Question of Nuance.* Belfast, Blackstaff Press.

O'Malley, P. (1990b) *Biting at the Grave.* Boston: Beacon Press; Belfast, Blackstaff Press.

Ó Maoláin, C. (1993) *Register of Research on Northern Ireland.* Coleraine, Centre for the Study of Conflict, University of Ulster.

Osborne, R. et al. (1993) *After the Reforms: Education and Policy in Northern Ireland.* Aldershot, Avebury.

Patterson, H. (1989) *The Politics of Illusion: Republicanism and Socialism in Modern Ireland.* London, Hutchinson.

Pollak, A., ed. (1993) *A Citizen's Inquiry: the Opsahl Report on Northern Ireland.* Dublin, Lilliput Press.

Purdie, B. (1990) *Politics in the Streets: the Origins of the Civil Rights Movement in Northern Ireland.* Belfast, Blackstaff Press.

Roche, P. J. and B. Barton, eds (1991) *The Northern Ireland Question: Myth and Reality.* Aldershot, Avebury.

Rolston, B., ed. (1991a) *The Media and Northern Ireland: Covering the Troubles.* London, Macmillan.

Rolston, B. (1991b) *Politics and Painting: Murals and Conflict in Northern Ireland.* London, Associated University Presses.

Rolston, B. (1992) *Drawing Support: Murals in the North of Ireland.* Belfast, Beyond the Pale Publications.

Rolston, B. (1993) *Fortnight: The Index, Nos. 1–300.* Belfast, Fortnight Publications.

Rolston, B. et al., eds (1983) *A Social Sciences Bibliography of Northern Ireland, 1945–1983.* Belfast, Queen's University.

Rooney, E. (1993) *Women and Community Politics in Northern Ireland.* Coleraine, Centre for Research on Women, University of Ulster.

Rubenstein, M. (1993) *Fair Employment Case Law.* Belfast, Fair Employment Commission.

Shannon, M. O. (1991) *World Bibliographical Series, vol. 129: Northern Ireland.* Oxford, Clio Press.

Smith, A. and S. Dunn (1990) *Extending Inter School Links: an Evaluation of Contact Between Protestant and Catholic Pupils in Northern Ireland.* Coleraine, Centre for the Study of Conflict, University of Ulster.

Smith, A. and D. Murray (1993) *The Chance of a Lifetime.* Coleraine, Centre for the Study of Conflict, University of Ulster.

Smith, A. and A. Robinson (1992) *Education for Mutual Understanding: Perceptions and Policy.* Coleraine, Centre for the Study of Conflict, University of Ulster.

Smith, D. J. and G. Chambers (1991) *Inequality in Northern Ireland.* Oxford, Clarendon Press.

Standing Advisory Commission on Human Rights (1989, 1990, 1991, 1992) *Fourteenth Report* to *Seventeenth Report.* London, HMSO.

Stringer, P. and G. Robinson, eds (1991) *Social Attitudes in Northern Ireland 1990–91* edition. Belfast, Blackstaff Press.

Stringer, P. and G. Robinson, eds (1992) *Social Attitudes in Northern Ireland, the Second Report.* Belfast, Blackstaff Press.

Stringer, P. and G. Robinson, eds (1993) *Social Attitudes in Northern Ireland, the Third Report.* Belfast, Blackstaff Press.

Sugden, J. and A. Bairner (1993) *Sport, Sectarianism and Society in a Divided Ireland.* Leicester, Leicester University Press.

Sugden, J. and S. Harvie (1993) *Sport and Community in Northern Ireland: a Governing Body Perspective.* Unpublished Central Community Relations Unit Report.

Whyte, J. (1990) *Interpreting Northern Ireland.* Oxford, Clarendon Press.

Wilson, D. and S. Dunn (1989) *Integrated Education: Information for Parents.* Coleraine, Centre for the Study of Conflict, University of Ulster.

Index